THE IDEA OF
THE CLERISY IN THE
NINETEENTH CENTURY

THE IDEA OF
THE CLERISY IN THE
NINETEENTH CENTURY

BEN KNIGHTS

Staff Tutor, Department of Extra-Mural
Studies, University of Durham

CAMBRIDGE UNIVERSITY PRESS

Cambridge
London   New York   Melbourne

Published by the Syndics of the Cambridge University Press
The Pitt Building, Trumpington Street, Cambridge CB2 1RP
Bentley House, 200 Euston Road, London NW1 2DB
32 East 57th Street, New York, NY 10022, USA
296 Beaconsfield Parade, Middle Park, Melbourne 3206, Australia

First published 1978

Printed in Great Britain by
Western Printing Services Ltd
Bristol

Library of Congress Cataloguing in Publication Data
Knights, Ben, 1947–
The idea of the clerisy in the nineteenth
century.
Bibliography: p.
Includes index.
1. English prose literature – 19th century –
History and criticism. 2. Authors, English –
19th century – Political and social views.
3. Great Britain – Intellectual life – 19th century.
4. Learning and scholarship – Great Britain.
5. Education, Humanistic – Great Britain.
I. Title. II. Title: Clerisy in the nineteenth
century.
PR778.S47K5   820'.9'35   77–80840
ISBN 0 521 21798 9

CONTENTS

Beside the humanity that the poet succinctly depicts as 'Minds turned to the world and heedless of the heavens' it was possible until the last half-century, to discern another, essentially distinct, which (up to a point) acted as a brake on the first. I mean that class of men whom I shall call the *clercs*, gathering under that title those whose activity does not in its essence aim at practical goals, and who, finding their satisfaction in the practice of art, of science or of metaphysics (in short in the possession of unworldly wealth), announce in one way or another, 'My kingdom is not of this world'. In fact over the two thousand years up to our time I see an uninterrupted procession of philosophers, of divines, of writers, of artists, of scientists (one might include nearly all such practitioners of the period) whose tendency constitutes a formal opposition to the realism of the masses. Take the specific case of political passions: the *clercs* oppose them in two ways. In one, totally free from these passions themselves, they give (like a da Vinci, a Malebranche or a Goethe) an example of devotion to a completely disinterested spiritual activity, and foster belief in the supreme value of that form of existence. In another, as moralists themselves and based on the conflict of human egoism, they inculcate (like an Erasmus, a Kant or a Renan) the adoption in the name of humanity and justice of an abstract principle superior to and directly opposed to those passions. Doubtless – and even though they founded the modern state to the degree that it is superior to individual selfishness – the action of these *clercs* remained above all theoretical. They did not prevent hatreds and slaughter on the part of the laity. But they did prevent the people at large from making a religion out of its aspirations, from thinking itself important in attempting to realise them. One can say that, thanks to them, humanity has for two thousand years performed evil but honoured goodness. That paradox is the glory of the human race, and the crack through which civilisation was able to slip.

Julien Benda, *La Trahison des clercs*

The ancient Poets animated all sensible objects with Gods or Geniuses, calling them by the names and adorning them with the properties of woods, rivers, mountains, lakes, cities, nations, and whatever their enlarged & numerous senses could percieve.

And particularly they studied the genius of each city & country, placing it under its mental deity;

Till a system was formed, which some took advantage of, & enslav'd the vulgar by attempting to realize or abstract the mental deities from their objects: thus began Priesthood;

Choosing forms of worship from poetic tales.

And at length they pronounc'd that the Gods had order'd such things.

Thus men forgot that All deities reside in the human breast.

Blake, 'The Marriage of Heaven and Hell'

PREFACE

The writing of this book fell into several phases, and incurred more debts than I can or should briefly acknowledge. Even to speak of debts creates the misleading impression of discrete and measurable additions to one's personal stock. But some acknowledgements demand to be made. The project first took shape under the stimulus and with the encouragement of Professor Raymond Williams, and continued under the guidance of my research supervisor, Professor Graham Hough. Many of my fellow graduate students deserve thanks for their vivid contributions to the period of continuing education out of which the original version grew. I would name especially Dr John Carroll and Dr Heather Glen. In its later phases, the book fed upon the conversation or advice of Cambridge colleagues – Dr John Barrell, Dr Jonathan Culler, Dr Leslie Hill, Mr Raymond O'Malley, Dr Wilbur Sanders – and students. Many of them helped far more than they themselves perhaps realise. Finally, a book which asks for a reassessment of the transactions between intellectual enterprise and practical living owes most to non-specialists: to those who by their companionship and example radically enlarged the experience behind the text. My especial thanks go to Janet, my wife; to Lionel and Elizabeth Knights, my parents; and to John Myer, who generously opened up to me the world of primary education.

Unfortunately, John Colmer's edition of Coleridge's *On the Constitution of the Church and State* was published too late for me to use. For all defects of scholarship and presentation I in my impatience am alone responsible.

BEN KNIGHTS

Durham
July 1977

1

INTRODUCTION

The idea of the clerisy, of the intellectuals as a distinct and socially beneficial group, has been an active one in this century. Characterisation of 'the intellectuals' has been considerably influenced by instances of political intervention – the Dreyfus case, the Spanish Civil War, the Vietnam War and so on. But the inclusive idea of the clerisy as a body whose field of competence was no less than the life of the mind in general has fallen victim to that very specialisation which was to have been one of its own tasks to overcome. The influence in England in the 1930s and 1940s of Mannheim's prescriptive theory of the social role of the intelligentsia was a case of residual attraction.[1] Yet Mannheim's is a less heroic, less nostalgic account than we find in Julien Benda's *La Trahison des clercs*, where there are still affinities of tone and aspiration with the nineteenth-century theorists. Probably, few would hold Benda's ideas today. If we seek a type of the intellectual speaking to the world today we tend to go to the technical scientist, or the economist. But I believe that ideas akin to Benda's still have an attenuated currency in the hinterland of contemporary educational and social thinking. I have undertaken these historical studies as a contribution to critical thinking about the idea and its implications. It is not the least of reasons for interest on the part of one who teaches English Literature that literary criticism inherited its own share of nineteenth-century arguments for the clerisy. Leavis's *Mass Civilisation and Minority Culture* has a pre-history that would be obscured if we thought that Matthew Arnold's 'criticism' could only be glossed as 'literary criticism'.

Early in the nineteenth century, the idea of the educated man became problematic. That is to say, those who thought about such things ceased to be able to rely upon the available structures of thought to provide a place for those whose characteristic occupation was cultural. Neither 'clergyman' nor 'man of letters' provided quite the right category. The discussion about the character of the highly educated man and his relationship to his society is basic to the matter of this book. Explicitly or implicitly all the writers dealt with here were concerned with the educated man as a social being and one whose very education (in a society where such education was the prerogative of a few) implied social responsibilities. Thus they contribute to a larger discussion – not in itself my subject here – of the educational or moral role of the governors, a discussion which may be amply evidenced from the debates on the Reform Bills of 1866 and 1867. Plato had suggested that perhaps the only thing for a philosopher to do in the Athens of the early fourth century B.C. was to take refuge from the storm and cultivate his own mind. Tempted as they sometimes were, the writers with whom this study is concerned preferred to work upon society, though not, it is true, directly in politics or social movements. Here Benda is well in the tradition. The intellectual should work indirectly: as an M.P., Mill – like the philosophic radicals before him – clearly regarded his political activities as simply an expression of his intellectual work. Thus our writers seem at first to adumbrate the separate worlds of Weber's *Politics as a Vocation* and *Science* (Wissenschaft) *as a Vocation*. But in fact they do not, since at the root of the theory of the clerisy was a conviction not merely that there was no discontinuity between the life of the mind and the practical life of society, but that the latter was vitally affected by the former. So the acceptance of Weber's contention that 'scientific' pleading on behalf of practical stands 'is meaningless in principle because the various value spheres of the world stand in irreconcilable conflict with each other'[2] would be a terrible defeat. The educated man's field of operation is the national intellect and culture, and he is a member of a fraternity whose education gives it a common intellectual nourishment, and which is enabled to grapple with all problems by virtue of its mental training. I shall examine the notion of liberal education in chapter 6. Here I would merely point out that in the nineteenth century liberal education was quite normally seen as leading to social position. It is significant that a number of writers claim the rank of 'gentleman' for the man of liberal education. Here is an extract from a letter from Coleridge to James Gillman (the son of his host at Highgate).

And what is a liberal Education? That which *draws* forth and trains up the germ of free-agency in the Individual, Education, quae *liberum* facit, and the man, who has mastered all the conditions of *freedom* is *Homo Liberalis* – the classical rendering of the modern term, *Gentle*man – because under the feudal system the *men of family* (Gentiles, generosi, quibus *gent* erat, et genus) alone possessed these conditions.[3]

In this study we shall be concerned with what men of letters have to say about themselves, with how they imagine and justify their activity. We shall necessarily be concerned with the character they desire for themselves or project on behalf of the ideal man of letters, so in examining these projective characters we are not straying far from our subject. The man of letters inherits, then, the title of gentleman. But what is the new *liber homo* free from? The answer is that he is to some extent freed from the pressures of historical necessity. The intellectual's attempt to make himself feel that he is not conditioned began in the nineteenth century and survived in Mannheim's paradoxical belief in the potentialities of the unattached intelligentsia. For reasons that I shall try to explain later, conditioning by the blind forces of society and history is identified with threatening pressures within the self, so that self-knowledge and the mastery that is believed to arise from it are seen as the road to freedom. Coleridge's letter continued:

For believe me, my dear young Friend: It is no musty old Saw but a Maxim of Life, a medicinal Herb from the Garden of Experience ... that He alone is *free* & entitled to the name of a Gentleman, who knows himself and walks in the light of his own consciousness.

And in a note on the brutality and political untrustworthiness of 'the people', he remarked that 'He alone is entitled to a share in the government of all who has learned to govern himself.'[4] We shall see that the ideal held out for the man of letters is one of inner balance, the *Tüchtigkeit* that Arnold sought. Carlyle (his selfhood more in danger, perhaps, than Arnold's) carried the idea even further – into a fascination with renunciation, with *Selbsttödtung*, the mortification of the flesh. 'Deny thyself; whatsoever is *thyself*, consider it as nothing.'[5] This is important, for the thread we are tracing leads us to the ideal of purity (conceived as the renunciation of the sensible world) that was one of the great secularisations achieved on behalf of culture by nineteenth-century theorists. Whether you are to discover or to preserve man's spiritual goods, you must be pure – so said Coleridge, Carlyle and Matthew Arnold; Mark Pattison, too, preaching in Lincoln College Chapel on the necessary connection between philosophy and asceticism. In arguing for the transcendent allegiance of culture, the theorists of the clerisy put forward a model both of the transcendent (the realm of order and security) and of the worldly (the chaotic, the sensual, the determined) that – if we still find it even partially acceptable – we should learn to question. The link with character may be illustrated from Matthew Arnold's 'best self' as applied both to the individual and to the state. We might well query the relationship between *Tüchtigkeit* and that best self 'which is not manifold, and vulgar, and unstable, and contentious, and ever-varying, but one, and noble, and secure, and peaceful, and the same for all mankind.'[6] There is a considerable affinity of aspiration between the men of letters who mapped out ideals for the social role of the educated man. This is the ground for the theory of the literary elite. Before we come to the theory itself, however, we must look briefly at the matrix of thought within which it was typically articulated.

The idea of the clerisy emerges from the aftermath of the French Revolution, a fact of dual significance for its history. Its exponents were as apt as Tory propagandists to assert the values of order and of social stability. Further, the Revolution had attracted attention to the social activities of intellectuals, since it was already a commonplace that they had played a substantial part in bringing it about. An interest in the social implications of literary activity gave rise to a rudimentary sociology of culture and knowledge. I am alluding to a tendency to see literature, including philosophy, and history, as being shaped by the period and social circumstances in which it was written, as well as exerting its own influence on the social character. A social approach to literature is evidenced in Isaac D'Israeli's 'Essay on the Character of the Literary Man' (1795), and is apparently quite acceptable by the time Bulwer wrote his *England and the English* in 1833. Comparable assumptions lie behind Arnold's theory of the conjunction of the man and the moment, and similar ideas behind Mill's discussions about the suitability of certain periods to philosophical or poetic writing.[7] A corollary to this tendency of thought is the claim that the clerisy helps create the conditions in which alone literature can be vital. Existing in unhappy equilibrium with this aspect of the historicism of the age is a set of related beliefs – more an order of aspiration than formulated theory – concerning hierarchy, order, and the 'real' or transcending nature of values. I shall examine these subjects in some detail later, and here should merely say that they represent a constellation of notions about the way in which the universe is ordered and the conditions under which it becomes intelligible. We must explore the connection between legislating at a theoretical level for the conditions of intellectual life and the emphasis on form, limitation, and control, on order seen not as emerging from but as preceding the creative act. Socrates countered the Sophists on the grounds that ideas were real, had an existence beyond the words that labelled them and beyond the historical conditions in which they happened to be manifested. The enterprise of saving certain values, principles, and metaphysical concerns in a world felt to be hostile to the concerns of the mind was essentially similar. Truth – especially moral truth – it could be argued, is not dependent on temporary historical conditions or on the development of natural science. It is a paradox which we should be aware of today that necessary claims for the continuity of experience with the past (even if they no longer appear to depend on metaphysics), and equally necessary claims for the cultural importance of tradition should so easily fit into a constellation of ideas that emphasises a normative order and a hierarchy of values which is seen as beyond historical alteration.

We are now the heirs of a degree of specialisation unknown to (even if dreaded by) the nineteenth-century theorists of the clerisy. I do not mean what a glance at, say, the *Edinburgh Review* or *Westminster Review* during their great years would disprove – that a variety of subjects were unknown to readers of the period. Rather, I would suggest that the sophisticated affairs of the mind were seen as vitally interrelated, and as bearing directly upon the social health – the morality indeed – of the nation. Culture and morality were finally one. Therefore the guardians of culture were the guardians of morality, an assertion which amply accounts for the seriousness with which the proponents of the literary elite took their task. All our writers could have agreed, in some sense, with the assertion of Saint-Simon's followers that 'For us, religion, politics, morality, are only diverse names for the same thing.'[8] We run the risk of a lack of historical sympathy unless we see that to discuss literature, ethics, or the life of the mind as separate from each other already implies a discontinuity where our writers (without consciously attempting a synthesis) saw a continuity. From Coleridge to the younger Arnold, our writers took for granted that morality – the rules for a viable social life – and the healthy, disciplined life of the intellect were but aspects of the same acceptance of form and order.

The danger inherent in their attitude (as in that of their successors) is that the belief in order easily turns into a legitimation of the existing order on the grounds that at least it *is* an order.

I have touched very briefly on the mental landscape in which we find proposals on behalf of a clerisy. I shall now sketch the salient proposals, warning that we shall find nothing approximating to an exact programme shared by all our writers. We start from the common position that the powers that be in society are not really powers at all, but are engaged in a mere mime of government. They do not know society's true needs and are consequently, at anything but a superficial level, impotent. The partiality or incapacity of the established powers is a theme on which all our writers play variations. The corollary – that there has historically been or that there ought to be a group in society which sees more clearly, describes the permanent and truly important behind the ever-shifting, untrustworthy phenomena, and consequently knows society's needs better than its ostensible rulers – becomes the central assertion of the clerisy argument. There is undoubtedly some truth here: indeed it is presumably a truism that in any state of society there will be some who understand more profoundly than others, whose proposals (even if met with general incomprehension) are more radical. But it is a bigger step from here than is often assumed to the proposition that we can say prescriptively of whom such a group is likely to consist, and what the nature of its operation in society will be. Our nineteenth-century writers argue the importance to social health of a spiritual power identified (as, more recently, Professor Northrop Frye has done) with the literary and philosophic class.[9] To be sure, its members were not to be philosopher-rulers; indeed, they felt that politics were only of secondary importance. They were to work on that substance of national life upon which political institutions were based – its opinions, its language, and its conceptions of ethical action. We may be reminded here of Shelley's assertion that the 'great instrument of moral good is the imagination; and poetry administers to the effect by acting upon the cause'. But mention of Shelley's claims for poetry illuminates by contrast an important point: the theorists of the clerisy are not talking about creative writers as such, or, except incidentally, about the imagination in its relation to the disposition of human energies in society. True, they were inclined to agree with Carlyle's version of Schiller that 'genuine literature includes the essence of philosophy, religion, art; whatever speaks to the immortal part of men. The daughter, she is likewise the nurse of all that is spiritual and thus exalted in our character',[10] and the poets were included in the literary and philosophic class, but they get no special attention as the forgers of the uncreated conscience of their race. Indeed, in the world of the theorists we find a surprisingly general uneasiness towards the creative writer, ranging from Arnold's proposed moratorium on creative literature, to the ambivalence of Carlyle and Mill towards 'fictions'. Who, then, was the clerisy to comprise? We are used to a situation in which intellectuals are specialists, where they first of all fall on one side or the other of that division between the humanities and the natural and mathematical sciences which has been an effective barrier for a century. But the spiritual power as identified with the intellectual class is made up of those capable of passing the boundaries of specialisms and of achieving insight into their various claims 'transmuting and integrating all that the separate professions have achieved in science or art – but, with a range transcending the limits of professional views or local or temporary interests applying the product . . . to the strengthening and subliming of the Nation itself'.[11] Such men would thereby achieve something that Comte in France and Mill in England had hoped sociology (based upon a suitable philosophy) would achieve – the integration of specialisms within a comprehensive and practical study of the human world. Whether seen as established or as self-constituted, the clerisy was to comprise those who had the capacity to assimilate particular sciences to the study of men in relation both to the transcendent and to each other.

What we are observing is the creation of an ideology for the intelligentsia, comprising an ideal character and an ideal role in relation to society as a whole. This may be a mediating role (like that of Coleridge's clerisy), a challenging role (as with Mill), or a renewing and conserving role (as with Arnold). There is thus a common insistence that, while the intellectuals stand apart from the existing classes and preoccupations of society, their activity is a precondition of social health. In no case do our writers (themselves members of a remarkably unalienated intellectual class, a class that never seems to have felt totally at war with the established order in its society) approach a concept like Marx's: 'The ideas of the ruling class are in every epoch the ruling ideas. . . . The class which has the means of material production at its disposal, has control at the same time over the means of mental production.' And it never seems to have crossed their minds that thinkers 'make their chief source of livelihood the perfecting the illusion of the (ruling) class about itself'.[12] Once again, there is a striking parallel with Mannheim's free-floating intelligentsia.

There are more elements of the theory of the clerisy. One of these was a theory of mind, or, more exactly, a disposition towards a theory, the disposition being supported and satisfied by those impulses that had been regularised into an epistemology by Kant, and whose appropriation by philosophy was regarded by many of Kant's followers as his central achievement. I mean the disposition to regard the mind not as a passive recipient for sensation, but as active, working upon and imposing its own modes upon the chaotic phenomenal world. With varying degrees of explicitness, proponents of the clerisy proposed epistemological doctrines suggested by this kind of insight. They quoted Proverbs to the effect that 'Without vision the people perisheth', and we should understand that vision was a creative and ordering vision, the imposition of meaning upon the chaos of experience. The clerisy was to do for society something that society, unaided, could not do for itself. It was to render susceptible of comprehension the raw matter of experience under the headings of transcendent principles. Thus the clerisy was to act as the active mind of society. Even when the claim was not as overt as this, the clerisy was still conceived as the link between the sensuous understanding – for which it was true that *nihil in intellectu quod non prius in sensu* (there is nothing in the mind which is not previously in the sense(s)) – and the realm of reason.

Many efforts were made to characterise the group whose responsibilities were of this kind. Thus, it was not just of its time, the victim of contemporary needs. It was a trans-historical group of *lumières*. Carl Becker has pointed out the 'uses of posterity' for the *philosophes* of the eighteenth century: the judgment of the court of history provided a kind of secular immortality for those who had worked long and earnestly to further the good of the human spirit.[13] Those nineteenth-century intellectuals who theorised about their own role also needed to be remembered, needed to be able to project the approval of their sub-group into the future, and to console themselves with the thought that (however little acclaim they might receive in their generation) they would be remembered as those who had in their day had charge of the light:

To whom, then, do we owe our ameliorated condition? To the successive few in every age (more indeed in one generation than another but relatively to the mass of mankind aways few) who by the intensity and permanence of their action have compensated for the limited sphere within which it is at any time intelligible, and whose good deeds posterity reverence in their results.[14]

There is an important sense in which all who write feel the need for an enduring community of understanding. Goethe, to whose example so many looked in the nineteenth century, had registered this need, and by the time Brougham gave his Rectorial Address at Glasgow in 1825 the notion of the secular immortality of great spirits had become a commonplace. It is clear that the later positivist calendar of saints is merely a development of an existing trend, attacked by Newman in his onslaught on Peel and Brougham.[15] Behind the aspirations that led to such doctrines was the haunting possibility that you might work unseen and misunderstood, unable to look forward to posterity's rectifying judgment on your work – the predicament of the unknown Theresas of the preface to *Middlemarch*.

The community of spiritual endeavour connects past, present, and future. The stress on the importance of continuity and tradition to the well-being of the national culture asked that attention be paid in turn to those who had preserved and handed on philosophy and literature. As we hope to be remembered so should we remember, and Coleridge noted that one effect of the preponderance of the commercial spirit was the neglect not only of the 'austerer studies', but also of the old philosophers. In return for this piety, those who had gone before provided an essential term of our cultural continuity, became an aristocracy of spirit –

> the kings of thought
> Who waged contention with their time's decay,
> And of the past are all that cannot pass away –

without whom memory in individual and history in collective consciousness would be void and without form. We shall see that this is a major theme in the articulation of the intellectual's self-consciousness, and, further, that it is connected with that earnestness which is such a salient feature of the clerisy of the period. For those who are truly concerned with spirit bear a great burden. Matthew Arnold copied a saying of Bunsen's into his Notebook: 'The aim is to understand myself and the age, to apprehend what is the prime need of each, and to minister according to our ability to that need.'[16] All the proponents of the clerisy, obsessed (like so many of their contemporaries) by history, and drawing from their recognition of the need for continuity the lesson of the value of tradition, asserted earnestness as an intellectual imperative.

From asserting the historical community of meaning to describing the group responsible for that community was no long step. But, that group once postulated, a common form of discourse was necessary so that the guardians could discuss the problems of society without mistaking the essential affinities of the problems under discussion. It is clear that during the nineteenth century the concept of the 'disciplines' became increasingly problematic: you could not but be aware of the fissiparous tendencies of the world of mind, of the fact that not only the natural sciences but also economics, historical science, philology, philosophy, even theology, were showing an alarming tendency to march off from the core of moral concerns that had long been assumed as an intellectual centre, and to set up as semi-autonomous 'subjects' with a technical language of their own. Much of the work of the advocates of the clerisy was in a sense a last-ditch defence of an idea of wisdom as based upon integrally related studies, an idea with its roots deep in renaissance humanism.[17] But the need for unity had only come to be discussed because fragmentation was well advanced. Thus the common centre of training in letters, the Greek and Latin classics (the model for philosophy and history as literature), had to be supported just because its claims to centrality were being called in question. The Erasmian unity of study and application was slowly and painfully giving way to the recognition of a plurality of worlds of discourse, as the members of the Metaphysical Society were to find in the 1860s and 1870s. The change was naturally alarming to those for whom the moral continuity of the life of the mind with the practical life of society was a deeply held conviction.

The proponents of the clerisy started from the premise that community and culture were in serious danger. They articulated a sense that the possibility of a single structure of values was in doubt; that while natural science was extending the realm of the ethically meaningless, and historical science implying that convictions and values were but relative, knowledge was becoming so vast as to exclude a personal grasp on more than a fraction of it. The point may perhaps most economically be made by setting alongside each other two statements made roughly a hundred years apart by leading thinkers of the day. The first comes from Samuel Johnson's *Rambler*, the second from John Stuart Mill's experimental diary for 1854.

The manner in which external force acts upon the body is very little subject to the regulation of the will.... But our ideas are more subjected to choice; we can call them before us, and command their stay, we can facilitate and promote their recurrence, we can either repress their intrusion, or hasten their retreat. It is therefore the business of wisdom and virtue, to select among numberless objects striving for our notice, such as may enable us to exalt our reason, extend our views, and secure our happiness.[18]

Scarcely any one, in the more educated classes, seems to have any opinions, or to place any real faith in those which he professes to have.... It requires in these times much more intellect to marshall so much greater a stock of ideas and observations. This has not yet been done, or has been done only by very few: and hence the multitude of thoughts only breeds increase of uncertainty. Those who should be the guides of the rest, see too many sides to every question. They hear so much said, or find so much that can be said, about everything, that they feel no assurance of the truth of anything.[19]

The symbolic universe had, so to speak, got out of control, and the large-scale philosophic and literary enterprises of the period might almost be seen as engendered in defiance of the possibilities of limitless scepticism. Developing subjects shrugged off the claims of mutual coherence.

An almost defiant assertiveness finds an analogy in the Victorian novel. If we assume with the structuralists that the novel constitutes a 'model for intelligibility'[20] we can unravel implicit epistemologies without doing violence to the imaginative quality of the text. While experiments with point of view were carried on, and would indeed ramify at the end of the century in an atmosphere of increasing doubt about the possibility of coherent knowledge of the world, it is noteworthy that the premise of Victorian fictional worlds is not yet a sceptical one. The rational mind of the author and of the reader can organise the relevant data; the social world at large can provide subject matter. Truth is many-sided (the extension of sympathy was an imperative of the novel), and misunderstanding – whether arising from ignorance, from prejudice, or from social inexperience – can in principle be resolved. Enormous pedagogic confidence characterises the novelists of the period. Belief in the possibility of comprehensive understanding, seen by Nietzsche as a comforting illusion, was evinced in fiction and in philosophy, as in narrative history, and went along with a residual faith in consecutive prose and logical argument. Syntax witnesses to the possibility of attributing meaning to what happens in the world. But teleology, after all, requires that God or someone be watching, since it is true of a pattern of significance that to be is to be perceived.

Those whose practice concerned knowledge were becoming painfully aware of a paradox inherent in Baconian thought – the divisions of knowledge prospered. But as they progressed, the practitioners of each could no longer see the others. At the same time (and in part as a result of the state of the intellectual life) divisions in society were becoming ominous. But here were the guardians of culture, the national treasury of valuations and meanings, without a coherent philosophy, and with the most various notions of how to set on a new footing the spiritual life upon which the material life rested. They accepted the historical doctrine of alternating eras of stability and disintegration, and asked how the next age of order was to be attained. Their diagnoses turned on the inadequacy of the available modes of thought to the current intellectual and social situation. It is no exaggeration to say that even when, like Mill or Arnold, they professed and called themselves liberals, one of their central preoccupations was with the inadequacy of the predominant form of liberalism. Liberalism attracted attention as the most widely active of the available socio-political doctrines. Even Mill, liberal theorist as he was, saw that the enlightenment and the dispositions of thought which descended from it were inadequate to plot the intricacies of social dynamics. Society, the clerisy theorists asserted, had a deeper unity, with more complex laws of degeneration and of re-creation than was dreamed of in enlightenment philosophy. We see here an aspect of that recurrent nineteenth-century attack by intellectuals on bourgeois values: Carlyle has more in common with the other writers in this study than at first appears. Not surprisingly, even when they did not, like him, assert heroic counter-values, they had a predisposition towards an ideal aristocracy (Coleridge's 'ancient feeling of rank and ancestry') that should link the generations and humanise the society around it. It was in keeping with this intense awareness of the failings and dilemmas of liberalism that they should take issue with *laissez-faire*, above all in education, where the clerisy-road led to a confrontation with what John Burrow has called 'a dilemma in liberal culture itself. How are you to make people aware of the tradition which can both shape their energies into something coherent and by its plurality opens to them new possibilities unless you in some sense first impose it upon them?'[21] Coleridge, not himself a liberal, provided what proved to be a paradigmatic answer to the question of who was to supervise the national education.

Beyond the diagnosis of the poverty of liberalism lay an attitude to liberal democracy, referred to simply as the problem of democracy. Speculations were often far removed from the nature of the case, but they rationalised quite real fears. It was writers such as ours who started asking what happens to high culture in a democratic society. Generally, they feared that democracy threatened the highest cultivation of mind because it enshrined the values of the ordinary, the mediocre, because its wants were of the moment, unadvised by history, and heedless of the future. *Das Gemeine* (mediocrity) was the characteristic danger of democratic society, and it was a threat to more than just art or philosophy. In threatening the highest achievements of the human spirit it threatened the modes of thinking and acting that kept society healthy. Amid the encroachments of chaos, the function of the clerisy was to maintain a cosmos in which literature and history made sense and in which, consequently, human actions and aspirations would still have meaning. 'A strongly organized spiritual establishment' to quote a modern, prescriptive statement, 'would persistently diminish the importance of the ephemeral by maintaining links between the evanescent present and the durable past, the moral point of view would be taken up at a position from which a large tract of human history can be surveyed.'[22]

This area of concern usually provides the connection between the idea of the clerisy and the wider thought of those with whom we are dealing. Not one of them, it is worth pointing out, can be identified merely with the theory of the intellectual class; the notion of its value, on the other hand, is closely tied up with their characteristic preoccupations. This is the case even with Carlyle who abandoned the idea in the 1840s, going on to assert the primacy of the will in the individual and of the leader in society; or with Mill, whose 'enlightened opinion' is pretty tenuous by the time of *Representative Government*. The place of the idea in specific philosophies will concern us later. Here we should note that, whatever value they attributed to the philosophic class as arbiters of value, none of our writers saw the elite as having any coercive power. They saw it as working on society in diverse ways and through channels often hidden, making use of that press which in agonised moments they saw as a terrible agent of the 'plebification of knowledge'. The elite was, in its very existence, a precondition of society's health.

Here we are faced with a central problem: the place of the clerisy theory in the movement we know as secularisation. The concept is not, of course, one that our writers would use about their own work. Coleridge indeed, with his theological passion and his insistence that the Bible was the best guide to political skill, was attempting to redirect social activities towards religion. But from this distance we can gain much from the observation that effectively the work of the clerisy theorists was to invest culture with many of the attributes formerly ascribed to religion, to claim that philosophy and letters were essential to the life of the nation, or even that they were more genuinely religious than existing religious institutions. The process, which was remarked on and criticised by opponents from Newman to T. S. Eliot, can thus be seen in the context of European secular religions.[23] Even Mill, working from a non-religious position, invested the intellectual life of the nation with what we can only call spiritual attributes. In all, Carlyle's preoccupation with re-clothing the spiritual life roused sympathetic harmonies:

'But there is no Religion?' reiterates the Professor. 'Fool! I tell thee, there is. Hast thou well considered all that lies in this immeasurable froth-ocean we name LITERATURE? Fragments of a genuine *Church-Homiletic* lie scattered there, which Time will assort; nay, fractions even of a *Liturgy* could I point out. And knowest thou no Prophet, even in the vesture, environment, and dialect of this age? None of whom the Godlike had revealed itself, through all meanest and highest form of the Common, and by him been again prophetically revealed: in whose inspired melody, even in these rag-gathering and rag-burning days, Man's Life again begins, were it but afar off, to be divine? Knowest thou none such? I know him, and name him – Goethe.'[24]

We are dealing with the tendency to invest literature – again in its broadest sense – with religious attributes, the tendency to define the spiritual life of the nation in terms of the transcendent. As Renan said, and was later echoed by Arnold,

Science, art, and philosophy are valueless except insofar as they are religious. That is to say inasmuch as they furnish the spiritual food that religion used to but can no longer supply. 'One thing alone is necessary.' We should recognise this precept of the great master of morality as the principle of all noble life.[25]

There is a suggestion – sometimes more than a suggestion – that there can be no living culture without a priesthood: a suggestion amply developed by Renan himself. Even where the proponents of the clerisy do not, like Coleridge and Seeley, identify that body with the national church, they are still attracted by the notion that, since literature is taking on the social and moral functions of religion, it should likewise have its officers. The desire to give literature a special relationship with the transcendent and to endow it and its priests as the mediators between the phenomenal and the noumenal became deeply embedded in our culture during the nineteenth century.

The proponents of the clerisy unwittingly illustrate the fact that once you have postulated an order (even if that order is only to be realised in the distant future) your advocacy becomes necessary to yourself, so that what was perhaps proposed in opposition to the existing order gathers force as an orthodoxy. If you go further, and postulate a group of minds who alone can (things being as they are) apprehend such a cosmos, you will tend to change – even if your plans are not effectively realised – and begin to find the lineaments of the ideal in the wildest approximations that reality affords. You will change, to borrow Leszek Kolakowski's terms, from jester into priest, albeit the priest of an ideal order. In theory you will be in favour of the revivification of reality. But since creative forces are apt to be anarchic, contradiction-riddled, and incomprehensible in the available languages, you are liable not to recognise them when they appear, or even to join the forces opposed to them. In these terms we can explain not only the frequent ambivalence of the clerisy theorists towards imaginative literature but also the ease with which clerisy theory lends itself to support of the *status quo*. In ways ranging from Carlyle's quasi-Calvinist distrust of 'fictions' to John Stuart Mill's positivist conviction that poetry was just a way of telling the truths already attained by discursive philosophy, the legislators of the unseen world circumscribed the place assigned to creative literature. Clearly, this is not fortuitous: the desire to place, to order, to legislate is but one moment of our understanding and creation of our world. Alone, it is incapable of the originality which might explode or render irrelevant its own formulations.

The image of those who are not comprised in the intellectual class is relevant. When in 1862 Arnold declared that we had not the word 'Philistine' in English, Carlyle had been using it for upwards of thirty

years. We might notice how curious the metaphor is in its implication that the user is one of the chosen people. This kind of arrogance
was undoubtedly common among the German student societies
(themselves the heirs of the *Tugendbund* – the anti-Napoleonic
league), in whose slang this usage originates. Our writers, it is true,
diagnosed many deplorable aspects of their society. But we need to
ask whether the sectarianism of enlightenment is inseparable from
such an enterprise, whether the Calvinist inheritance that is marked
in Carlyle, and to a lesser extent in Ruskin and others is merely an
accidental conjunction.

To see questions like these in perspective, we must glance at the
psychological needs to which the theorists of the clerisy bear witness.
I shall claim that these men acted as registers of a psychic condition
inherent in their society and heightened in them by their own study
of the history of culture. We find in their writings many hints of a
deeply rooted dread of personal disintegration in the face of uncontrollable forces. Working from the assumption that any group's
projections about itself and its society will be deeply intertwined
with its reading of its own personality, I shall argue that one source
of emotional dynamic for the clerisy theorists was the fear that
reason was a precarious defence against drives and needs by which
the conscious self was threatened, against elements of the self to
which, as heirs of the Romantics, they were bound to grant prominence. The intellectual life thus becomes regulative, especially in a
society whose authority structures appeared to be in doubt, and there
are times when the drive towards a clerisy looks like a crusade
against some of the cultural and social implications of Romanticism.
'Will society be regenerated by its Intellect in spite of its Passions?'
asked Pattison. 'What security have we that the sleeping volcano of
Passion will not flame forth with irresistible violence? That the
ocean of Imagination, and False Opinion, will not break in, submerge a continent, and sweep away every trace of the Palace of
Truth?'[26] The advocates of the clerisy formulated for the intellectual
an ideal (whether lived up to or not) of minimal contact with the
phenomenal world, and consequently of withdrawal from direct
relationships: it was presumably something like this that Trilling
had in mind when he spoke of the modern intellectual 'abstracting
himself from the life of the family' as part of his effort to make
himself feel that his life was not conditioned; or Lawrence when he
censured the intellectual's hatred of household tasks.[27] The with-

drawal was felt to be necessary if indirect relationships through scholarly work were to be possible.

In an age of cheap domestic labour, the clerisy theorists worked to legitimate a situation in which the intellectual could make himself feel that his life was not conditioned; where he would tend to overlook the socio-economic basis of his own position, to dislike servitude yet want to be waited on, to reject his society's values yet profit psychically or socially by their acceptance. Praise or blame is irrelevant, but we should not give up the attempt at explanation in a matter of such profound importance to our own cultural condition. For I shall argue further that our writers typified an attitude towards those classes that seemed to constitute the objective correlative of their own uncontrollable elements. The dread – rational enough in its way – of unruly forces (in society those who have not learned to inhibit their impulses, and who live, like small children, for the minute alone, in what Arnold once called 'thraldom to the passing moment'[28]) has its own irrational springs in those who have not integrated their childhoods or unruly energies into their own lives; especially if they are (rightly) conscious that the continuing enhancement of the life of people in society requires an awareness of history, of meanings and evaluations that have more than a dragonfly existence. The fear of the many-headed monster springs in part from the identification of the appetites with the mob, and of democracy with the rule of appetite. In a profound sense, right reason in the individual and in society are one: the democratic character-type is to be shunned.

'In fact,' I said, '[he who is dominated by appetite] lives for the pleasure of the moment. One day it's wine, women and song, the next bread and water. ... Next he takes to politics and is always on his feet saying or doing whatever comes into his head. ... There's no order or restraint in his life, and he reckons his way of living is pleasant, free and happy.' A very good description of one who believes in liberty,' he commented.[29]

The *Republic*, which Rousseau asserted was 'point un ouvrage de politique, comme le pensent ceux qui ne jugent des livres que par leurs titres: c'est le plus beau traité d'éducation qu'on ait jamais fait',[30] is not, as we shall see, irrelevant. Before going on to examine some specific English thinkers, we must take a further look at some currents of thought which tended, directly or by implication, to reinforce the importance of the intellectual class.

MIND IN HISTORY

In this section we must take a closer look at some interconnected
ideas about history, politics, and education which were being elaborated on the Continent (especially in Germany) in the late eighteenth
and early nineteenth centuries. While this is not the place to attempt
a systematic account of these ideas, I have a twofold object in intro-
ducing them: first, to suggest the nature of the interest that English
thinkers on these subjects took in Germany (even where what they
gathered bore little resemblance to what German philosophers had
actually said), and second, to discuss in a morphological rather than
a genetic manner certain ideas and arguments for the comparative
light they shed on the subjects of this book. My concern with
questions of genesis, influence, or reaction is therefore limited.
I shall be at least equally concerned with typological affinities or
contrasts between theories of education and culture.

From the end of the eighteenth century, outside observers began
to take a serious interest in cultural developments in Germany.
In England, Coleridge, Crabbe Robinson, and Carlyle (among
others) acted as intermediaries for German literature and thought,
and Madame de Staël's influential work of popularisation, *De
l'Allemagne*, evaded Napoleon's censorship by being published in
England (first in French, and in English the next year, 1814).[31]
An image of Germany – based, it is true, on a highly eclectic
acquaintance with German writers – gained currency. This image
credited Germany with the development of a philosophy that presented a radical challenge to the materialist enlightenment, and that
consequently provided an example and encouragement to those
who, dissatisfied with Lockean man, Newtonian nature, and Paley's
God, felt themselves called upon to do battle with the eighteenth-
century legacy in thought and politics. For Carlyle, as for Madame
de Staël, German thinkers were attempting to inspire man towards
higher ends, to absolve him from the bondage of sense, to seek
within the mind inherent principles of moral action, and to reassert
the spiritual nature of man in the face of materialist determinism.
They proposed goals that rose above the realm of mere animal satisfaction, and offered a history of man's progress towards salvation.
For all interested onlookers, German writers composed, in the
politically and socially divided condition of Germany in the eighteenth century and under Napoleonic rule, a cultural common-

wealth filled with promise for the power of mind and letters over present circumstances. For the 'Philosophical system, adopted in any country, exerts a great influence over the direction of mind; it is the universal model after which all thought is cast; – those persons, even, who have not studied the system, conform, unknowingly, to the general disposition which it inspires'.[32] At the heart of this philosophical renaissance lay a new epistemology, heralded as a victory for human independence, which, as Carlyle put it, 'in direct contradiction to Locke and all his followers, commences from within and proceeds outwards; instead of commencing from without . . . and endeavouring to proceed inwards'.[33] I propose to examine first the idealist theory of knowledge and secondly the new movement in historical studies in so far as they found a response among the English thinkers with whom we shall be concerned.

Madame de Staël and Carlyle were in the fashion, both in looking at German philosophy as a spiritual renewal and in treating epistemology as central to that renewal. Both were less impressed by Kant's critical achievement than with the positive possibilities latent in his critiques. Both believed that he was a constructive metaphysician, and Carlyle declared his unwillingness or inability to discriminate between Kant's work and that of his followers.[34] By implication, therefore, they identified with those thinkers who built systems on Kant's foundations – with Fichte, Jacobi, or Schelling – rather than with the master himself. The eclecticism and confusions of English disciples of German idealism have long been a subject for comment among scholars,[35] and it is no part of my object to unravel them. I do, however, wish to emphasise the importance of idealism among those who advocate a clerisy. This may seem a strange assertion in a study which includes such a noted nominalist as John Stuart Mill. But even in Mill we find aspects of idealism at the points where his thought touches the kind of problems with which we are concerned. His 'intellectualism' – granting a predominant role in historical dynamics to the life of the mind – may well be seen as a surrogate idealism. As I intend to argue that we can meaningfully apply the term 'idealist' to elements in the work of proponents of the clerisy beyond the explicit idealists Coleridge and Carlyle, I should state what I take to be the broad characteristics of idealism, adding the warning that I am not describing formulated doctrine, but an *affectio quaerens intellectum*. This may be represented by the following tenets: (1) that the ideal forms are prior to the precarious and shifting phenomena of the material world; (2) that the sphere from which values emanate is harmonious and internally consistent; (3) that there is an essential affinity between the structure of the mind and the structure of the cosmos (or, on a smaller scale, the social organism); (4) that the finite mind, not being altogether the child of the sense world, can (under certain conditions) participate in the transcendent rational sphere. A disposition such as I have sketched is apt to come into prominence in a period of acute symbolic change: historical reality and the evanescence of symbolic structures once believed to be permanent, play on that very insecurity that seeks the assurance of an unchanging order. Society at large, with its material concerns, its presumed lack of foresight or memory, is taken to parallel the forces within the self which the regulative intellect keeps in check. 'The perfect frame of a man is the perfect frame of a state: and in the light of this idea we must read Plato's Republic', noted Coleridge.[36] The paradox of the idealism that attracted the proponents of the clerisy is that, while it urges the primacy of spirit over matter, and hence the possibility of human freedom, its allegiance is to a static order of truth. It thus ends up drawing tight the conceptual net over reality, and suggesting the superior value of unified modes of looking at the world. This is the same tendency, common in the Victorian age, which would read literature not as an experiment in mental activity but as the vehicle of 'truths', or philosophy less as a stimulus to thought than as a formal system.

English writers from Coleridge onwards, attached great importance to the distinction between two radically different modes of knowing, adapted by Kant's German successors out of his pure and practical reason, and converted into a higher and a lower faculty. Briefly, the importance of the distinction between the two modes was that the hypothesis of a higher kind of knowing (*Vernunft* – Coleridge's 'reason') through which truth could be directly apprehended, freed men from total dependence on naturalistically conditioned knowledge. The lower faculty (*Verstand* – Coleridge's 'understanding'), on the other hand, was that form of cognition that merely (for Kant's message has been distorted) deals with phenomena. As the form of cognition which generalises by reflection upon experienced sense data, its relationship to the world is the same as that of the human mind as a whole in Locke's theory. This distinction between the reason and the understanding, the mode of knowing the noumenal world and the mode of knowing the phenomenal world, allowed Jacobi's successors an escape from a world of absolute phenomena, and, holding out the possibility of freedom through knowledge, permitted a reaffirmation of the cognitive scale inherent in Platonism.

Any theory of knowledge implies a theory of education. Further, a mode of thought on one subject (particularly such a pervasive subject as that of the nature and limits of human knowledge) will often stimulate or confirm thinking about subjects which might appear to lie outside its own boundaries. Sometimes the subsequent parallels will be such that one can suspect an underlying structural affinity between the activities. Such is the case with the distinction between *Vernunft* and *Verstand*, which tends to generate or at least reinforce the division of mankind into different sorts of knowers, those who operate merely at the lower level, and the superior sort who can operate at both levels, irradiating understanding with reason. As Fichte pointed out,

[the] noble mind can indeed understand the thought of the ignoble, for we are all born and fashioned in Egoism, and have all lived in it, and it needs struggle and effort to destroy this old nature in us; but the ignoble cannot know the thoughts of the noble, because he has never entered the world to which they belong, nor traversed it as his world has of necessity been traversed in all its extent by the noble. The latter surveys both worlds, the former only that which holds him captive.[37]

Fichte's noble minds were to lead humanity along the path of salvation. Let us turn to our second subject, the new movement in historical studies.

In the nineteenth century, history was to become the exemplary discipline, and historical explanation the approved principle in study, whether of social institutions, of biology, of psychology, of theology, or of language. The reasons for this wholesale adoption of history as the key science are obscure, though, tarred with the same brush ourselves, we might guess that behind it lay the desire to make sense of and to exert some kind of intellectual control over the changes and discontinuities in the symbolic and social order of Europe. From the late eighteenth century, German writers had pioneered historical science both as an empirical study – historical scholarship as we know it was to a considerable extent the invention of those years – and as a philosophy devoted to the discovery of what Thomas Arnold (one of the first English exponents of the new history) called the 'deepest principles of past and present'.[38] Even where there was no direct influence, the new history worked along the lines laid down by Vico in *The New Science*. 'The nature of institutions is nothing but their coming into being at certain times and in certain guises',[39] he had written, and his successors set out to give a genetic account of institutions, and to investigate the dynamics of historical change. Implicit in the whole approach is a spirit of relativism, a withholding of immediate moral judgment on the past in the light of the present, in favour of inquiring into the reasons why things were as they were when they were. Out of this attitude comes a further tendency to treat historical periods as different from each other, and different, above all, from the present. The right activity for the historian is therefore not merely to ransack the past for examples or for stories of great men, but to enter sympathetically into the spirit of the age under study. Going with these imperatives for research, was a concern with the discovery of historical laws. It was this 'ideal history of the eternal laws which are instanced by the deeds of all nations in their rise, progress, maturity, decadence, and dissolution'[40] that constituted the true relevance of the past for the present. Consciousness of history thus became a kind of moral imperative, since meaningful social action presupposed an enlightened awareness of the nature of historical development, and of the perils your society was likely to have to face. Above all, it entailed awareness of the conflicts between classes underlying the surface phenomena of change. Progress might be history's law, but it was also an imperative; to play your part in social improvement you had to understand what was really happening, to recognise that history was a process of developing moral awareness, analogous with the growth of the individual from dependent childhood to moral adulthood. The new history challenged philosophers in three ways. By insisting on the unavoidable nature of change it offered a superior role to those who could subject the flux to interpretative categories; by offering a relativist account of institutions it endorsed a need for moral and cultural absolutes; by insisting on teleology it provided a course over which the enlightened portion of mankind could lead its followers.

Before examining some theories of the learned man and his social activities, we must investigate the blending of two concerns which for convenience we have just treated separately. Let us return briefly to Plato's description of the philosopher-ruler in the *Republic*. In the history of ideas we should not treat doctrines as though they were detachable from the period and culture in which they were formulated. But with due caution, and recognising that we can never wholly recapture the sense in which those words were used, we may grant that the appeal of Platonism has been perennial, and that Plato's statement of the doctrine of the philosopher-ruler is clear and explicit enough to be treated as representative of much subsequent thinking. So I return to the *Republic* in order to draw attention to a relevant aspect of what his most notorious modern critic has called 'the spell of Plato'. In the *Republic* the doctrine of the philosopher-ruler is clearly central. We have to recognise the dependence of the political upon the epistemological argument. The image of the cave will recur in this study; the philosophers have the right to tell society the way it should go, because they alone have access to the higher, immutable reality which is truth. In this context the famous argument for the convergence of knowing and being occurs. It has two consequences. One is that there is a hierarchy of knowing: the lower its objects in the scale of reality, the lower the kind of knowledge. The second consequence concerns the mass of people: as they know only the 'twilight world of change and decay', they are not capable of government. The potential state is conceived as a work of art which only those who have perceived the divine blueprint can create.

I believe that theories of the clerisy always rest upon theories of knowledge, and I hope to illustrate this later in nineteenth-century terms. Fundamental to the Platonic state of mind in any period is the conviction that change is always for the worse, and that the untidiness of history and the chaos of sense impressions cannot represent the *real* world. Reality must be sought in the domain of thought, among the ideas or forms. Whatever the translation, the enduring essentialism is there: the constructs of the mind are seen not as empirical and convenient but as devolving from the changeless ideal world. Matter is of inferior importance in the universal scheme. Whatever Coleridge might say about the division of mankind into born Platonists or born Aristotelians, the Aristotelian doctrine of 'substance' and 'accident' ministers to the same tendency: universals are real, but the contingent shapes they assume belong to an inferior order of reality. The more the concept can be dissociated from its material embodiment, the purer and, consequently, the more worthy of serious study it is. The epistemological hierarchy matches the ontological hierarchy. Our true lover of knowledge naturally strives for truth, and is not content with common opinion, but soars with undimmed and unwearied passion till he grasps the essential nature of things with the mental faculty fitted to do so, that is with the faculty which is akin to reality, and which approaches and unites with it, and begets intelligence and truth as children, and is only relaxed from travail when it has thus reached knowledge and true life and satisfaction.[41]

Surely this lingers behind many late eighteenth-century accounts of the faculty of 'reason'. Those with access to the eternal are rightful governors. As Socrates asks, knowing what answer he will get,

If philosophers have the ability to grasp eternal and immutable truths, and those who are not philosophers are lost in multiplicity and change, which of the two should be in charge of the state?

The converse is obvious:

So philosophy is impossible among the common people.
Quite impossible.
And the common people must disapprove of philosophers.
Inevitably.[42]

A strong ambivalence towards the political realm appears. For the true philosopher

whose mind is on higher realities, has not time to look at the affairs of man, or to take part in their quarrels. . . . His eyes are turned to contemplate fixed and immutable realities, a realm where there is no injustice but all is reason and order, and which is the model he imitates.[43]

But he must be compelled to govern, for the object of our legislation is

not the welfare of any particular class, but of the whole community. It uses persuasion or force to unite all citizens and make them share together the benefits which each individually can confer on the community; and its purpose in fostering this attitude is not to enable everyone to please himself, but to make each man a link in the unity of the whole.[44]

He is a desirable governor precisely because his allegiance is not to the everyday but to the higher world. Plato asks for his ruler the benefits both of mystic intuition and of secular domination. This seems to me unfair. The vision of the beautiful whole is too tempting; the road from persuasion to force, or the wish to exert force is fatally easy. In this politics of ultimate ends lies the answer to Popper's question how it is that the philosopher who will 'never willingly tolerate an untruth' can calmly prepare to propagate lies of supposed social utility. He is in love with 'the knowledge that reveals eternal reality, the realm unaffected by change and decay'.[45] By comparison the ordinary realm of human ventures must seem pretty trivial – so trivial that lying propaganda told for society's own good is but a venial sin. The philosopher is passionately committed to the true reality, while ordinary men, whose soul is sense, are inescapably committed to illusion. The object of true knowledge is purged of material adulteration, while the social world is portrayed in images of disorder and decay, as subject to the twin dangers of the mob and of sensual appetite. The historical world is beneath the philosopher's notice.

To the apparent contradiction between the new history and rationalist philosophy, the philosophy of history supplied a resolution. In the late eighteenth century, secular teleological interpretations of history came into fashion. Thus the threatening consequences of the new science – its attention to mundane detail, and its doctrine of fundamental change – appeared to be met by history itself. A large enough view of world history would show particularity and change itself in perspective, elucidating the meaning behind the phenomena; in this secularised theodicy, even evil men or destructive events would be seen to have played their part in the cunning of reason. Idealist historicism spelt the end of traditional theology: with his usual modesty, Fichte remarked that he knew the theologians' arguments, 'but I also know my own theory . . . too well not to perceive that it altogether supersedes the whole present theology, with all its pretensions'.[46] For the philosophic observer there is the lure of a stable viewpoint through comprehension of the processes of the absolute mind, to which a thousand years are but as a day. This is not the place for a discussion of the philosophies of history of Herder, Schelling, or Hegel, but I wish to draw attention to one aspect of this accommodation of history to rationalism which particularly concerns us.

Plato's theory of knowledge could be visualised as an ascending scale. Implicit in the histories of salvation which catalysed the idea of the clerisy was the projection of this scale on the temporal plane.[47] The history of the human race (recapitulated by each society in its turn) began from a childhood of dreams and delusions, and advanced through submission to external authority to a millenarian state of blessedness at present beyond the imagination of all but a few. The success of the ontogenetic metaphor, and the passion in intellectual circles for treating life as a process of *Bildung*, turned history into a colossal process of education. Towards the end of his life, in 1780, Lessing published his *Die Erziehung des Menschengeschlechts*, in which, in a mildly theistic manner, he proclaimed the parallelism between the education of the race and of the individual, and explained that the general path led from the authority of revelation to the autonomy of reason. Religious belief was, in fact, a relative stage in mankind's advance towards maturity, though those who felt they had outgrown the need for religious sanctions should nevertheless wait for their slower brethren to catch up. Lessing's argument and the scope of his *Erziehung* (education) clearly fulfilled a need, and, elaborated and extended, became widely diffused in late eighteenth- and early nineteenth-century Germany. Its relevance to our study is manifest. True radicalism, it was held, must start from the identity of history and education: the 'revolutionary desire to realize the Kingdom of God is the flexible starting point of progressive education and the principle of modern history', remarked Friedrich Schlegel.[48] Theories of the role of the learned as the vanguard and educators of humanity were not slow to arise in Germany where national unity existed at the level of culture alone. German writers prided themselves on belonging to a cultural commonwealth which rose above political and social barriers. Cultural and linguistic nationalism, forged in the struggle against French culture, gained new significance in the struggle against French political domination.

Fichte's *Addresses to the German Nation* (1807) constitute a practical act of the philosopher applying himself to a task which is at once educational and political. In 1774 Klopstock had published his *On the German Republic of Scholars*, a somewhat fantastic vision of a Germany organised under its scholar teachers, which had considerable influence on Hölderlin, Fichte, and even Goethe, sceptical as in some ways he was about cultural nationalism.[49] But the highest development of the idea of the scholar (*Gelehrter*) was left to Fichte's evangelical fervour. His account of the role of the scholar teacher, depending as it does on his philosophy of history, draws out every elitist implication of the nascent historical idealism. Fichte's Erlangen lectures *On the Nature of the Scholar* (1805) were known to Carlyle; indeed, they appear to be the only Fichte he read, but from them he gleaned much that seemed to endorse his own ideas. These lectures were the second series that Fichte had given on the subject. In 1794, in his radical youth, he had tried to infuse the unruly students of Jena with a sense of mission by means of his course *On the Vocation of a Scholar*. Very much a product of the time – not for nothing was Fichte to be suspected by the authorities of revolutionary sympathies – they argued that the aim of society was the 'perfect equality of all its members',[50] and that the true vocation of the scholar teacher was 'the most widely extended survey of the actual advancement of the human race, and the steadfast promotion of that advancement'.[51] The elite forms the advance guard of humanity. So far John Stuart Mill could have agreed. But even this early in Fichte's career, the scholar's vocation was conceived in weighty, quasi-religious terms:

The words which the founder of the Christian Religion addressed to his disciples apply with peculiar force to the Scholar – 'Ye are the salt of the earth; if the salt have lost its savour, wherewith shall it be salted?' – if the chosen among men be depraved, where shall we seek for moral good?[52]

The thought must occur to each of us, Fichte added, that 'I am the Priest of Truth'. By 1805, when he was lecturing at Erlangen and Berlin, this theme had drowned the rest. The world was not what it seemed to the 'uncultivated and natural sense of man', for the concealed foundation of all appearances was the 'Divine Idea'. The end of men's life on earth, he explained in his lectures on the *Characteristics of the Present Age*, was that they 'may order all their relations with FREEDOM according to REASON'.[53] This was, needless to say, a remote end. At present we were only in the third age (characterised by liberation from external authority and indifference to truth) of the five ages of universal history, and the Divine Idea was accessible only to the scholar who had, through a rigorous self-cultivation inspired by 'an all-engrossing love for the Idea', become the agent of reason in history. He was thus the mediator between the Idea and the everyday world, since 'common observation . . . is quite blind to the Idea'.[54] An enormous disdain for those who were not scholars developed:

No one . . . should intermeddle in the direct guidance and ordering of human events, who is not a Scholar in the true sense of the word. . . . With labourers and hodmen it is otherwise: – their virtue consists in punctual obedience, in the careful avoidance of all independent thought, and in confiding the direction of their occupations to other men.[55]

It will be seen that Fichte followed out the logic of his historical idealism. The sequel was an irritable insistence on the holiness of the scholar and his vocation: he had been sent into the world 'that the

eternal counsel of God in this universe may through me be seen of
men in another, hitherto unknown light.'[56] He would shun the world
of transitory appearances, saying to himself 'I am eternal, and it is
below the dignity of the eternal to waste itself on things that perish.'
Conscious of his sacred mission, he would avoid contact with the
'vulgar and ignoble', and repudiate jesting. In the complete scholar
personal life would be extinguished in the life of the idea,[57] and
Fichte delineated a hierarchy of scholars, of which the top rank
would be occupied by those who mediated between the pure spiritu-
ality of thought and the 'material energy and influence' which that
thought acquired through the work of scholars more directly involved in the affairs of the mundane world.

New and exciting ideas about history and progress have merged
in Fichte's account of the scholar teacher and his role. And they
have merged under a presupposition that there must be an aristocracy of spirit, performing its function in a world subject to law.
Fichte's thought generates little bands of saviours – everything 'great
and good upon which our present existence rests ... has an existence
only because noble and powerful men have resigned all enjoyments
for the sake of Ideas'.[58] The thinkers whom we have been reviewing
set about transmuting on behalf of the intellectual caste notions
derived from the aristocratic culture which prevailed in eighteenth-
century Germany. From middle class (or even, like Fichte, from
artisan class) backgrounds, they must often have felt themselves outsiders. Wilheim Meister – here, surely, speaking for Goethe himself –
spoke, like many intellectuals of the period, of self-cultivation as his
purpose in life, but went on to say how difficult this quest was for the
burgher:

> personal cultivation is beyond the reach of any one except a nobleman.
> [The nobleman] does and makes, the [burgher] but effects and procures; he
> must cultivate some single gifts in order to be useful, and it is beforehand
> settled that in his manner of existence there is no harmony and can be none,
> since he is bound to make himself of use in one department and so has to
> relinquish all the others.[59]

On achieving – often with difficulty – eminent positions, German
intellectuals were naturally inclined to adopt patrician notions.
Fichte, in particular, found that since the mass felt reluctance for
the life of the idea, it would require external authority for a long
time to come. And since in this transitional age the former powers
were passing away, he visualised the revolution as bringing in the

rule of the intellectuals, themselves free from external constraint.[60] The mantle of the aristocracy was to descend upon the scholars. The harbingers of this state of affairs adopted a tone consonant with the dignity which history was keeping in store. 'The realm of the sciences', Schelling remarked, 'is not a democracy, still less an ochlocracy, but an aristocracy in the best sense of the word',[61] and he observed further that if

anything could arrest the rising tide that ever more visibly is wiping out the barriers between the superior and the inferior – even the rabble has begun to write, and every plebeian aspires to be a critic – then it is philosophy, whose natural motto is *Odi profanum vulgus et arceo.*[62]

This dual attitude must be remembered: the pursuit of philosophy is the means of raising society, but ought to remain the preserve of the few.

Education in an extended sense, the diffused process of leading society away from that pure 'thoughtlessness' which was its natural state, was the implied solution to more than one problem of political theory.[63] The notion that governments had an ethical duty to improve their subjects – in itself agreeable, presumably, to any of the so-called 'enlightened' despots of the age – was by the end of the century taking an educational form. The image of the educational community, paternally organised for the benefit of its members, spreads from Pestalozzi's *Leonard und Gertrud* to Robert Owen's New Lanark. The thought struck Froebel during his musings at Göttingen that 'politics itself was in its essence but a means of uplifting man from the necessities of Nature and of life to the freedom of the spirit and of the will'.[64] Similarly, even if we do not father 'totalitarian democracy' on Rousseau, we must recognise that the famous distinction between the *volonté générale* and the *volonté de tous* and his suggestion that on occasion a man must be 'forced to be free', created a crux with serious implications for political as well as educational theory. His successors had to ponder the means by which the mere aggregative will could become the rational will. Of the thinkers with whom we shall be dealing, Coleridge, Arnold, and Mill made distinctive contributions to the debate. Within the politico-educational tradition the realisation of society and the perfecting of man presupposes a pedagogic process in which a leading part will inevitably be played by the enlightened.

Two concepts that were developed in the German thought of the period and that were to prove formative in educational thinking remain for brief consideration: the concepts of dialectic and of mediation. By dialectic I mean nothing more esoteric than the reading of intellectual processes in terms of the relationship of opposites which are, despite their conflict, mutually necessary. We may glance back at an English source.

The Earl of Shaftesbury's speculations on aesthetics and on the nature and role of the cultivated man were influential in eighteenth-century Europe. At the heart of his philosophy was what he called 'our sovereign remedy and gymnastic method' of internal soliloquy. Philosophy, he claimed, ought not to be a matter of esoteric speculation, but the knowledge of human nature and of yourself which followed from conducting an unremitting internal dialogue.[65] What Shaftesbury proposed for the individual virtuoso, his German successors were inclined to attribute to the human mind. One incentive to do so was restlessness under Kant's insistence on the limitations of the intellect: ambitious thinkers could not stomach the thought that only contradictions could emerge from the attempt of the human mind to apply its science to objects beyond the bounds of experience. The Kantian inheritance, nevertheless, seemed to offer a range of binary concepts between which relations might be established. The relevance of this to our immediate concerns is that social and intellectual processes were seen in a new way: not as mere accumulation or linear development, but as resulting from the tension or strife between opposed principles – such complementary but jarring pairs as stalk the pages of Coleridge and Matthew Arnold. They are not merely satisfactory modes of description; they are inherent properties of the subjects of discussion.

Schiller's exciting work *On the Aesthetic Education of Man* is the first example of the elaboration of this approach to educational and intellectual matters. Published in instalments in 1794, it forms an instructive contrast with his friend Fichte's *Vocation* lectures of the same year. To Schiller, reason and nature, moral freedom and physical necessity, unity and multiplicity, personal identity and the otherness of the ambient world, did not stand in irreconcilable conflict with each other. Neither did human development demand the suppression of one term in the interests of the other. For a human being or a society to thrive required the recognition of the complementary nature of opposed drives. In the absence of cultivated sense-awareness, intellect was impoverished – reason and nature both had their legitimate claims: 'Hence it will always argue a still defective education if the moral character is able to assert itself only by sacrificing the natural. And a political constitution will still be very imperfect if it is able to achieve unity only by suppressing variety.'[66] Dialectical play between opposites became a formative notion in some theories of the clerisy, from Coleridge's opposition of permanence and progression to Mannheim's ideology and utopia. The unattached intelligentsia mediated between the conservative and progressive terms.

The idea of mediation arises out of the positing of polarities which characterises dialectical thought. If the polarities are to be related or integrated there must be some third term in which they meet and interpenetrate. In Schiller's *Aesthetic Letters* this term was provided by aesthetic play, in which man's two basic drives could counterbalance each other and thus bring about his freedom. In Coleridge and his followers the clerisy acts as both horizontal and vertical mediator, mediating both between the noumenal and phenomenal worlds and, within society, between the forces of permanence and of progression. Without it, society would not only be divided against itself, but also adrift, without chart or guide. Dialectic can of course be resolved, and rare indeed are the thinkers who look forward to no permanent resolution. Shaftesbury's practical philosophy, as I noted, prescribes internal dialogue. To further this end, in his customary tone of judicious pleasantry, he tells the fable of Appetite, the elder brother, Reason, the younger brother, and Will, the top or football between them. But the aim of the dialogue is not, it turns out, the stimulus of the dialogue itself, but the victory of reason. Like Arnold, and in strikingly similar terms, Shaftesbury proposes a 'better' and an 'ignoble' self. Every one, he says, is convinced of the reality of the better self, but

[the] misfortune is, we are seldom taught to comprehend this self by placing it in a distinct view from its representative or counterfeit.[67]

This he proposed to do. Philosophy turns out to be the friend of honesty and morality in subjecting to questioning the desires of the ignoble self which present themselves in the guise of fancies or lawless imaginings. Upon the 'bottom' of pleasure in being honest and moral,

let me try how I can bear the assault of Fancy, and maintain myself in my moral fortress against the attacks which are raised on the side of corrupt interest and a wrong self.[68]

Examples of rational questioning follow, and end in inevitable dismissal of what (in a significant turn of phrase) Shaftesbury called the 'lady fancies'. What, one wonders, becomes of a dialogue where the presumption of rightness is so complacently on one side? To make his point, Shaftesbury employs a rhetorical question:

Can there be strength of mind, can there be command over myself, if the ideas of pleasure, the suggestions of fancy, and the strong pleadings of appetites and desire are not withstood, and the imaginations soundly reprimanded and brought under subjection?[69]

Dr Johnson would have approved. So would many exponents of the clerisy, drawn back from antinomian temptations to an eighteenth-century psychology of discrete faculties, and apt to resolve the dialectic in favour of the 'higher' term. Moral purity – understood as triumph over the promptings of the animal self – becomes the goal of the philosopher, and the ground of his relationship to the mass of his fellows. Morality, observed Schelling, liberates the soul from alien, material elements:

True knowledge turns away from mere reflections of the infinite in the finite, towards being-in-itself or primordial knowledge, requiring complete resolution of the particular in the universal, i.e. moral purity of the soul. Conversely, there is no true ... morality without the soul's being at home in the world of Ideas. A man who has not purified his soul to the point of participating in primal knowledge has not attained moral perfection: the pure universal appears as something outside himself.[70]

From such imperatives – attractive as they were to theorists of the clerisy – certain consequences follow.

The first of these, to which the quotation from Schelling points, is the rooted suspicion of material nature, including all the biological and economic processes by virtue of which human life exists. If we are bent on expelling nature as far as possible from ourselves, we shall be unlikely to regard the natural world as a suitable subject for the highest study, and are likely to cherish contemplation rather than activity as the highest good. Coleridge confided to his Notebook the thought that there is 'something inherently mean in action. Even the creation of the universe disturbs my Idea of the Almighty's greatness – would do so, but that I conceive that thought with him creates.'[71] This ambivalence towards the material world is all the more striking in one with Coleridge's eye for the particular, and informed curiosity about the science of his day. But it indicates an attitude which denies the natural sciences any but an inferior or specialised significance in education and culture. Schelling, writing on the subject of university studies, insists over and over again on the necessity of subordinating the study of the particulars of science to the universal ideas manifested through them. He starts from a proposition that might seem to anticipate Popper's work on scientific inquiry: 'there is no reason for regarding the experimental investigation of nature as superior to theory, for only theory guides it; without theory it would be impossible to "put nature to the question" '.[72] But where Popper's logic requires a kind of dialectic between hypothesis and observation in the course of which hypothesis may be disproved, but can never become anything other than hypothesis, Schelling rises above observation in favour of intuiting the form. Thus, for example, the more general the view from which the anatomist 'derives the genesis of forms and the less closely modelled on individual cases, the sooner will he grasp the extraordinary simplicity of so many natural structures'.[73] High speculation, with its emphasis on the philosopher's self-sufficiency and dignity, must not sully itself with the empirical study of nature or practicality.

R. Hookyas has recently challenged the received idea that modern science is the lineal descendant of the Greek spirit of inquiry. In his seminal study, *Religion and the Rise of Modern Science*, he suggests that the rationalist tradition overestimated the value of speculation and correspondingly underestimated the value of manual work and technical skill.[74] Thus, fusion with the Biblical and Christian attitude towards labour was a precondition for the rise of experimental science. Certainly, a patronising attitude towards *techne* characterised the rationalists with whom we are dealing, and they did much to legitimate a situation in which natural science was (and is still, by a series of long-institutionalised suspicions and associations) debarred from its rightful place in general culture.

By a curious irony, which has gone largely unnoticed in debates about the 'two cultures', natural science has not been the only area of cultural endeavour to fall under the suspicions of the prospective clerisy. They also entertained ambivalent feelings towards art. If abstract thought was the highest mental activity of which men were capable, then the thought least dependent on concrete images was to be most highly prized. Even the poets fell, as we have noted, under suspicion. I have already spoken of the projection upon a temporal plane of the Platonic scale of knowledge. One consequence of this theory was the assumption that poetry, like myth, was a characteristic of the primitive mind. Consequently it represented a stage of human thought which the enlightened had already grown out of. Vico asserted an identity between the thought of poets, primitive peoples, and children. The more advanced a people, the more abstract its thought. The argument is central to the second book of *The New Science* ('Poetic Wisdom'), where we find the predictable identification between image and sense on the one hand, and abstraction and intellect on the other.[75] Human history is the progress towards a higher kind of cognition. The argument about language and thought found an heir in positivism. In the tradition with which we are dealing, the distrust of poetry and of the non-verbal arts is sustained by a repudiation not only of the sense world, but also of fantasy, the mental representative of the lawless self, and by the consequent inclination to assert the magisterial powers of intellect. Kant, whose ethical imperative is, after all, one of constraint, of compelling your own adherence to the categorical imperative, devoted some interesting pages of the 'Critique of Aesthetic Judgement' to the manner in which the sublime can be presented to our minds. The appreciation of sublimity is a moral act; we cannot call anything sublime unless it awakens our consciousness of intellectual strength:

the sublime must in every case have reference to our *way of* thinking, i.e. to maxims directed to giving the intellectual side of our nature and the ideas of reason supremacy over sensibility.

We have no reason to fear that the feeling of the sublime will suffer from an abstract mode of presentation like this, which is altogether negative as to what is sensuous. For though the imagination ... finds nothing beyond the sensible world to which it can lay hold, still this thrusting aside of the sensible barriers gives it a feeling of being unbounded; and that removal is thus a presentation of the infinite.... Perhaps there is no more sublime passage in the Jewish law than the commandment: Thou shalt not make unto thee any graven image, or any likeness of any thing that is in heaven or earth, or under the earth &c. This commandment can alone explain the enthusiasm which the Jewish people, in their moral period, felt for their religion when comparing themselves with others.... The very same holds good of our representation of the moral law and of our native capacity for morality.[76]

It was this imperialism of the abstract intellect that Hazlitt censured in contemporary philosophers, and to which he felt with bitterness that Wordsworth and Coleridge had sold out.[77] But to the codifiers of consciousness, the artistic impulse with its springs in fantasy and its realisation in images of the sensible world was bound to be suspect. Schiller envisaged aesthetic activity (in the broadest sense) as consisting in experimental and liberating play, for 'man only plays when he is in the fullest sense of the word a human being, and he is only fully a human being when he plays'.[78] Schelling, by contrast, wished to know what philosophers, who aim at truth by way of intellectual intuition, not by the eye of sense, could have to do with art, 'whose sole purpose is to produce visible beauty and whose products are merely deceptive images of truth or wholly sensual'. His answer was:

I speak of art in a more sacred sense – of the art which, in the words of the ancients, is an instrument of the gods, herald of divine mysteries, unveiler of the Ideas. It is that preternatural beauty whose inviolate light illumines only pure souls, which is as hidden to the sensible eye as pure truth itself. The philosopher is not interested in what the vulgar call art. To him, art is a direct and necessary expression of the absolute, and only insofar as this can be demonstrated has it any reality to him.[79]

Purged of sensual contamination, and illuminating only pure souls (it should plainly not make a practice of dining with publicans and sinners), art attracted only in so far as it was inviolate. If art was to be set apart like this, the fate of ordinary human activities was likely to be even worse. The kind of culture for which the clerisy would stand excluded base life, and thus courted its own impoverishment. Ultimately it risked institutionalisation as a special activity, a free-floating criticism of the world.

In a similar way, the goal of the philosopher was independence from the demands of vulgar reality. Unlike Schiller, the clerisy theorists proposed to weight the dialectic, and hankered after a resolution in favour of the 'higher' term. The result was to set up two models of mental life: one – a higher, speculative, moral type, insulated as far as possible against the encroachments of image, sense, and fantasy – characterised the elite. The other – a lower type, practical and limited – was attributed to the mass, whose only hope of salvation lay in obedience to the moral code sponsored from above. The model for mind and the model for society are one, and preference should be given to contemplation, rather than to activity; to speculative, rather than to practical thought; to high seriousness, solemnity even, rather than to play.

The tendency to suspend the dialectic, perceptible in Coleridge,

Carlyle, or Arnold, has repercussions for the concept of mediation. For in the presence of higher and lower terms, enlightenment becomes a one way process, the luminescence of the higher irradiating the lower faculty. In the last of the *Aesthetic Letters*, Schiller proposed the notion of the 'third state', the aesthetic realm, parallel to the imagination in the individual, in which the mutual inter-penetration of the formal, rational drive and the natural, instinctual drive could be carried on. There, duty must respect nature; the claims of unity those of multiplicity; and knowledge, ceasing to be a monopoly of the schools, could become a common possession of human society. This was a description of a social possibility, even though, as a realised fact, the third state existed, 'like the pure Republic, only in some few chosen circles'.[80] When the 'third state' is metamorphosed into the clerisy, the concept of mediation has been thoroughly institutionalised. A comparable contrast exists between Schiller's aesthetic education, and an education based on books. Under the new dispensation, the mediators, like Fichte's *Gelehrter*, take on an awful dignity comparable to that of the artist as inspired teacher of Romantic mythology; Hölderlin objected to Schiller's play theory, finding it incompatible with his own conception of the prophetic and religious mission of the poet.[81] Shelley was drawn into a vast overestimate of what it was possible for poetry to achieve in the social world. The principle is the same as that underlying the theory of the clerisy: the pure, ideal world is mediated to the impure, real world through mediators who assume a dignity commensurate with their quasi-sacred mission. It is a principle with enormous attraction, even (paradoxically) for those who were inspired by the dialectical model for mind and education. The attribution of transcendent importance to one term of the dialectic constitutes a heritage which we cannot afford to take at its own valuation. Improbable as it may seem, a study of the clerisy ideal in its first century of development may have implications for theories of learning and education that are only indirectly related to the subject of that study.

2

THE IDEA OF THE CLERISY:
SAMUEL TAYLOR COLERIDGE

I hold it the disgrace and calamity of a professed statesman not to know and acknowledge, that a permanent, nationalized, learned order, a national clerisy or Church is an essential element of a rightly constituted nation, without which it wants the best security alike for its permanence and its progression; and for which neither tract societies nor conventicles, nor Lancasterian schools, nor mechanics' institutions, nor lecture bazaars under the absurd name of universities, nor all these collectively can be a substitute.

Coleridge, *On the Constitution of the Church and State according to the Idea of Each*

It is not merely because he gave us the word that Coleridge figures first in a study of the idea of the clerisy in nineteenth-century England. In his last completed work, *On the Constitution of the Church and State according to the Idea of Each*, he gave a wide-ranging account of the clerisy and its relations to society. But the idea was germane to his most central thinking, and in his work, his aspirations, and dilemmas we can watch the theory growing, and sense what needs it was supposed to answer. Individual as his theory is, its study is an essential preliminary to the study of the clerisy theme in the nineteenth century, for his response to problems which in fact survived him was in a sense paradigmatic. Above all, Coleridge's argument on behalf of the clerisy must make us aware of the inter-connection of philosophy, theology, and social theory within educational politics. Let us not forget his own words: 'Of this however we may be certain . . . that our minds are in a state unsusceptible of Knowledge when we feel an eagerness to detect the falsehood of an adversary's reasonings, not a sincere wish to discover if there be Truth in them.[1] While asking questions about the nature of Coleridge's projected order, we must be aware of the fertility of his insights, and even, paradoxically, of the dependence of those insights on the very theory which we wish to criticise.

37

HARMONY OR DISSOLUTION?

In June 1817, the Prime Minister, Lord Liverpool, received a letter from Coleridge, by then domiciled with the Gillmans at Highgate. Social tensions, following the end of the Napoleonic Wars and the subsequent economic depression, were increasing: sterner measures were in train for the control of the radical press, the army was standing by to put down insurrections, and Cobbett had fled to the United States. Coleridge wrote to strip down the affairs of the nation to their essential principles. As R. J. White pointed out, the letter is a classic instance of Coleridge's sense of the interconnectedness of things. His science, his philosophy, and his sociology are inextricable from each other.

As long as the principles of our Gentry and Clergy are grounded on a false Philosophy, which retains but the name of *Logic*, and has succeeded in rendering Metaphysics a term of opprobrium, all the Sunday and National schools in the world will not preclude Schism in the middle & lower classes. The predominant philosophy is the keynote.[2]

The national health required the acceptance of what Coleridge was beginning to call the 'dynamic philosophy' – that system of thought which he had been working towards with the help of the writings of Kant, Fichte, and Schelling, since his German visit in 1799, and which he saw as a continuation of the great Platonic tradition. The mechanical philosophy which it should replace was, he argued, inimical to social life because it located life not in the whole but in the parts, and viewed institutions as artificial contrivances of convenience. The consequence was the disaster of natural rights theory, of which Coleridge shared Burke's opinion:

The independent atoms of the state of nature cluster round a common centre and make a convention; that convention becomes a constitution of government; then the makers and the made make a contract, which ensures to the former the right of breaking it whenever it shall seem good to them, and assigns to the governed an indefeasible right of sovereignty over their governors, which being withstood, this one-sided compact is dissolved, the compages fall abroad into the independent atoms aforesaid, which are then to dance the Hayes until a new constitution is made for them. For, as Mr. Locke and Major Cartwright sagaciously observe, an atom is an atom, neither more nor less, and by the pure attribute of his atom has an equal claim with every other atom to be constituent and demiurgic on all occasions.[3]

Amusing, after the second *Treatise of Civil Government,* but not
exactly open to what a Cartwright might be trying to achieve.
'The predominant philosophy is the keynote.' Coleridge linked the
mechanistic nature of enlightenment thought with its individualism
and its materialism, and saw these blooms as rooted in the common
soil of associationist psychology. But enlightenment thought had had
its day, and one had now to work one's way back to the recognition
that life was not to be predicated of parts, but of wholes. The thesis
of the primacy of speculative philosophy, with its implied correlative
– the importance of the speculative philosopher – must be seen in the
context of what Alfred Cobban rather misleadingly called the 'revolt
against the eighteenth century'.[4] Cobban's simplification of both
eighteenth century and revolt, as well as the implied chronological
watershed, is nevertheless well grounded in the self-images of those
whom he studied. For Coleridge, as for Burke, the age of reason (so
called) ended quite logically in the excesses of the French Revolution.

The primacy of speculative philosophy runs through Coleridge's
work, and is the premise upon which his own practice as a prophetic
social commentator is based. Two examples may clarify the point.
The breakdown of Roman politics in the era of the triumvirates and
civil wars was one with the dearth of philosophy:

The eye which was the light of the body had become filmed and jaundiced.
The only two nations which possessed intellect, and with that intellect the
power of communicating order and civilisation were corrupted and became
the vilest of the vile.[5]

Or again, he asserted that:

the history of all civilised nations . . . the recorded experience of Mankind
[attests] the important fact – that the Taste and Character, the whole tone
of Manners and Feeling, and above all the Religious (at least the Theological) and the Political tendencies of the public mind, have ever borne
such a close correspondence, so distinct and evident an Analogy to the
predominant system of speculative Philosophy . . . as must remain inex-
plicable, unless we admit not only a reaction and interdependence on both
sides, but a powerful, tho' most often indirect influence of the latter on the
former.[6]

It would be a travesty of Coleridge's thought to say that he ana-
chronistically asserted a kind of philosophical determinism at a time
when the political economists had already drawn attention to the
importance of material wealth in creating the national life. The

Coleridge who involved himself in the struggle for the passage of
Sir Robert Peel's child labour bill, or whose letters show him concerned in the debate over the Corn Laws, was not one to overlook
the economic foundations of society. But his very awareness of the
importance of economic activity seems to have bred a correspondingly great emphasis on the intellectual activity that was to keep
economic life in its proper, subordinate place. The formation of a
just understanding of the parts of the national life in relation to one
another depended on the currency of a life-giving philosophy among
the higher classes.

Characteristic of the imbalance between elements of the national
life was the development of civilisation at the expense of cultivation.
Coleridge's distinction between the two must be seen in the context
of other complementary pairs of terms to which the dialectical
nature of his thought gave rise. Like other pairs of opposites
(Coleridge was at pains to distinguish between opposites, which were
complementary, and contraries, which were essentially different
from each other) – reason and understanding, genius and talent,
imagination and fancy – it represents another aspect of that
Entzweiung which Kant's successors strove to overcome. The 'permanent distinction and the occasional contrast, between cultivation
and civilisation', between material progress and moral culture, was
one which all Coleridge's successors retained.[7] The distinction served
not only in criticising the contemporary world but as an aid to
reflection on history, since periods could be characterised in terms of
the predominance of civilisation or culture. We must remember the

momentous fact, fearfully as it has been, and even now is exemplified in a
neighbour country, that a nation can never be too cultivated, but may easily
become an over-civilised, race.[8]

First publicly made in 1808, the distinction remained central to
Church and State over twenty years later. Civilisation

is in itself but a mixed good, if not far more a corrupting influence, the
hectic of disease, not the bloom of health, and a nation so distinguished
more fitly to be called a varnished than a polished people; where this
civilisation is not grounded in *cultivation*, in the harmonious development
of those qualities and faculties that characterize our *humanity*.[9]

England was in danger of becoming permanently enamoured of
civilisation, and hence wasting in disease. Yet to represent the threat
thus was to take the actual course of material development as the

only possible type of such development; thus the corrective to existing civilisation was envisaged not as an alternative form of civilisation but as cultivation.

In the place of the philosophy of the enlightenment we should put the 'dynamic philosophy', whose acceptance would be – the musical image is insistent – a return to harmony, to a recognition of the essential interconnectedness of things. Towards the end of his life Coleridge once said, as reported by his nephew:

All harmony is founded on a relation to rest – a relative rest. Take a metallic plate and strew sand on it; sound an harmonic chord over the sand, and the grains will whirl about in circles and other geometrical figures, all, as it were, depending on some point of sand relatively at rest. Sound a discord, and every grain will whisk about without any order at all, in no figures and with no points of rest.

The clerisy of a nation, that is, its learned men, whether poets, or philosophers, or scholars, are these points of relative rest. There could be no order, no harmony of the whole without them.[10]

The development of the idea of the clerisy is inseparable from the war against mechanist philosophy and associationist psychology, a campaign which Coleridge found prefigured in Plato's confrontation with the sophists. For Plato

taught the idea, namely the possibility, and the duty of all who would arrive at the greatest perfection of the human mind, of striving to contemplate things not in their phenomenon, not in their superficies, but in their essential powers, first as they exist in relation to the other powers, then as they exist in relation to the other powers co-existing with them, but lastly and chiefly as they exist in the Supreme Mind, independent of all material division, distinct and yet indivisible.[11]

We shall return to the image of Plato and his reinstatement of universals. Here I must insist on the political dimension of Coleridge's thought. Continued adherence to a false philosophy threatens society with dissolution in asserting the state as an artificial contrivance for meeting the needs of an aggregate of individuals. But the state, asserts Coleridge, is no such thing:

It is high time, My Lord, that the subjects of Christian Governments should be taught that neither historically nor morally, in fact or by right, have men made the state; but that the state, and that alone makes them men.

Depend upon it, whatever is grand, whatever is truly organic and living, the whole is prior to the parts.

Who does not know what a poor worthless creature man would be if it were not for the unity of human nature being preserved from age to age through the godlike form of the state?[12]

The state is defined in terms of its ultimate end. There is, however, a corollary, though one on which Coleridge was chary of insisting. If the state fails in its moral and educational duty towards its citizens, it absolves them of their obligation to the state. Thus, in speaking of Henry VIII's alienation of the church lands (in Coleridge's terms, the 'Nationalty'), he speaks of them as dedicated to 'the potential divinity in every man, which is the ground and condition of his *civil* existence, that without which a man can be neither free nor obliged, and by which alone, therefore, he is capable of being a free subject – a citizen'.[13] The theory of the minimal state is therefore self-destructive. The alternative to a recognition of the state's ethical role to humanise its citizens is the continuance of a state of affairs which will lead straight to social dissolution and the naked struggle of particular interests. Let us continue by examining the alternative to this stark possibility.

THE DYNAMIC PHILOSOPHY

To examine Coleridge's philosophy is a notoriously perilous exercise. I cannot hope, even if I wished, to emulate all those commentators who have unravelled Coleridge's thought.[14] What I want to do is something rather different: to suggest some of the drives evidenced by his thought, and their connection with the putative role of the clerisy. This will mean taking issue to some extent with the immensely suggestive accounts of his thought given by Walter Jackson Bate and Thomas McFarland. For Bate claims that the

overriding philosophical interest of Coleridge, from the time that he became a disciple of David Hartley . . . until the end, was in unity of interpretation, unity of feeling, unity of relationship of every sort, but with no sacrifice of the claims of diversity. At the same time this lifelong hunger for unity . . . is counterbalanced in Coleridge by his openness to the obdurate detail, the unexpected nuance, the resistant qualification, and by his eagerness in every case to rescue it into a higher synthesis.[15]

And McFarland that

Coleridge's endeavour was always towards system. But this orientation was first of all the need to connect rather than the need to complete.[16]

Coleridge's tendency was indeed towards unity, towards connection in ever greater wholes. But I shall argue that his tendency was, increasingly as he grew older, to retreat from the obdurate detail towards the sphere from which he could, so to speak, legislate for the world by the means of thoughts; to escape the menacing power of the particular by subsuming it within a larger conception.

Now, Coleridge's dynamic philosophy is a form of idealism and begins with Kant, in whose work he had immersed himself. ('I reverence Immanuel Kant with my whole heart and soul', he once wrote.)[17] But like so many of Kant's followers, Coleridge could not believe that he had meant to stop where he did. Kant was, he held, really a constructive metaphysician.[18] Left where it was, the great Critique stopped short at a dualism that offered no real challenge to the Lockes, Condillacs, and Hartleys of this world, for Kant had failed to follow his trail to its transcendental end. Fichte, whom Coleridge soon learned to reject, did, nevertheless provide the missing link. He 'has the merit of having prepared the ground for and laid the first stone of, the *Dynamic Philosophy* by the substitution of Act for thing'.[19] Now Coleridge had a starting place for a philosophy based on a theory of mind and the world as process.

We can rarely be so keenly aware of the unity of impulse of Coleridge's mature thought as when studying the connection between his social writings, his scientific speculation, and the articulation of the dynamic philosophy with which his letters show him engaged from the beginning of the second decade of the nineteenth century. All plurality is mediated through the oneness of God – 'The eternal identity of Allness and Oneness'. This is a principle that obtains throughout the created universe. Matter itself is describable in terms of relationship, and the relationship between subject and object is another one whose joint product is something other than either of the two taken separately. His thought is dialectical to the very pith. It is worth quoting part of a long letter written to Gillman about the time when Coleridge was beginning his engagement with the philosophy of life.

The sum of all . . . is; that in all things alike, great and small, you must seek the *reality* not in any imaginary *elements* . . . all of which considered as other than elementary relations . . . are mere fictions. . . . The Alphabet of Physics no less of Metaphysics, of Physiology no less than of Psychology, is an Alphabet of *Relations*, in which N is N only because M is M and O, O. The reality of all alike is the A and Ω, far rather that Ineffable which is neither Alpha separately, nor Omega separately ... but the Identity of both.[20]

All that suggested the interdependence of related energies was grist to Coleridge's mill. He seized on recent investigations of the nature of electricity and magnetism, and assured Lord Liverpool that recent chemical discoveries 'almost force upon the senses the facts of a mutual penetration and intus-susception, which have supplied a series of experimental proofs that in all pure phenomena we behold only the copula, the balance, or indifference of opposite energies'.[21] His thought, I have suggested, was dialectical, but the dialectic was imperative as much as descriptive. So long as we grounded ourselves on a false philosophy – a philosophy, that is, that denied the dialectical relationships between what would thus be falsely assumed to be discrete phenomena – the human mind would be adrift in the universe, and society correspondingly atomised. The affinities between mind and world were for Coleridge a liberating discovery. But so long as the predominant philosophy (or 'anti-philosophy') denied this common ground of relationship, social life could not be led back to the state of harmony in which mutual duties and obligations, and the subordination of the parts to the whole would be recognised.

Above all, the community would acknowledge its relationship to its God. Coleridge's social thought is theistic, and while religion was not philosophy, it was nevertheless the goal towards which all true philosophy aspired:

True Philosophy begins with the τὸ Θεῖον in order to end in the ὁ Θεος; takes its root in Science in order to blossom into Religion.[22]

The growth of the whole community towards vital religion must be fostered. The interconnection of religion and philosophy involved a social thesis:

This I shall, I hope, shew: that as religion never can be philosophy, because the only true philosophy proposes religion as its end and supplement, so on the other hand there can be no true notions of religion among men at large without just notions of philosophy in the higher classes.[23]

Coleridge's ideal community was actively involved with its God:

Religion, true or false, is and ever has been the centre of gravity in a realm, to which all other things must and will accommodate themselves.[24]

The dynamic philosophy was the only one that could make creative sense of the natural and social worlds:

By celestial observations alone can even terrestrial charts be constructed scientifically.[25]

The formative core, the hope that released Coleridge's intellectual energy, was the desire for unity, for a monistic vision in which all discrete phenomena might be subsumed in a greater whole. This is what had tempted him in Spinoza, but Spinozism was pantheism, and pantheism terrified Coleridge because, as McFarland has well demonstrated, he was so tempted by it. Pantheism was, he came to argue, tantamount to atheism.[26] But a monism of the spirit, in which all matter would turn out to be but an expression of the activities of spirit, was different, and towards the achievement of such a philosophy Coleridge strove for the last twenty-odd years of his life, struggling with what was to become the much described but never completed *Magnum Opus*. For he was possessed by what Lovejoy has called a 'metaphysical pathos', and, cruelly unfair as Carlyle's portrait of the Highgate Coleridge is, it contains some truth.[27] We may not agree with Carlyle that Coleridge used a version of Kant to introduce orthodox theology through the back door. As Hort recognised, theologians have much to learn from Coleridge's orthodoxy, if that is what it is.[28] But we may sense that he distanced the world by means of the very speculations through which he sought to encompass it. Much discussion of his thought has taken it as though it were intended empirically, and as though his insights could be appropriated without regard to the metaphysical strivings out of which they arose. The approach has been valuable in so far as it has de-mystified Coleridge, and directed attention to the seminal quality of so much of his thought.[29] Yet the spirit in which Coleridge undertook his metaphysical pursuits is not absent from what appears as his pragmatic thought, and his metaphysics are consequently unavoidable in any discussion of his educational and social prescriptions. Without being guilty of irresponsible reductivism, we might suggest that his metaphysical drive represents a striving after assurance that the philosopher, if he works faithfully, may be at home in the universe, that he may be spared a fragmented and partial existence, and partake in the energy of the whole:

The ground-work, therefore, of all true philosophy is the full apprehension of the difference between the contemplation of reason, namely, that intuition of things which arises when we possess ourselves, as one with the whole, which is substantial knowledge, and that which presents itself when, transferring reality to the negations of reality, to the over-varying frame-work of the uniform life, we think of ourselves as separated beings. . . . By the former, we know that existence is its own predicate, self-affirmation, the one attribute in which all others are contained, not as parts but as manifes-tations. It is an eternal and infinite self-rejoicing, self-loving, with a joy unfathomable, with a love all-comprehensive. It is absolute; and the abso-lute is neither singly that which affirms, or that which is affirmed; but the identity and living copula of both.[30]

The alternative, Coleridge insisted, was to be caught in a rigid subject–object dualism, a philosophy of death in whose sight infinitely numerous particles jostled and whirled.[31] His own philosophy, on the other hand, was one of freedom. We must investigate the nature of this claim.

One excellence of the doctrine of Plato, or of the 'Plotino-Platonic Philosophy, Coleridge noted,

is that it never suffers, much less causes or occasions, its Disciples to forget themselves, lost and scattered in sensible Objects disjoined or *as* disjoined from themselves. It is impossible to understand the Elements of this Philo-sophy without an appeal, at every step round of the Ladder, to the fact within, to the mind's Consciousness – and in addition to this, instead of lulling the Soul into an indolence of mere attention . . . [it] rouses it to acts and energies of creative Thought & Recognition.[32]

It was this philosophy that Coleridge proposed to bring back, and in this enterprise his desire to fortify consciousness, to avoid being 'lost and scattered in sensible Objects', meets us at every turn. A passive mind had no way of defending itself against sensory input, nor against the stream of association by which Coleridge was, as his Notebooks show, perpetually fascinated and repelled. The very vivid-ness of his interest in dream and the twilight processes of the mind, and his developed awareness of the irrationality of the inner self, bred a corresponding revulsion and fear of violation by forces from outside that self, and a consequent desire to fortify the autonomous reason. That is why, despite the enormous value of his theory of mind as active and creative, his epistemology is always in danger of one-sidedness, of weighting the dialectic in favour of a repressive ration-ality. The mind's activity is defensive. Let me try to substantiate this. In 1795 he was still a follower of Hartley, and playing with the idea of the passiveness of mind, which registers the impressions sense input makes upon it. In 'The Aeolian Harp', the harp (a splendid image for a mind played upon by external breezes) is likened to 'some coy maid half yielding to her lover'. As the image expands, one wonders how far the mind, like the nature of which it formed a part, might welcome this infringement and thus tempt to repeat the wrong.

> Full many a thought uncalled and undetained,
> And many idle flitting phantasies,
> Traverse my indolent and passive brain,
> As wild and various as the random gales
> That swell and flutter on this subject Lute!

The point here is not the pantheistic drift from which Sara was invoked to recall her husband to the path of orthodoxy, but rather Coleridge's consciousness of the mind's possible subjection. His idea of the active nature of mind is ambiguous: it is active both because Coleridge sees the limitations of the prevailing sensationalism, but also in order to protect itself against invasion by forces outside its own control. His developed epistemology embodies a defensive requirement.

Whatever position one takes up on the question of how far Coleridge was an original thinker who built on German foundations, or an unoriginal thinker and incompetent plagiarist, one can still credit him with having made a distinctive contribution to English thought. In the discussion of cognition, this takes the form of adapting for use within an English context the epistemological theories which we have already discussed in chapter 1. In doing so he brought out the affinities between individual and social processes of perception. In terms of the organic metaphor there is an identity between the rightly constituted human mind and the rightly constituted state, an identity which was, of course, fundamental to Plato's *Republic*. The notion of the clerisy is implicit in the organic metaphor that Coleridge found so pregnant in the description of the state, that is 'the nation, dynamically considered':[33]

With, perhaps, one exception (that of the *Word* for the Son of God), it would be difficult in the whole compass of language to find a metaphor so commensurate, so pregnant, or suggesting so many points of elucidation, as that of the body politic, as the exponent of a State or Realm.[34]

An examination of Coleridge's social writings shows how close are his conceptions of communal and individual cognition. The reason, as implying the possibility of moral action, was the way out of the deterministic impasse, the promise that a being could act independently of manipulation by the material world. Coleridge often seems close to dethroning the understanding ('the faculty of means to medial ends'):[35]

> [... of the understanding in and of itself] the peripatetic aphorism, nihil in intellectu quod non prius in sensu, is strictly true.... The eye is not more inappropriate to sound, than the *mere* understanding to the modes and laws of spiritual existence. In this sense ... I assert that 'the understanding or experiential faculty, unirradiated by the reason and the spirit, has no appropriate object but the material world in relation to our worldly interests'.[36]

The understanding requires to be irradiated by the reason, which is 'not a faculty but a light', and which works through the understanding.[37] In *Aids to Reflection* Coleridge provides a scheme reminiscent of the divided line of the *Republic*, 510.[38] Reason cannot be identified with the workings of individual consciousnesses – we can speak without tautology of the human understanding, but not of human reason, for there 'neither is nor can be but one reason, one and the same'. The terrible mistake, the 'Queen-Bee in the hive of error',[39] is to rely on understanding alone. As will become clear, Coleridge regards his scheme of the mind as prescriptive rather than descriptive, not as a description of how the mind works, but of how it ought to work. There are people who live unillumined by reason, just as there have been whole historical periods when reason was in abeyance. The eighteenth century was one such period when the understanding (which can only attain to conceptions, not to ideas) was let loose on the whole terrain of human enterprise. Coleridge's generation was having to live with the consequences, and society stood badly in need of those who could attain to the knowledge of ideas:

> In every direction, they advance, conquering and to conquer, Sea and Land, Rock, Mountain, Lake and Moor, yea Nature and all her Elements, sink before them, or yield themselves captive! But the *ultimate* ends? Where shall I seek for information concerning these? By what name shall I seek for the historiographer of REASON? Where shall I find the annals of *her* recent campaigns? the records of her conquests?[40]

If I am right, this extremely simplified account of Coleridge's epistemology is pertinent to the clerisy. For through it Coleridge postulates two levels of self, the noumenal and the phenomenal, and they are not selves that are necessarily integrated in every individual.

In asking, with Lovejoy,[41] in what sense freedom may be predicated of the noumenal and supratemporal ego, we are also to ask in what sense bondage may be predicated of its empirical and temporal counterpart.

As a prelude to the discussion of the tyrannical character-type, Plato's Socrates sketched the nature of immoral desires:

[the] sort that emerge in our dreams, when the reasonable and humane part of us is asleep and its control relaxed, and our bestial nature, full of food and drink, wakes and has its fling and tries to secure its own kind of satisfaction. As you know, there's nothing too bad for it and it's completely lost to all sense and shame. It doesn't shrink at the thought of intercourse with a mother or anyone else, man, beast or god, or from murder or sacrilege. There is, in fact, no folly or shamelessness it will not commit.
    – That's perfectly true.
But a man of sound and disciplined character, before he goes to sleep, has wakened his reason and given it its fill of intellectual argument and meditation; his desires he has neither starved nor indulged, so that they sink to rest and don't plague the highest part of him with their joys and sorrows, but let it alone to pursue unhampered its quest for knowledge of past, present and future.[42]

Of such desires, invading his waking life, the tyrannical character was in fact the slave. Today we are accustomed to the picture of Coleridge craving love yet unable to establish satisfying relationships, desperate to succeed and yet incapable of achievement, the self-conscious victim of hypochrondria, laudanum, and neurotic terror. The general picture is sustained in grisly detail by his Notebooks and Letters, but it is not my task to identify and evaluate the psychological processes involved.[43] He was acutely sensitive to the fragility of mental equilibrium, and his theory of mind – which is simultaneously a theory of social mind – was erected to discipline and subordinate the realm of fantasy and appetite which, Plato had believed, the rational man could curb even in his sleep. Coleridge, we must assume, identified the empirical self with the fearful, cowed, fantasising self. Consequently, he identified the ascendancy of the understanding – the cognitive faculty pertaining to the ordinary self – with the ascendancy of animality and vice. Hence some pages of parsonical rhetoric which have alternately bored and puzzled his commentators. Thus of the eighteenth century again:

the Human Understanding ... was tempted to throw off all show of reverence to the spiritual and even to the moral powers and impulses of the soul;

and usurping the name of reason openly joined the banners of Antichrist, at once the pander and the prostitute of sensuality, and whether in the cabinet, laboratory, the dissecting room, or the brothel, alike busy in the schemes of vice and irreligion.[44]

The theme of reason is the theme of self-discipline, of the mastery of the spiritual over the sensible being, the hegemony in fact – for the theme is recurrent – of the 'best self'. The

dignity of Human Nature will be secured, and at the same time a lesson of humility taught to each individual when we are made to see that the universal necessary laws and pure IDEAS of Reason, were given us, not for the purpose of flattering our Pride and enabling us to become national legislators; but that by an energy of continued self-conquest, we might establish a free and yet absolute government in our own spirits.[45]

On a social plane, Coleridge illustrated the desiccating results of the ascendancy of materialism from the character of the French, and of pure reason (here equivalent to 'understanding') from the French Revolution. Sensuality, he maintained, with a Victorian touch, was the predominant characteristic of the French nation: 'o! that I could find a France for my Love, but ah! spite of Paschal, Madame Guyon and Moliere, France is my Babylon, the Mother of Whoredoms in Morality, Philosophy, Taste'.[46] He was not alone. Madame de Staël, who, like Coleridge, enjoyed categorising the attributes of nations, saw French intellectual life as manifesting empiricism and materialism devoid of the veneration for customs which kept the English from drawing the logical conclusions of their scepticism. Materialism and scepticism led straight to immorality and solipsism. They had already done so in France, where, she asserted with a somewhat cavalier regard for logic, the moral theory based on interest and bolstered with materialist epistemology had been the excuse for profligacy.[47] Liberation, Coleridge held, was to be attained through the 'energy of self-conquest', the establishment of a repressive supremacy of the 'higher' over the 'lower' self. It need not be doubted that this imperative would have entailed a tragic rejection of some of the very sources of Coleridge's own power. Thus he urged the pedagogic value of tracing words to their origin because it led to the ability to 'use the *language* of sight without being enslaved by its affections', and continued that to 'emancipate the mind from the despotism of the eye is the first step towards its emancipation from the influences and intrusions of the senses, sensations and passions generally'.[48] Needless to say, Coleridge never achieved his programme, but its existence as an imperative coloured his work.

Coleridge's active theory of mind was, I have argued, in some sense defensive. To say so, let me repeat, is not to deny value to his insights. But we are concerned here to examine the nature and consequences of his model for mind. Wherever we may decide the explanation lies, he was attracted by the idea of a philosophical activity remote from the fearful pressures of day-to-day reality. One of Aristotle's central claims on behalf of the contemplative life had, after all, been that it reduced one's dependence upon the outside world:

> The wise man . . . must have the necessaries of life. But, given an adequate supply of these, the just man also needs people with and towards whom he can put his justice into operation; and we can use similar language about the temperate man, the brave man, and so on. But the wise man can do more. He can speculate all by himself, and the wiser he is the better he can do it.[49]

In exploring the consolation of philosophy, Coleridge gave up that vividness of perception which we find in his best poetry; that reaching out, even in depression, to the object of his observation. McFarland has suggested, in the context of his discussion of the philosophies of 'I am' (loosely, idealism) and of 'it is' (loosely, realism), that the 'Heart's blood of poetry is transferred from the realm of "it is" '.[50] I would rather say that poetry is born of a tension between 'it is' and 'I am', a tension that implies a willingness to expose the self to an affective relationship with the object without shrinking from the potential irony or pain of that interaction. But Coleridge, in the midst of appalling suffering, seems to have become increasingly incapable of such a relationship. In 1818 he wrote to William Collins: 'Poetry is out of the question. The attempt would only hurry me into that sphere of acute feelings, from which abstruse research, the mother of self-oblivion, presents an asylum.'[51] The research to which he was now devoted was the *Magnum Opus* which he keeps describing in his letters, that 'great work on the *Logos* Divine and Human, on which I have set my Heart, and hope to ground my ultimate reputation' to which the *Biographia* was but a preface.[52] If one stimulus to the construction of Coleridge's model had been the desire to overcome fantasy, another was the wish to avoid one more component of phenomenal being – exposure to change and uncertainty. Ideas are ahistorical.

When he came to write *Church and State*, Coleridge defined an idea as

that conception of a thing which is not abstracted from any particular state, form or mode in which the thing may happen to exist at this or that time; nor yet generalised from any number or succession of such forms or modes; that which is given by the knowledge of *its ultimate aim*.[53]

Aristotelian *entelechy* and Platonic idea merge. It was undoubtedly illuminating to look at institutions in the light of their idea (ideas were, after all, 'truth powers of the mind'), but the net effect was opposed to historicity, as may be seen from that passage of the same work where Coleridge weaves an unsteady path between a discussion of the ideal and the actual church. His metaphysics led to an escape from history through reference to the 'fontal mirror of the idea'; in assuring the mind of its own potency, it risked the enfeeblement of the actual by dissolving its strangeness. Coleridge's more directly historical thought illustrates this tendency, for in practice the ideas turn out more and more to constitute a way of directing the many back to the one, or subordinating incarnation to the spirit. *The Statesman's Manual* and *Church and State* are among the best instances of Coleridge practising that reference to ideas to which a liberal education was to lead men, but in both appears the paradox that his enterprise of showing forth the dynamic, of going beneath the surface of events, ends up offering static principles – whether the political truths that he found in the Bible, or the principles of justice involved in the establishment of the national church. He tended in fact to resolve his characteristic preoccupation with 'multeity versus unity' in favour of the One, which looms through his later work.[54] The system was never finished, but the struggle to do so is deeply symptomatic. Let us quote William James on the subject of the appeal of Hegelianism:

Probably the weightiest contribution to our feeling of the rationality of the universe which the notion of the absolute brings is the assurance that however disturbed the surface may be, at bottom all is well with the cosmos – central peace abiding at the heart of endless agitation. This conception is rational in many ways, beautiful aesthetically, beautiful intellectually ... and beautiful morally, if the enjoyment of security can be accounted moral. Practically it is less beautiful ... in representing the deepest reality of the world as static and without a history, it loosens the world's hold upon our sympathies, and leaves the soul of it foreign. Nevertheless, it does give *peace*, and that kind of rationality is so paramountly demanded by men that to the end of time there will be absolutists, men who choose belief in a static eternal, rather than admit that the finite world of change and striving, even with a God as one of the strivers, is itself eternal.[55]

Coleridge's philosophical drive was towards unity, towards a sphere beyond historical change, where division would be no more. His idealism represented a need for an immutable world whose existence would guarantee intellectual freedom from natural pressures, from the crushing burdens of inhabiting a body. This is the connection between his postulate of the higher self and his reluctance to acknowledge variety as an ultimate attribute of the universe. He speaks of the 'principles of truth' (to which his own age is indifferent) 'that belong to our permanent being, and therefore do not lie within the sphere of our senses'.[56] For the phenomenal being, subject to whatever inner or outer weather which happened to prevail, the noumenal self constituted a bridgehead in the transcendent world. Reason was the 'sole principle of permanence amid endless change'.[57] Lazerowitz has argued (in a manner very similar to that of William James) that the function of such a statement as that all change is unreal 'is to ward off anxiety by strengthening an unconscious belief that threatening changes will not happen in our lives'.[58] At the risk of reductivism, I want to insist on a strategy of explanation which will not explain away Coleridge's metaphysics, but which seeks to gain insight into his civic theory of mind. While his theory of mind counselled resistance to the turbulent forces which, given their head, might prove to dominate life, he was attracted towards monism because it appeared to offer a bulwark against the perils of historicity.

Coleridge's pursuit of his moral and intellectual imperatives had its consequences. His retreat from the obdurate detail was in itself a retreat from poetry, especially from a poetical practice that had produced its best work from self-observation. How contemptible the older Coleridge might at times have thought such an enterprise is brought home by a short poem on the subject of self-knowledge from the last year of his life, in which he turned away from his beloved maxim – know thyself – to ask

> What is there in thee, Man, that can be known?
> Dark fluxion, all unfixable by thought,
> A phantom dim of past and future wrought,
> Vain sister of the worm, – life, death, soul, clod –
> Ignore thyself, and strive to know thy God![59]

Commitment to the physical self and the physical world was equivalent to enslavement by passion, guilt, and dread. One victim of this increasingly charged phase of Coleridge's thought was the doctrine of the imagination. Until the time of *The Statesman's Manual*, the imagination was an integral component of the reason – understanding model of the mind. The 'completing power which unites clearness with depth, the plenitude of the sense with the comprehensibility of the understanding',[60] it was the faculty which made possible the operation of the mind upon data. As is well known, Coleridge had developed the notion of *Einbildungskraft* which he found in Kant's Third Critique – a mediating faculty between the pure and practical reason, without which concepts would be empty and percepts blind. His development of this idea culminated in the claim in the *Biographia* that the primary imagination was the 'prime agent of all human perception, and ... a repetition in the finite mind of the eternal act of creation'. Yet this was, I believe, the highwater mark of Coleridge's theory of the imagination. He never retracted the doctrine, but the concept ceases to be a key one in his thought, as Shawcross recognised years ago in his edition of the *Biographia*:

[As] with increasing age his sense of aloofness from external things grew stronger, and his inward life gained in vividness and depth, he realised more and more the paramount importance of emphasising and appealing to the purely spiritual consciousness. ... Thus imagination, as the faculty of mediate vision, is thrust into the background, while reason, the faculty of direct access to truth, claims a more exclusive attention.[61]

Craving the 'verbal necromancy of metaphysical proof',[62] Coleridge edged away from his own theory of creative mind. A reading of *Church and State* after a reading of parallel passages in the *Friend* will, I think, suggest limitations on R. J. White's suggestion that he spent his life after 'The Ancient Mariner' 'showing that the way of Creative Genius was the way of ordinary humanity'.[63] The discipline of mind becomes a struggle towards intuiting an immutable and invulnerable world. For the modifying power, active in all human perception, is exchanged a more esoteric vision; for creation, revelation. The decline of imagination parallels another retreat within Coleridge's theory of cognition.

Coleridge's account of cognition turns out to have a less than universal application. Ideas are formative and creative; they manifest themselves through the phenomena about which our minds tell us. But it is the privilege of the few to possess an idea: of the generality of men, it might be more truly affirmed that they are possessed by it.[64]

Consciousness of the possession of a higher faculty constitutes a just claim to superiority on the part of those who cultivate it. In *The Statesman's Manual* Coleridge hinted at his 'master thought':

The first man, on whom the light of an IDEA dawned, did in that same moment receive the spirit and credentials of a Law-giver: and as long as man shall exist, so long will the possession of that antecedent knowledge (the maker and master of all profitable Experience) which exists only in the power of an Idea, be the one lawful qualification of all Dominion in the world of the senses.[65]

The Kantian recognition of the ideality of our differentiation and organisation of experience is being curtailed in the interests of the possessors of ideas, to whom alone, presumably, 'profitable experience' is possible. The ability to grasp the particular in the universal and the universal in the particular is dependent on the noumenal freedom of the thinking subject. In the *Second Lay Sermon* Coleridge had lamented the public desuetude of philosophy in the following terms:

An excess in our attachment to temporal and personal objects can be counteracted only by a pre-occupation of the intellect and the affections with permanent, universal, and eternal truths.[66]

To be limited by the finite was to exist but partially, but it was a form of existence to which, it seems, the mass of mankind were to be condemned. By a blatant irony, the dynamic philosophy ends up supporting the idea of an organic, static society whose salvation was to be achieved through the disinterestedness of the pure minority.

REGENERACY AND PHILOSOPHY

There is a sense in which, as John Beer has remarked, Coleridge spent his life in a search for a communion of true spirits. The Pantisocracy and his later idealisation of seventeenth-century Anglican divines represent aspects of this search.[67] He had cultivated a style of prophetic utterance for addressing the nation, and had early toyed with the idea of what it would feel like to belong to the elect. In doing so he forged a link between regeneracy and philosophy that was to remain germinal in his thought. As early as 1795 he had thought of a self-style that combined purity, the transcendence of

partiality and passion, and aspirations towards the adoration of the
One:

> And blest are they
> Who in this fleshly World, the elect of Heaven,
> Their strong eye darting through the deeds of men,
> Adore with steadfast unpresuming gaze
> Him Nature's essence, mind and energy!

It is curious how many of Coleridge's perennial aspirations can be
seen thus early in his career, and the recognition may excuse lengthy
quotation from this bombastic verse:

> There is one Mind, one omnipresent Mind,
> Omnific. His most holy name is Love.
> Truth of subliming import! with the which
> Who feeds and saturates his constant soul,
> He from his small particular orbit flies
> With blest outstarting! From himself he flies,
> Stands in the sun, and with no partial gaze
> Views all creation.

Superstition has obscured this truth, and Coleridge will protest
against it:

> But o'er some plain that steameth to the sun,
> Peopled with Death; or where more hideous Trade
> Loud-laughing packs his bales of human anguish;
> I will raise up a mourning, O ye Fiends!
> And curse your spells, that film the eye of Faith,
> Hiding the present God; whose presence lost,
> The moral world's cohesion, we become
> An Anarchy of Spirits! Toy-bewitched,
> Made blind by lusts, disherited of soul,
> No common centre Man, no common sire
> Knoweth! A sordid solitary thing,
> Mid countless brethren with a lonely heart
> Through courts and cities the smooth savage roams
> Feeling himself, his own low self the whole;
> When he by sacred sympathy might make
> The whole one Self! Self, that no alien knows!
> Self, far diffused as Fancy's wing can travel!
> Self, spreading still! Oblivious of its own,
> Yet of all possessing! This is Faith!
> This the Messiah's destined victory![68]

Commentators are apt – in some ways rightly – to trace Coleridge's
thought through successive fields of influence: Hartley, Spinoza,

Kant, Schelling. But in this particular study we need to recognise
that certain of his preoccupations were formed early ('Religious
Musings' dates from his revolutionary period, and before he had
discovered German thought) and, nourishing themselves upon his
different philosophical diets, retained a constant identity. The
conflation of true philosophy with moral purity in a campaign
against a false philosophy (seen here in a religious context) was to
fuse with the theory of mediation. Where Coleridge's cultural theory
is concerned we would do well not to overlook continuity. Writing
some thirty years later to James Gillman, Coleridge spoke of independence, the 'up-hill road to manly principles' as he had recently
called it.[69] His jocoseness produced a revealing metaphor. The
fifteen-year-old James could, he said, choose '*which* of the two you
consider to be your true and proper Self, the Caterpillar (that is,
your present *boy*-nature) or the Butterfly (that is, the Man which is
growing within you)'. He must dread getting stuck at the stage of
childish wilfulness. If the boy regarded the

mere *Larva* as his true and only *Self* . . . if he resolves neither to know or
care about any Self but his present and immediate Havings, Likings, and
Cravings, the consequence . . . *must* be, that he will not retain his Caterpillar Life and State of Being an hour longer on this account, but will pass
into a poor lame starveling lop-sided Butterfly, dragging and trailing his
soiled and tatterdemalion wings along the ground, which instead of being
the means and organs of Elevation and Liberty – the means of at once
rising in the world, and of becoming his own Master – are an additional
Burden.[70]

Contradicting the caterpillar became an imperative. The real life of
nations, like that of the individual, entailed reducing dependence
upon the natural world and material development, and the struggle
within the self paralleled the struggle of the few against the mortal
tendencies of people at large.

To whom then do we owe our ameliorated condidition? To the successive
Few in every age . . . who by the intensity and permanence of their action
have compensated for the limited sphere, within which it is at any time
intelligible; and whose good deeds posterity reverence in their results.[71]

The attributes of the 'higher' mental faculty are fostered upon
the few, and those of the 'lower' upon the many. History showed
that the noble structures raised by the few were 'gradually under-
mined by the ignorance and profligacy of the many'. Unlike the
Pantisocrats, the few ought not to opt out of society, for theirs is the

task of mediation, and upon their purity and disinterestedness the possibility of social humanisation rests. A footnote in *Church and State* is telling:

Ideas . . . or the truths of philosophy, properly so called, correspond to sub-stantial beings. . . . To adopt the language of the great philosophic Apostle, they are *spiritual realities that can only spiritually be discerned*, and the inherent aptitude and moral preconfiguration to which constitutes what we mean by ideas, and by the presence of *ideal* truth and *ideal* power, in the human being. They in fact constitute his *humanity*. For try to conceive a *man* without the ideas of God, eternity, freedom, will, absolute truth, of the good, the true, the beautiful, the infinite. An *animal* endowed with a memory of appearances and of facts might remain. But the man will have vanished, and you have instead a creature, more subtle than any beast of the field, but likewise cursed above every beast of the field: upon its belly must it go and dust must it eat all the days of its life. But I recall myself from a train of thoughts little likely to find favour in this age of sense and selfishness.[72]

The ideas are still the truth powers of the mind, but we cannot necessarily predicate their possession of all men. We can – and there is a sub-textual suggestion that some do – turn our backs on them, in which case God's curse on the Serpent applies to us. All men, we have seen, are not conscious of the ideas. Between society and the pit stand the few, and if not the pit, then at least barbarism: 'Alas! dear Sir! what is mankind, but the *Few* in all ages? Take them away, and how long, think you, would the rest differ from the Negroes or New Zealanders?'[73] We have next to explore the relevance of the ideas we have been tracing to Coleridge's educational and social prescriptions.

EDUCATION AND THE NATIONAL CHURCH

In considering Coleridge's idea of the national church, we must pay attention to his theories of education as well as his theories of society. We have already considered his letter to Lord Liverpool, where he asserts that we have neglected to our cost what he elsewhere calls the 'austerer studies', and that the road to social regeneration leads through the re-education of the 'higher classes' and then, in turn, of the middle classes. In his writings at large he has much to say about the nature of the educational process, and what he says may still stimulate thinking about education in our own time. But before endorsing his prescriptions or adopting his stance, we should recog-nise that the most important form of education – the liberal education of which we have seen him speak to James Gillman – was the education of the higher classes, and it was to the education of such that most of his thinking on the subject applies. Of it he spoke in terms of a recurrence to

a more manly discipline of the intellect on the part of the learned themselves, in short a thorough re-casting of the moulds, in which the minds of our Gentry, the characters of our future Landowners, Magistrates and Senators are to receive their shape and fashion.[74]

In the context of these social priorities we must read the famous 'Essay on Method', with its insistence that we must 'prepare and discipline the student's intellectual and moral being'.[75] True education must awaken the mind to a consciousness of its own powers, and at times Coleridge seems pretty close to Froebel, an affinity hinted at in his epistemological theory that knowledge arises from the operation of the mind upon experience. Froebel wrote that

it seemed to me that everything which should or could be required for human education and instruction must be necessarily conditioned and given, by virtue of the very nature of the necessary course of his development, in man's own being, and in the relationships amid which he is set.[76]

And in a similar vein, Coleridge wrote of the dreadful sight of

young men the most anxiously and expensively be-school-mastered, be-tutored, be-lectured, any thing but *educated* ... perilously over-civilised, and most piteously uncultivated! And all from inattention to the method dictated by nature herself, to the simple truth that, as the forms in all organised existence, so must all true and living knowledge proceed from within; that it may be trained, supported, fed, excited, but can never be infused or impressed.[77]

Through this education from within, an intuition of the unity of knowledge would be gained, and in another letter Coleridge explained to James Gillman that the

philosopher considers the several knowledges and attainments which it is the Object of a liberal Education to communicate or prepare for, as springing from one Root, and rising into one common Trunk, from the summit of which it diverges into the different Branches and ramifies, without losing its original unity.[78]

But we must insist that this higher form of education, the only form of education that truly deserved the name, was the education of the higher classes, without which all schemes for reform were futile.

In 1812 Coleridge wrote of parliamentary reform that

I fear, I fear, that it is a hopeless business & will continue so till some
fortunate Giant-mind starts up & revolutionizes all the present Notions concerning the education of both Gentry and Middle Classes. While this
remains in statu quo, I suspect that good Dr. Bell's scheme carried into
full effect by the higher Classes may suggest to a thinking man the Image
of the Irishman on the Bough with his face towards the Trunk sawing
himself off.[79]

He was himself enthusiastically – at least for a while – in favour of
Bell's monitorial education scheme (this 'incomparable machine, this
vast moral steam-engine'),[80] and cited approvingly his friend Sir
Alexander Ball's opinion that the 'dangers apprehended from the
education of the lower classes, arose . . . from its not being universal'.[81]
We are faced therefore with the question of what he considered the
role of lower-class education to be. The answer is, I think, twofold.
Firstly, a modicum of education is the right of all men. The Bible
should not be withheld even from the poorest – indeed it is all the
book-learning needful for them. To this extent, Coleridge never
forgot his parting injunction of his Bristol lectures of 1795: 'Go
preach the GOSPEL to the poor.'[82] Then Coleridge's thought never
entirely lost its revolutionary progressivism, and we would be
wrong to think that his social model was entirely static. The state,
we have noted, promised humanisation to all, and, if it failed in its
educational duty, then men could not be citizens and could own no
obligation to the state. It owed them the kind of knowledge

necessary for all in order to their CIVILITY. By civility I mean all the
qualities essential to a citizen, and devoid of which no people or class of
people can be calculated on by the rulers and leaders of the state for the
conservation or preservation of its essential interests.[83]

In the *Second Lay Sermon*, Coleridge had laid down the ends of the
state, in a passage which he reproduced with modifications in
Church and State. These were to 'make the means of subsistence
more easy to each individual'; to 'secure to each of its members the
hope of bettering his own condition or that of his children', and the
'development of those faculties which are essential to his humanity,
that is, his rational and moral being'. But we must not confuse this
education with the wider education and fortifying of consciousness
which pertained to the higher classes. The rider, which Coleridge
retained with only slight alterations in *Church and State*, is crucial:

Under the last head we do not mean those degrees of intellectual cultivation which distinguish man from man in the same civilized society, but those only that raise the civilized man above the Barbarian, the Savage, and the Animal.[84]

And at the end of chapter VII of *Church and State*, where Coleridge expressed his regrets and apprehensions about the present age, he adapted and extended a passage from the *Friend*. Arguing against liberals and utilitarians, he accused his opponents of wishing for 'general illumination':

You begin, therefore, with the attempt to *popularise* science: but you will only affect its *plebification*. It is folly to think of making all, or the many, philosophers, or even men of science and systematic knowledge. But it is duty and wisdom to aim at making as many as possible soberly and steadily religious; – inasmuch as the morality which the state requires in its citizens for its own wellbeing and ideal immortality, and without reference to their spiritual interests as individuals, can only exist for the people in the form of religion.[85]

These passages do much to clarify the sense in which Coleridge intends general education.

Secondly, Coleridge's idea of general education was prudential. The working classes should be educated (up to a point) because – education having advanced as far as it had – it was safer to finish the job, and do it in a religious spirit, than to leave it to demagogues and agitators. His hatred for 'Cobbetts and such like animals' was enduring. From a 'popular philosophy and a philosophic populace, Good Sense deliver us'.[86] Education of the people at large was, he sometimes felt, a matter of expediency:

Reflections and stirrings of the mind, with all their restlessness, and all the errors that result from their imperfection, from the *Too much*, because *Too little*, are come into the world. The Powers that awaken and foster the spirit of curiosity are to be found in every village: Books are in every hovel. The Infant's cries are hushed with picture books: and the Cottager's child sheds his first bitter tears over pages, which render it impossible for the man to be treated or governed as a child. Here as in so many other cases, the inconveniences that have arisen from a thing's having become too general are best removed by making it universal.[87]

Nevertheless, religious and Biblical education are not intended to lead on to speculation or civic responsibility. Instead, the working man is to discover the

sufficiency of the Scriptures in all knowledge or requisite for a right performance of his duty as a man and a Christian. Of the labouring classes, who
in all countries form the great majority of the inhabitants, ... more than
this is not generally desirable. 'They are not sought for in public counsel,
nor need they be found where politic sentences are spoken. It is enough if
every one is wise in the working of his own craft: so best will they maintain
the state of the world'.[88]

The education of the people as a whole is a matter of polity. Within
the whole, the organic metaphor insists, different members have
different functions, and (unless their function is government or
teaching) need but be 'wise in the working of their own crafts'.

The shift to a holistic idea of the state can be charted by referring
back to Coleridge's early periodical, *The Watchman*, whose aim was
'That All may know the TRUTH; And that the TRUTH may make
us FREE!', and in whose prospectus he argued that 'a people are
free in proportion as they form their own opinions. In the strictest
sense of the word, Knowledge is Power.'[89] Yet although Coleridge's
sense of educational priorities changed radically over the next twenty
years, one component of his theory remained constant. That was the
mission of the educators, for with this mission his conception of his
own social role was bound up. In 1796, after the collapse of *The
Watchman*, and at a time when a career as a Unitarian preacher
was still very much a possibility, he wrote to his friend, the revolutionary Thelwall, 'I am not *fit* for *public* Life; yet the Light shall
stream to a far distance from the taper in my cottage window.'[90]
And the year before, in 'Religious Musings', he had spoken of the
rise of freedom out of science:

> O'er waken'd realms Philosophers and Bards
> Spread in concentric circles: they whose Souls,
> Conscious of their high dignities from God,
> Brook not Wealth's rivalry! and they, who long
> Enamoured with the charms of order, hate
> The unseemly disproportion.

Science, or systematic knowledge, and especially speculative philosophy, retained its social role, as we have seen, in his thought. And
so, necessarily, did those who were entrusted with its maintenance
and the diffusion of its blessings. In this context Coleridge's profound interest in German thinkers, even his tendency to plagiarise
from their work, takes on additional significance. For, like Madame
de Staël or Carlyle, he was impressed not only by German erudi-

tion, but by the pioneering work of creating a new spiritual philosophy.

Coleridge's educational programme demanded the re-education, or rather the education, in a more disciplined, permanent, and far-reaching fashion of the higher classes. But the members of the higher classes, even when educated to the requirements of the 'Essay on Method', would not, of course, form the clerisy. The education in civility of the lower classes and the liberal education of the higher rested upon a common ground. That ground was the active existence of the clerisy, and to the specific development of that idea in Coleridge's later years we must now turn our attention.

The burden of this chapter has been the argument that Coleridge's idea of the clerisy – although not fully developed until his last years – was active in his thinking all along. From an early age he looked to an elite to purify and revivify society, hoped that he himself might play such a mediating part, and developed a theory in which speculative philosophy was essential to the cultivation, ultimately even the existence, of the nation. His struggles with epistemology forced his attention to pedagogical issues. It would indeed have been possible for him to develop a theory of an intellectual elite without recourse to other than German materials. But in fact there were two other important stimuli. One was his high regard for the Hebrew prophets ('protectors of the Nation and privileged state moralists')[91] and his conviction that the Bible should be expounded prophetically. The other was his growing commitment to the Anglican Church, in which, he believed, despite the historical conflation of the national church and the church of Christ, certain essentials had been maintained. Historically, the church had provided a home for the national clerisy. This held advantages for men of letters, and even by the time of the *Biographia* he was observing that 'the church presents to every man of learning and genius a profession in which he may cherish a rational hope of being able to unite the widest schemes of literary utility with the strictest performance of professional duties.'[92] But the chief advantages were for society as a whole, and in a passage which he reproduced in *Church and State* he wrote as follows:

That to every parish throughout the kingdom there is transplanted a germ of civilisation; that in the remotest villages there is a nucleus round which the capabilities of the place may crystallize and brighten; a model sufficiently superior to excite, yet sufficiently near to encourage and facilitate imitation; this, the unobtrusive, continuous agency of a Protestant church establishment, this it is which the patriot and the philanthropist, who would fain unite the love of peace with the faith in the progressive amelioration of mankind, cannot estimate at too high a price.[93]

Memories of Ottery St Mary haunt Coleridge's intellectual odyssey. The church provided a model for an intellectual establishment upon whose value to society he had long brooded in terms which he could find among the common stock of Renaissance humanism.[94] But more than that, it provided a model for diffusion, for the means of spreading the benefits accrued through speculative and scholarly activity. The history of education 'has been this: from the schools to the pulpit, not by any long circuit but directly, to the common people'.[95] The existence of a national clerisy had been one of the characteristic features of the period of English cultural efflorescence of the sixteenth and seventeenth centuries to which he looked back so fondly, and the style of whose Anglican divines he had attempted to adopt. The clerisy as an audience for the intellectual achievements of its own members was contrasted with the 'public' – usually a derogatory term – and its disappearance was shown to be a feature of that dead time that began in 1688: 'After the Revolution, the spirit of the nation became more commercial than it had been before; a learned body, or clerisy, as such, gradually disappeared, and literature in general then began to be addressed to the common miscellaneous public.'[96] We might profitably compare the argument, with its embryonic sociology of literature, with Arnold's account of the functions of criticism and of academies. The appeal of the church to Coleridge was strong; one more attraction, and another overlap with the idea of the elite, was the very separateness of its ministers: while serving the world, their eyes were not fixed exclusively upon it. He felt that the purity of the few must be safeguarded; the accommodations demanded by popular education could be dangerous:

There are, in every country, times when the few who know the truth have clothed it for the vulgar, and addressed the vulgar in the vulgar language and modes of conception, in order to convey any part of the truth. This, however, could not be done with safety, even to the *illuminati* themselves in the first instance; but to their successors habit gradually turned lie into belief, partial and *stagnate* truth into ignorance, and the teachers of the vulgar (like the Franciscan friars in the South of Europe) became a part of the vulgar.[97]

The search for truth must be carried on free from contamination, but at the same time, in order that the purifying consequences of that search might be nationally effective, they must be presented in terms of morality and religion to the nation at large. The Church of England provided the requisite model. But Coleridge now had to discriminate between the church of Christ – the '*sustaining, correcting, befriending* Opposite of the world'[98] – and the national church, and we can observe him doing this, both in his letters and other writings, from around 1820.[99] The matured theory of the clerisy which we find in *Church and State* arose from the accommodation of his development of German idealist philosophy to English cultural conditions. As such it is specifically English and Coleridgean, and even the industry of Professor Fruman can find no immediate German source for it.[100] Coleridge's relative security and stability after settling at Highgate did not, it is true, permit him to finish his *Magnum Opus*. But they did permit him to precipitate, to make public in the form of a social theory, an idea of the intellectual life in its social and moral bearing that had sustained him throughout his career as a consolatory and reassuring vision.

The ostensible reason for writing and publishing *Church and State* was to intervene in the debate on Catholic emancipation. However, the Test Act had been repealed in 1829, the year before the book was published, and it is clear that the debate provided Coleridge with the occasion to say something he was wanting to say in any case. There was also a concern with the growing Reform crisis which – although it does not appear on the surface of Coleridge's work – means that we can usefully compare *Church and State* to Arnold's *Culture and Anarchy*. As the 'last relic of our nationalty', the Church of England retained an essential role in preventing social dissolution, and the *Table Talk* shows Coleridge horrified by reports that the church was to suffer despoliation.[101] Social dissolution, beginning as philosophical and moral blindness, became political in the accepted sense. 'What', he had once demanded in a letter about the 'Anti-magnet of social Disorganization and *Dissoluteness*', 'are the clergy doing?'[102] Since society was not – could not be – a mere conglomeration of self-fulfilling individuals, the dissolution of the body politic (a 'constituted realm, kingdom, commonwealth, or nation ... where the integral parts, classes or orders are so balanced or interdependent, as to constitute more or less, a moral unit, an organic whole'[103]) would in itself terminate the progressive humanisation of its erstwhile members. The reconstitution of the clerisy was the only hope.

The social model within which the clerisy was to act was in essence the dialectical one which had long appealed to Coleridge. He invoked one of his favourite images, the bar magnet, to illustrate it. The agricultural interest and the possessors of land constituted one pole, the mercantile, professional, and personal interests the other.[104] The interaction of these forces of permanence and progression constituted the state. In the absence of either, the state would cease to exist. We must, however, remember that he is talking about the idea of the state, not about realised actuality. While his philosophy of history asserts that it is towards the realisation of this idea that national history has been moving ('sometimes with, sometimes without, not seldom, perhaps, against, the intention of the individual actors, but always as if a power, greater, and better than the men themselves, had intended it for them' – the cunning of reason is an inescapable feature of philosophies of history), there is no inevitability about the final realisation. Imbalance between the two forces is a distinct possibility, and had indeed, according to Coleridge, been a factor in the social condition into which England fell after 1688. The point needs to be emphasised, since it is the clerisy that creates a possibility of continued balance and interaction. This is what I mean when I claim that in his theory, the members of the clerisy act as horizontal mediators; their activity is a precondition of the healthful opposition of powers.

The existence of imbalance was a problem to which Coleridge had addressed himself, in the *Second Lay Sermon*, as early as 1817. There he had asserted that the underlying causes of the present distress were 'resolvable into the overbalance of the commercial spirit in consequence of the absence or weakness of the counterweights'.[105] Then, he had hurried through the 'natural counterforces' in order to concentrate on the influence of religion. But on the way he enunciated a programme which he was to fulfil in *Church and State*. An excess in our 'attachment to temporal and personal objects can be counteracted only by a pre-occupation of the intellect and the affections with permanent, universal, and eternal truths'. The ascendancy of unchecked commercialism, in other words, shares a fundamental identity with the ascendancy of the unleavened understanding, for he had left himself no means of discriminating between the effects of commercialism in particular, and those of attachment to material objects in general. Coleridge's epistemology and his social theory are inseparable. The subject led him on, but he explained: 'I must not permit myself to any more on this subject, desirous as I am of shewing the importance of a philosophic class, and of evincing that it is of vital utility, and even an essential element in the composition of a civilised community.'[106] This desire he achieved in *Church and State.*

Without the clerisy, the dialectic would fall apart. Coleridge used the example of the ancient Greek democracies which fell into dissolution from an excess of the 'permeative' over the organised powers, 'the permeative powers deranging the functions, and by explosions shattering the organic structures, they should have enlivened'.[107] Basic to his theory was the notion of the 'nationalty' the national heritage of land, set aside for the good of the nation, illegitimately possessed in the middle ages by the church, and much of it later, and wrongfully, alienated. This nationalty was intended in the idea for the maintenance of the national church, a body different from the church of Christ, which he discussed later on. The national church was the 'third estate of the realm', and its object was 'to secure and improve that civilization, without which the nation could be neither permanent nor progressive'.[108] The order which was to carry on this civilising and mediating work was to be divided into a larger and a smaller body. The smaller was to

remain at the fountain heads of the humanities, in cultivating and enlarging the knowledge already possessed, and in watching over the interests of physical and moral science; being likewise, the instructors of such as constituted, or were to constitute, the remaining more numerous classes of the order.

The latter were to be distributed throughout the nation

so as not to leave the smallest integral part or division without a resident guide, guardian and instructor; the objects and final intention of the whole order being these – to preserve the stores, to guard the treasures, of past civilisation, and thus to bind the present with the past; to perfect and add to the same, and thus to connect the present with the future; but especially to diffuse through the whole community . . . that quantity and quality of knowledge which was indispensable both for the understanding of [their] rights, and for the performance of the duties correspondent.

In such fashion the clerisy was to irradiate the body politic much as the reason was held to irradiate the understanding. Higher education did not pertain to the mass of the people, but the civilising effects of the speculation and scholarship carried on by the inner clerisy – so to speak – were to be mediated to society at large by the distributed clerisy. The learning which they represented was fundamental to the national vitality.

THE CLERISY of the nation, or national church, in its primary acceptation and original intention comprehended the learned of all denominations; – the sages and professors of the law and jurisprudence; of medicine and physiology; of music; of military and civil architecture; of the physical sciences; with the mathematical as the common *organ* of the preceding; in short, all the so called liberal arts and sciences, the possession and application of which constitute the civilization of a country, as well as the Theological. The last was, indeed, placed at the head of all; and of good right did it claim the precedence. But why? Because under the name of Theology . . . were contained the interpretation of languages; the conservation and tradition of past events; the momentous epochs, and revolutions of the race and nation; the continuation of the records; logic, ethics, and the determination of ethical science, in application to the rights and duties of men in all their various relations, social and civil; and lastly, the ground-knowledge, the prima scientia as it was named, – PHILOSOPHY, or the doctrine and discipline of *ideas*.

Many of Coleridge's perennial concerns have crystallised here, in a forcible statement of the relevance to national well-being of the kind of intellectual work to which he was himself devoted. Only instead of being scattered and divided, out on the edge of things, and limited in its influence, the clerisy has come home. The sociological dimension of his thought insisted that the clerisy be provided for: in a rightly constituted society, the clerks would not be driven from temporary shelter to temporary shelter and from financial expedient to financial dependence. His readers were left to decide how best the lesson might be applied in the nineteenth century in the light of Coleridge's account of Henry VIII's failure. For Henry had had the opportunity of restoring the lands wrongfully – sacrilegiously indeed – alienated from the nationalty, but had failed to take it. If he had, the land should have been distributed for the maintenance (1) of the universities and 'great schools of liberal learning'; (2) of a pastor in each parish; (3) of a school-master in each parish who should assist the pastor, and in due course succeed him. It is this practical element in his thought that sets Coleridge's idea of the clerisy apart from, say, Arnold's idea of the critics. The former wanted to know in detail how his elite was to work upon society and how it was itself to be maintained.

From the description of how the clerisy ought to have been organised, Coleridge turned (as should not surprise us) back to the reason and the understanding. The 'commanding knowledge, the *power* of truth, given or obtained by contemplating the subject in the fontal mirror of the Idea, is in Scripture ordinarily expressed by Vision'. And, he repeated, 'Where no vision is, the people perisheth'. Yet ordinary people, we have seen, were incapable of vision in this sense. The absence of a functional clerisy therefore deprived the nation of that leavening of reason that alone could bring about the humanisation of its members, and we lived 'under the dynasty of the understanding'. In such a condition – and the terms in which he speaks of it parallel Arnold's distrust of 'machinery' – true freedom was impossible, for the understanding pandered merely to material need. Coleridge's model of the mind underwrites and sustains his model of society. The French Revolution had failed, he long ago claimed, because the French were 'too sensual to be free'. 'The Sensual and the Dark rebel in vain, Slaves by their own compulsion.'[109] The 'New Heaven and the New Earth' consists in an interior condition, 'Undreamt of by the sensual and the proud'. The clerisy, mediating reason, is the *sine qua non* of genuine society.

In a recent lecture, Donald MacKinnon has spoken of the irony of Coleridge's descent into a 'complacent Anglicanism', and, more broadly, of his falling for a kind of sectarianism in arrogating to himself absolute moral judgment. He sought the triumph of the ideas with which he had identified himself at the expense of their corruption.[110] Where his educational and social thought is concerned, we may, I believe, speak of another irony. That is that we have a theory of mind and of education of a wonderful fruitful sort, a psychological intelligence of enormous power which becomes committed to a limiting desire to separate the faculties of mind. In weighting the proposed dialectic in favour of the so-called 'higher' faculty, it impoverishes intellect, and (while appropriating the higher form of intellectual health for the few) sustains class society by proposing a merely partial and dutiful notion of intellectual health for the many. Dialectical interplay resolves into the subordination of one faculty to another, and the dynamic philosophy ends up supporting an organic and largely static idea of the state.

The pathos of unity and infallibility had absorbed Coleridge. The clerisy represented unity in a divided and divisive world by reason of its foothold in the noumenal world, and he invested it with

those attributes which he apparently desired for himself. The cultivation, of which it was to be the agent, represented the passage
beyond striving to a state of communication with a world of surety,
a condition which permitted interpretation of the multitudinousness
of the real world within the framework of the ideas firmly anchored
in the changeless. Back in about 1797 he had copied into his
Notebook a quotation from Jeremy Taylor; he used it again in the
philosophical twelfth chapter of the *Biographia*, and it might serve
almost as a motto to his thought: 'he to whom all things are one,
who draweth all things to one, and seeth all things in one, may enjoy
true peace and rest of spirit.'[111] The pursuit of the synthesis in which
all the details might be safely subsumed became all-absorbing;
Coleridge's thought on the subject of the clerisy is the precipitation
of a mind that had ceased to regard the essential unity – whether of
knowledge, or of the transcendent world, or of the idea of church
and state – as merely provisional. The theory of the clerisy in
nineteenth-century England thus starts with an inheritance of idealism in both the everyday and the philosophic senses. And at a purely
practical level this inheritance could lead to some remarkable over-
sights.

   In describing his own philosophic progress, Coleridge spoke of his
indebtedness to the mystical tradition which he saw represented by
George Fox, Jakob Boehme, and William Law. In doing so, and in a
passage whose relevance is in no way diminished by Fruman's
observation that it is lifted from Schelling's *Natur-Philosophie*, he
made some interesting admissions:

Whoever is acquainted with the history of philosophy during the last two
or three centuries cannot but admit that there appears to have existed a sort
of secret and tacit compact among the learned not to pass beyond a certain
limit in speculative science.... Therefore the true depth of science, and
the penetration to the inmost centre, from which all the lines of knowledge
diverge to their ever distant circumference, was abandoned to the illiterate
and the simple, whom unstilled learning and an original ebulliency of spirit
had urged to the investigation of the indwelling and living ground of things.
These then, because their names had never been inrolled in the guilds of the
learned, were persecuted by the registered livery-men as interlopers on their
rights and privileges. All without distinction were branded as fanatics and
phantasts.... And this for no other reason but because they were the
unlearned, men of humble and obscure occupations. When, and from
whom among the literati by profession, have we ever heard the divine
doxology repeated, 'I thank Thee O Father ... because Thou hast hid

these things from the wise and prudent, and has revealed them unto babes'? No! the haughty priests of learning not only banished from the schools and marts of science all who had dared draw living waters from the fountain, but drove them out of the very Temple, which meantime the 'buyers, and sellers and money-changers' were suffered to make 'a den of thieves'.[112]

When he came to formulate the idea of the clerisy, Coleridge would have done well to reflect on this very danger. For he gives no reason to think that his own clerisy would not be capable of a similar, or even greater treason.

3

THE HERO AS MAN OF LETTERS:
THOMAS CARLYLE

All this, of the importance and supreme importance of the Man of Letters in modern Society, and how the Press is to such a degree superseding the Pulpit, the Senate, the *Senatus Academicus* and much else, has been admitted for a good while; and recognised often enough, in late times, with a sort of sentimental triumph and wonderment. It seems to me, the Sentimental by and by will have to give place to the Practical. If Men of Letters *are* so incalculably influential, actually performing such work for us from age to age, and even from day to day, then I think we may conclude that Men of Letters will not always wander like unrecognised Ishmaelites among us!

Carlyle, 'The Hero as Man of Letters'

The germ of Coleridge's idea of the clerisy, I have argued, is to be found in his projection of his own social role. Carlyle's man of letters arises, I believe, by a similar process. The ideal springs from and returns to his conception of himself as a man of letters working to overcome his age. He belongs in this study both because of his immense influence and because through his work we can see – the more clearly because of its relative crudity, and its constant repetitiveness – a configuration of ideas and aspirations about the intellectual life in its relation to the phenomenal and the non-phenomenal worlds. In claiming, however, that Carlyle helped to develop the theme of the clerisy (he did not himself use Coleridge's word) we are talking about the younger Carlyle: the most explicit document for our purposes, the lecture on 'The Hero as Man of Letters' was given in May 1840 when he was forty-five. Nevertheless, while it is a commonplace that Carlyle's thought became more authoritarian as he grew older, the authoritarian strain was growing during the period when his own chosen heroism was that of letters. The hero ideal is deeply intertwined both with his early radicalism, and with his projection of the man of letters. Carlyle, as R. H. Horne noted as early as 1844, often spoke with a forked tongue.[1]

In dealing with Carlyle we need to be aware of the autobio-graphical or auto-projectional nature of much of his writing: through various guises he tried out different roles, tried on, so to speak, the clothes of fictional characters (Wotton Reinfred, Teufels-dröckh), or historical characters (Schiller, Abbot Samson, Samuel Johnson, Cromwell) through whom he could discover what it felt like to be called from obscurity to an unwilling spiritual pre-eminence. Heroism was the characteristic of these men, as also of those who accepted their spiritual authority.[2] It was the courage to discover your own nobility in a world of shams, and it was more important than the particular historical guise in which it appeared. The hero 'can be Poet, Prophet, King, Priest or what you will, according to the kind of world he finds himself born into. I confess, I have no notion of a truly great man that could not be *all* sorts of men.'[3] The problem was how to work as best you could, how best to tap the energy that Carlyle believed to be sublimated wrath.[4] Increasing frustration with the man-of-letters role led Carlyle further and further into the idea of an impregnable great self, into the bullying exasperation of the *Latter Day Pamphlets* or of 'Shooting Niagara'. The wise and good conceived as heroes remain constants in his thought, but the idea overlaps only partially with that of the man of letters. That it does so at all puts forcibly before us the link between advocacy of a clerisy and the longing for a world of con-sistent values as a source of prescription.

The overlap is, however, of a significant kind: Carlyle developed his idea of heroism (and heroism for him was, to the end, a form of spiritual authority) in the course of working out the role of the man of letters. Greatness was a spiritual property, the power to realise in the world the values gained from a sphere more real than the historical and mutable world could ever be. We shall have to return to the discussion of what Carlyle meant by the primacy of the spiritual over the material, as also to the part great men were to play as mediators between the seen and unseen worlds. For the moment enough is suggested by the opening contention of the lectures *On Heroes and Hero Worship*:

They were the leaders of men, these great ones; the modellers, patterns, and in a wide sense creators, of whatsoever the general mass of men con-trived to do or to attain; all things that we see standing accomplished in the world are properly the outer material result, the practical realisation and embodiment, of Thoughts that dwelt in the Great Men sent into the world: the soul of the whole world's history, it may justly be considered, were the history of these.[5]

There can, however, be no doubt that the first articulation of this thesis was in connection with his own calling as a man of letters. The accretion of other heroisms is first of all experimental – in terms of potential autobiography – and later in earnest, as, frustration increasing, the various masks of Carlyle's personal drama rigidify in monotonous expressions of contempt.

NO FIXED HIGHWAYS MORE

From the beginning of his public literary career, Carlyle was seeking a calling. In one sense he was also striving to make his life a continuous process of *Bildung*, though unlike his German counterparts he had a fairly limited sense of the possibilities of education.[6] It is no accident that from writing the *Life of Schiller*, in which he studied a literary vocation, he went on to investigate a young man's search for the meaning of his own life. His translation of *Wilhelm Meister* not only laid the foundations of his knowledge of Goethe, but it also provided a starting place for his own educational theory, suggesting (or reinforcing) that curious constellation of ideas represented by the belief which surfaces time and again in the Romantic era that silence, the stillness of the vocal and rational faculties, is the attribute of spiritual health, and talking or consciousness the sign of disease and decadence. More than forty years later, at his inauguration as Rector of the University of Edinburgh, it was to the tediously engineered education of young Wilhelm that Carlyle looked back:

Words are good, but they are not the best. The best is not to be explained in words. The spirit in which we act is the highest matter.... No one knows what he is doing while he acts aright; but of what is wrong we are always conscious. Whoever works with symbols only, is a pedant, a hypocrite, or a bungler.... The true scholar learns from the known to unfold the unknown, and approaches more and more to being a master.[7]

From *Meister*, Carlyle's relationship with Goethe, of which their correspondence is a curious and rather touching testimony, developed. Goethe became for Carlyle the archetypal hero as man of letters, and I would suggest that the reason why he was not included in the *Heroes* lectures was not the one given (that he was not well enough known in England – Mahomet was not either), but rather that Carlyle felt too close to his hero to make use of him in a series of popular lectures. Reverence adumbrates the renewed possibility not only of continued personal sanity, but also of spiritual order in the world at large:

> For it can never be forgotten that to [you] I owe the all-precious knowledge and experience that Reverence is still possible.... That you have carried and still carry such life-giving light into many a soul, wandering bewildered in the eclipse of doubt; till at length whole generations have cause to bless you, that instead of Conjecturing and Denying they can again Believe and Know; herein truly is a Sovereignty of quite indisputable Legitimacy, and which it is our only Freedom to obey.[8]

In an age of doubt, Goethe symbolised for many English intellectuals the possibility of triumph over the dissipation of knowledge.[9] He constituted a potent image for the possibility of meaningful devotion to the things of the mind. Carlyle further, and typically, found in him an image of sovereignty which fitted well with his belief – political as much as epistemological – in the authoritative nature of true knowledge. When Goethe died in 1832, Carlyle wrote that the sun had gone down, and in the years following he attempted to incorporate Goethe's role into himself. Teufelsdröckh, the jester through whom Carlyle could utter much that he meant in all serious-ness, made his first appearance in the very article in which he attempted to assess Goethe's work as a whole; he spoke (not for the last time) of that reverence for great men which was the type of man's search through the finite for the infinite. An almost fictional Goethe became a surrogate father for Carlyle, and one whose hero-ism as a sage Carlyle could himself carry on:

> For if I have been delivered from darkness into any measure of light, if I know aught of myself and my duties and destination, it is to the study of your writings more than to any other circumstance that I owe this; it is you more than any other man that I should always thank and reverence with the feeling of a Disciple to his Master, nay of a Son to his Spiritual Father.[10]

Under Goethe's aegis Carlyle achieved in 1827 a characteristic self-dramatisation:

> I look forward with cheerfulness to a life spent in Literature, with such fortune and such strength as may be granted me; hoping little and fearing little from the world; having learned that what I once called Happiness is not only not to be attained on Earth, but not even to be desired.[11]

In the guise of Teufelsdröckh, and using the editorial device to distance his comment, Carlyle played the role of the philosopher, perched high above his teeming 'Weissnichtwo', announcing through the clothes philosophy the tenets that were to remain his own.

Carlyle thus created for himself the role of spiritual authority, experimenting with various guises for the part. He is inescapable in this study because of the part he played in secularising the idea of spiritual authority. For him, all authority was authority over men's spirits, and the visible reality of our daily life was but the temporal vesture of the eternal order. He believed passionately in the ultimate moral order of the universe and the responsibility of the elect for its realisation in the human world. Further, he illuminated (because he was a cruder and less intrinsically interesting thinker than Coleridge) that Manichaean streak in those who adopted some version of the epistemology of *Vernunft–Verstand* and the related idea of the spiritual primacy of the elite. This assertion of spiritual authority was plainly one source of his appeal to the troubled young men of the 1840s and after. In a style more propagandistic than Coleridge's, more evangelical than Dr Arnold's, he proclaimed the exhilarating if fearful responsibility of those who were aware of the condition of the age. Edward Caird, the idealist philosopher, testified in 1892 that Carlyle was 'the greatest literary influence of my own student days'. He revived the 'old Platonic idea that the State had a social and ethical work to perform'. Even when the necessary criticisms have been made, 'we are forced to recognise that no English writer in this country has done more to elevate and purify our ideals of life, and to make us conscious that the things of the spirit are real, and that, in the last resort, there is no other reality'.[12]

Since Carlyle proposed the necessity of a spiritual authority, it is impossible to consider his development of secular morality or of the role of the man of letters without examining his attitude to one such existing authority, the Church of England. The most relevant document is his biography of John Sterling. To the old question as to what Sterling had done that could possibly rate a biography by Carlyle, the answer is, I think, sufficiently obvious. He had exemplified the problem of the sensitive educated young man trying to find a mission, and there can be no doubt that Carlyle identified, to some degree, with his problems. 'In Sterling's Writings and Actions, were they capable of being well read, we consider that there is for all true hearts, and especially for young noble seekers, and strivers towards what is highest, a mirror in which some shadow of themselves and of their immeasurably complex arena will profitably present itself.'[13] For Carlyle was involved in a movement whose concern was the duties of educated young men, a loose enough configuration of aspirations and one to which Carlyle lent a voice. Among other sources, his own 'Characteristics', *Heroes*, and *Life of Sterling*, Sterling's *Arthur Coningsby*, Disraeli's Young England writings, Kingsley's *Alton Locke* and *Yeast*, and F. D. Maurice's *Eustace Conway*, bear witness to a dilemma to which we shall have to return in chapter 6. All substantiate Disraeli's claim in *Sybil* that we 'live in an age when to be young and to be indifferent can no longer be synonymous'.[14] A rhetoric of uncertainty resolved or canalised spread abroad; it was, for example, Disraeli who asked whether the young men now in possession of the fundamental truth about their era would

remain brave, single, and true; refuse to bow before shadows and worship phrases; sensible of the greatness of their position, recognise the greatness of their duties; denounce to a perplexed and disheartened world the frigid theories of a generalising age that have destroyed the individuality of man; and restore the happiness of their country by believing in their own energies and daring to be great?[15]

Nor, in the context, was Disraeli's theatrical neo-feudalism an altogether surprising suggestion. Conviction of social mission had all the makings of a paternalistic spiritual (and hence also political) elitism.[16] To those caught in the intellectual and credal ferment of the 1830s, 1840s, and 1850s Carlyle said a lot, and many could have said with Froude, if not with the touch of the master's style, that 'I, for one . . . was saved by Carlyle's writings from Positivism, or Romanism, or Atheism, or any other of the creeds or no creeds which in these years were whirling about in Oxford like leaves in an autumn storm.'[17] To a perturbed generation, Carlyle appeared to hold out a radical critique of English social thought and a hope for the restoration of an organically integrated society through the beneficent operation of spiritual nobility. The ideas which were to legitimate imperial destiny later in the century were patented for use at home by conscientious and dedicated leaders of the blind.

What was a young man such as Sterling to do on leaving Cambridge? That there could be difficulty in finding out appeared to Carlyle one of the symptoms of the age. One answer, and the one accepted (eventually, and by default) by Sterling, was literature:

Of all forms of public life, in the Talking Era, it was clear that only one completely suited Sterling, – the anarchic, nomadic, entirely aerial and unconditional one called Literature.

For the

true Canaan and Mount Zion of a Talking Era must ever be literature, self-elected, indescribable *Parliamentum*, or Talking Apparatus, which talks by books and printed papers.[18]

But before Sterling reached this station there were the stumbling blocks of Coleridge and the Church of England.

It is important to an understanding of Carlyle's conception of the heroism of letters to see that Sterling's character was described in terms of power. The capacity to see further than others was some-times defined in terms of political power. In a revealing metaphor, Sterling was described as

a kingly kind of man; – whose 'kingdom', however, in this bewildered place and epoch of the world will probably be difficult to find and conquer!

Such was the world as it must have appeared to a young radical, and it is plain that for Carlyle it was a world to be overcome and forcibly subjected to the noble:

For alas, the world as we said, already stands committed to this young soul of being an untrue, unblessed world; its high dignitaries many of them phantasms and players' masks; its worships and worships unworshipful.[19]

In this pestiferous fog, Sterling had made the tragic error of listening to Coleridge and inclining to the church. *Sterling* is above all an anti-ecclesiastical document, written because Carlyle could not stand the official account by Archdeacon Hare, and it is bitter because, as a devout believer in spiritual authority, he felt deep antipathy for an institution whose claim to constitute such an authority was no longer remotely credible. Against Hare's story, he insisted that Sterling's theology, his curacy even, were mere excrescences on the surface of Sterling's life, and that his real needs (which had driven him to the church) lay within. Carlyle was incapable of writing anything that was not didactic, and the lesson was emphatically insisted upon; literature might serve these young men where the church, and, indeed, the accepted categories of political life, could not. On the rather tenuous thread of Sterling's life he hung both the possibilities of, and his objections to the Church of England for the public gaze.

Coleridge was a potential hero who had sold out; hence, I think, much of the bitterness which suffused Carlyle's much-quoted accounts of him. The sickly fruit of his spiritual laziness and *mauvaise foi* in endorsing the Church of England and its doctrines was still ripening. To assert this point, Carlyle even awarded Coleridge a place in the genealogy of the Oxford Movement: 'from his cloud Juno did not he too procreate strange Centaurs, spectral Puseyisms, monstrous illusory Hybrids, and ecclesiastical Chimeras, – which now roam the Earth in a very lamentable manner'.[20] Carlyle's variety of natural theology could, in any case, have no truck with orthodox theology. Here his position was one of historical relativism: there had been periods in which theology had been valuable, but now it was cant, and a cant which someone of Sterling's intelligence should have seen through at once. His strictures have their context in his ideas on what a church ought to be; priesthood, he had declared, was among the everlasting types of institution. But the form available in the existing church was completely unfitted for the present time and stood in the way of a just appreciation of what was going on in the world. Perhaps it was not surprising that such a 'vehement, trenchant, far-shining and yet intrinsically light and volatile soul' as Sterling's should be attracted to the church. But the failure to discriminate between true and false spiritual authority was a fundamental error:

To such lengths can transcendental moonshine, cast by some morbidly radiating Coleridge into the chaos of a fermenting life, act magically there and produce divulsions and convulsions and diseased developments. So dark and abstruse, without lamp or authentic fingerpost, is the course of pious genius towards the Eternal Kingdoms grown. No fixed highways more; the old spiritual highways and recognised paths to the Eternal now all torn up and flung in heaps, submerged in unutterable boiling mud-oceans of Hypocrisy and Cant.[21]

Carlyle objected not to Sterling's commitment to the clerks, but to his commitment to the Church of England. His belief in spiritual authority was unshaken. Had he not compared Samuel Johnson to the great churchmen of his day and found that 'the true Spiritual Edifier and Soul's father of all England was, and till very lately continued to be, the man named Samuel Johnson'.[22] To find out in what sense such a statement could be meaningful, we must recognise that for Carlyle true priesthood was an embodiment of the supremacy of the unseen over the material. If we examine what he meant by this supremacy, the identity of the hero will emerge more clearly. For it was the practice of this supremacy that priesthood, prophecy, or poetry shared with the literary class.

THE SUPREMACY OF THE UNSEEN WORLD

Carlyle's attitude to the relationship between matter and mind has a basic similarity to Coleridge's. More insistent and less given to qualification, he equated the triumph of mind with the kind of greatness of which great men were the examplars, and he set up a model for that breakthrough into majesty which so absorbed him in his fictional autobiographies:

There is something beautiful and moving in the aspect of a noble enthusiasm, fostered in the secret soul, amid obstructions and depressions, and at length bursting forth with an overwhelming force to accomplish its appointed end. . . . It seems the triumph, hardly contested, and not wholly carried, but still the triumph, of Mind over Fate, of human volition over material necessity.[23]

To overcome material necessity – and it is clear that for Carlyle this includes both material conditioning and inclinations from outside the known self – was a mental triumph of which the mass of people were simply incapable. In 'Signs of the Times' he yoked two doctrines that he found despicable – the determinism of 'circumstances of the time', and the belief that, collectively, 'little minds' were stronger than a 'great mind'. He continued: '*one* mind that has a higher Wisdom, a hitherto unknown spiritual Truth in him, is stronger . . . than *all* men that have it not; and stands among them with a quite ethereal, angelic power, as with a sword out of Heaven's own armory, sky-tempered, which no buckler and no tower of brass will finally withstand.'[24] A 'hitherto unknown spiritual Truth in him' is typical in that it suggests both the pre-existence of the truth at issue and a relationship between knower and known which is that of the receptacle to the spiritual substance. Some striking examples of the domination of matter by mind come from *Sartor*, where Teufelsdröckh repeatedly explains how our contrivances for overcoming nature and extending the empire of man – gunpowder, the printing press, the steam engine – are but the material apparitions of thought.[25] Carlyle obviously found the conceit comforting: through taking thought he too might be able to affect the world. Like Wotton Reinfred (the first of his autobiographical disguises) his sense of intellectual superiority over his coarse and bullying schoolfellows could now be exercised in a drama of triumph.[26] Halliday is clearly right in drawing attention to the curious episode in *Sartor* in which Teufelsdröckh, wrapped, like the Virgin Mary, in a blue cloak, puts to flight the intrusive Russian (representing 'savage animalism') on the North Cape.[27] Such passages suggest that the superiority of spirit over matter had a strong personal meaning for Carlyle. But there was more to it than merely legitimating his own existence as a writer and thinker. Like Coleridge (and I am not for one moment suggesting that Carlyle's development of the theme was as subtle or as suggestive as Coleridge's), Carlyle was excited by the distinction between *Vernunft* and *Verstand* which he understood in a very broad sense. 'Of the vast, nay in these days boundless, importance of this distinction, could it be scientifically established, we need remind no thinking man.'[28] Here again is the attraction towards participation in an unchanging world, a world serenely immune from the brutal and transient, though ultimately unreal phenomena of history. The context of inquiry and dissatisfaction in which this germinal theory of the mind appealed appears vividly in Carlyle's unfinished novel *Wotton Reinfred*. The philosopher (who, to judge by other indications, is based on Coleridge) speaks:

Understanding perceives and judges of images and measures of things ... reason perceives and judges of what has no measure or image. The latter only is unchangeable and everlasting in its decisions, the results of the former change from age to age; it is for these that men persecute and destroy one another; yet these comparatively are not worth the name of truth. They are not truth but only the ephemeral garments of truth.[29]

Carlyle's imaginative feeling for history (which leads him often enough into sympathetic accounts of different cultures and periods) is not to be allowed to infiltrate his reverence for spiritual authority. As an historian, he was torn between allegiance to a traditional, typological history and the influence of the new science. Greatness was the recognition of the divine spark of reason in your nature, and the determination to subdue the world to it. For Novalis, Carlyle wrote approvingly, 'the material Creation is but an Appearance, a typical Shadow in which the deity manifests himself to man'. Novalis had worked to 'preach and establish the Majesty of Reason, in that stricter sense; to conquer for it all provinces of human thought, and everywhere reduce its vassal, Understanding, into fealty, the right and only useful relation for it'.[30] Teufelsdröckh's history of thoughts – lacking any account of how thought became alienated as matter in the first place (Carlyle never seems to have come across Hegel) – was plainly imperative rather than descriptive.

A connection between Carlyle's idealism (the visible world is the vesture of the invisible) and his exploration of the importance of the intellectual emerges. What I am loosely calling his Manichaean outlook is central: the more the philosopher can reduce his dependence on the material world, the more force is his as the 'last forlorn outpost in the war of Mind against Matter'.[31] The man of letters, he had noted ruefully, 'is not wholly made of Spirit, but of clay and spirit mixed'.[32] He is therefore dependent on the material world: he needs food, shelter, company. Unlike the ordinary mortal, however, he must be discontented with this situation, and strive upwards; Carlyle was dogged by the fear of relapse into mere animalism. Literature in the broadest sense included the 'essence' of philosophy, religion, art, whatever spoke to the 'immortal part of man'. In the following passage, from the *Life of Schiller*, we can see how literature was adopted as the vehicle of the trans-material world. Further, we see emerging the configuration of sensual and mechanical, opposed to the spiritual and organic. The divine spark is entrusted not only to genius, but also to the servants and guardians of what genius has created. The boon literature bestowed was truth,

truth not merely physical, political, economical, such as the sensual man in us is perpetually demanding, ever ready to reward, and likely in general to find; but truth of moral feeling, truth of taste, that inward truth in its thousand modifications, which only the most ethereal portion of our nature can discern, but without which that portion of it languishes and dies, and we are left divested of our birthright, thenceforward 'of the earth earthy', machines for earning and enjoying, no longer worthy to be called the sons of Heaven. The treasures of Literature are thus celestial, imperishable, beyond all price: with her is the shrine of our best hopes, the palladium of pure manhood; to be among the guardians and servants of this is the noblest function that can be intrusted to a mortal.[33]

Carlyle has discovered his role, a role which demands purity and the renunciation of the sensible world. In a world bogged down at the level of sense – the fearful legacy of the materialist eighteenth century – the basic facts of man's existence on earth must be discovered and represented. If man again becomes aware of himself as a spiritual being, he will rediscover order in the universe. To bear this message requires a redefinition of the roles of prophet and priest, of the man who is sent (like Schiller, Goethe, or Teufelsdröckh) to 'body forth somewhat out of chaos'.

The idea of creation as the imposition of order, and of greatness as the establishment of order where there was none before is a constant in Carlyle's thought. It is as apparent in the chaos – cosmos opposition of the *Latter Day Pamphlets*, as in 'Signs of the Times' nearly quarter of a century before. Within the idea of creation we can see growing emphasis on the order which is created: spiritual power imposes order, but Carlyle was finally to invest spiritual power not in the man of letters, but in the man whose strength took political, even military form – a shift, in terms of his autobiographical adventures, from Schiller, Goethe, and Teufelsdröckh, via Abbot Samson, to Cromwell and Frederick the Great. With his increasing admiration for absolute power, the projected order too becomes absolute. Goethe had presented him with the notion of spiritual authority ruling the world:

It begins to be everywhere surmised that the real Force, which in this world all things must obey is Insight, Spiritual Vision and Determination. The thought is parent of the Deed, nay, is living soul of it, and last and continual, as well as first mover of it; is the foundation and beginning of man's whole existence here below. In this sense, it has been said, the Word of man (the uttered thought of man) is still a magic formula, whereby he rules the world.[34]

His intuition of the 'real Force' is not merely abstract: it bears directly on his own aims. While writing his review of William Taylor's book on German poetry, he wrote to Goethe: 'Were this 'Historical View' once off my hands, I still purpose to try something infinitely greater! Alas, alas! the huge formless Chaos is here, but no creative voice to say, 'Let there be Light', and make it into a world.'[35] While God remained silent, His emissaries might deputise. Goethe encouraged Carlyle in this ideal of the man of letters devoted to creation out of chaos, just as Dante had created Italy as a moral, cultural whole.[36] In the following passage from the 'Historic Survey of German Poetry' the place of literature in the general conception of the supremacy of mind is apparent. So too is the assimilation of 'poet' to 'thinker'.

Late in man's history, yet clearly at length, it becomes manifest to the
dullest, that mind is stronger than matter, that mind is the creator and
shaper of matter; that not brute Force, but only Persuasion and Faith is
the king of this world. The true Poet, who is but the inspired Thinker, is
still an Orpheus whose lyre tames the savage beasts, and evokes the dead
rocks to fashion themselves into palaces and stately inhabited cities. It has
been said, and may be repeated, that Literature is fast becoming all in all to
us; our Church, our Senate, our whole Social Constitution. The true Pope
of Christendom is not that feeble old man in Rome; nor is its Autocrat the
Napoleon, the Nicholas, with his half-million even of obedient bayonets:
such Autocrat is himself but a more cunningly-devised bayonet and military
engine in the hands of a mightier than he. The true Autocrat and Pope is
that man, the real or seemingly Wisest of the past age; crowned after
death; who finds his hierarchy of gifted Authors, his Clergy of assiduous
Journalists; whose Decretals, written not on parchment, but on the living
souls of men, it were an inversion of the laws of Nature to *dis*obey. In these
times of ours, all Intellect has fused itself into Literature: Literature,
Printed Thought, is the molten sea and wonder-bearing chaos, into which
mind after mind casts forth its opinion, its feeling, to be molten into the
general mass, and to work there; Interest after Interest is engulfed in it, or
embarked on it: higher, higher it rises round all the Edifices of Existence;
they must all be molten into it, and anew bodied forth from it, or stand
unconsumed among its fiery surges. Woe to him whose Edifice is not built
of true Asbest, and on the everlasting Rock; but on the false sand, and of
the drift-wood of Accident, and the paper and parchment of antiquated
Habit! For the power or powers, exist not on our Earth, that can say to that
sea, Roll back, or bid its proud waves be still.[37]

Traces of ambivalence about literature there are, but nevertheless
in this, his period of optimism about literature, Carlyle's theory was
to be his practice. The image of the light of society was for him a
magnetic image: Goethe, we remember, he had likened to the sun.
The image of light which, frustrated or pent up, becomes lightning,
stems from a kind of fantasy physics that recurs in his consciousness.
It affirms a kind of self-dramatisation. Wotton, jilted by the girl he
loved, complains in wording that inevitably recalls the first chapter
of John's Gospel, that she has preferred the darkness to light.
Carlyle's offering himself to society as light which, if rejected, will
return as lightning or volcanic fire, reminds one again of his affinities
with Nietzsche.[38] The great man, he said at the beginning of his
Heroes lectures, 'is the living light-fountain, which it is good and
pleasant to be near. The light which enlightens, which has enlightened the darkness of the world.'[39] The significance of this
ubiquitous image is twofold: for not only does it suggest that the

great man is sent by God (either as a gift or as vengeance), but also, in proposing an identity between insight, leadership, and retributive violence, it provides an imaginative vehicle for Carlyle's transition from self-characterisation as the light-bearer, to Thor, the thunderer; from Goethe's hopeful correspondent, to the author of 'Shooting Niagara'. It was well that Abbot Samson repressed his anger 'that it may become in [him] as noble central heat, fruitful, strong, beneficent; not blaze out, or the seldomest possible blaze out, as wasteful volcanism to scorch and consume'.[40]

Writing thus became the legitimate outlet for wrath. As historian (and historian, too, of the French Revolution, that cautionary tale of cataclysmic vengeance on inattentive rulers), as social thinker, and as philosopher he could work upon society as Samson (the same age when elected, as Carlyle when he wrote *Past and Present*, and even a little like Carlyle to look at)[41] worked upon his abbey with his 'clear-beaming eyesight': 'it is like *Fiat lux* in that inorganic waste whirlpool; penetrates gradually to all nooks, and of the chaos makes a *kosmos* or ordered world!'[42] Thus he brought about a 'total change of regimen, change of constitution and existence from the very centre of it; a new body to be got at, with resuscitated soul'.[43] Yet although Carlyle had outlined in 1840 the way in which heroism could be realised in letters, his doubts about literature grew. Around the time of the *Heroes* lectures he laid down a programme for himself in a letter to Sterling, who had urged him to start a periodical for the expression of his views. Carlyle (not, one feels, well fitted to work with collaborators) replied that he had no 'fighting regiment', but that the picture was not all black: 'failing all things, and failing all men, there remains the solitary battle (and were it by the poorest weapon, the tongue only, or were it by wise abstinence and silence and without any weapon), such as each man can wage for himself while he has life'.[44] From this time onwards, even as a man of letters (his bid to act as Peel's mentor was hopeless from the start), he marched steadily away from the literary ideal. His strong men were strong in immediately political ways; his images became more martial, and his pessimism about literature more marked, so that young men writing to him about their careers (they went on doing this to the end) were always advised against literature, the characteristic verbal anti-verbalism having added prose to poetry on the infernal index. 'Surely it is better for a man to *work* out his God given faculty than merely to speak it out?'[45] Behind this advice lies the disaster of Carlyle's life, his ambivalence, his self-doubt, and his contempt. Speaking to Froude, even before Jane Welsh's death, he remarked that if 'there be one thing for which I have no special talent it is literature. If I had been taught to *do* the simplest useful thing, I should have been a better and happier man. All that I can say is, that I have done my best.'[46]

Carlyle is in many ways an unattractive figure, and there is something peculiarly repellent about the pleasure he takes in his own verbal violence ('I vomited it forth upon them like wild Annandale grapeshot', he wrote to his mother about the lecture on 'The Hero as Prophet'), and in posing as a 'wild man' against a world which not only tolerated, but often liked him. In a letter to his brother John he characterised his *French Revolution*: 'I find on a general view that the book is one of the *savagest* written for several centuries. It is a book written by a *wild man*, a man disunited from the fellowship of the world he lives in, looking king and beggar in the face with an indifferent brotherhood and an indifference of contempt.'[47]

In all fairness we must remember that Carlyle had been, and to some extent remained, an outsider in literary London, but his posturing was scarcely calculated to lessen his isolation. The fortune of the man-of-letters ideal was closely allied to his changing hopes for his own achievement. Hope and despair about literature are counterpointed in his work, but, as he got older, the latter voice predominated. In 1833 he had written that literature is 'but a branch of religion, and always participated in its character: however in our time, it is the only branch that still shows any greenness'. Yet even in this essay the equation of silence and health was to hand, and he came close to a version of *Civilisation and its Discontents* as he verged on saying that all conscious knowledge is a 'symptom of derangement'. Throughout

the whole world of man, in all manifestations and performances of his nature, outward and inward, personal and social, the Perfect, the Great is a mystery to itself; whatsoever knows itself is already little, and more or less imperfect. Or otherwise, we may say, Unconsciousness belongs to pure unmixed life; Consciousness to a diseased mixture and conflict of life and death; Unconsciousness is the sign of creation; consciousness, at best, that of manufacture. So deep in this existence of Ours, is the significance of Mystery. Well might the Ancients make Silence a God.[48]

That any man had to speak was in itself a symptom of a diseased society; even more so was the babble of uncertain and critical voices

Carlyle heard around him. With such a disposition, the chances for a class of professional truth-tellers were poor. To the 'outlet of literature', the 'haven of expatriated spiritualism . . . do the windy aspirations, foiled activities, foolish ambitions, and frustrate human energies reduced to the vocable condition, fly as the one refuge left; and the Republic of Letters increases in population at a faster rate than the Republic of America'.[49] The truth-tellers were likely to be infected with the very disease they diagnosed; all whose vocation was not for strong silent action were suspect. The grandiose ambition for literary omnipotence bred a correspondingly bitter disappointment. Hero status proved beyond Carlyle's reach. Instead, he would cultivate the role of the wild man, of the bitter fool at the court of industrial society. Unfortunately, he lacked the good humour essential to the fool, and was incapable of severing his personal obsessions from his account of society. Both his considerable historical insight, and his measure of sociological imagination were lost in the intellectual pursuit of leadership and the ambiguous cogitations over the identity of might and right. Increasingly, his misanthropy rather than his sympathy informed his system. Spiritual authority had to be built upon the facts of the universe, not on shifting human concerns. We must return to the connection between spiritual authority and the absolute world, a world which in its stability, consistency, and hierarchy provides a source of consolation for superior souls fated to struggle in 'this wild death-element of Time'.

THE PROPHET AND THE PRIEST

Let us start with the question why the man of letters rather than the poet was chosen as the exponent in his age of the transcendent order. At the time of *Schiller*, as we have noted, Carlyle included the poets in the literary class. That Goethe was a poet was emphasised in the essays on his works and on his death. Dante and Shakespeare (heroes as poets) received a lecture in the 1840 series. Why, then was the man of letters our 'most important modern person'?[50] Where a Shelley had found the poet to be the unacknowledged legislator, Carlyle's emphasis gave the major influence to the non-fiction writer. Why was he so suspicious of poetry? Clearly, there is an element of Platonic distrust: poets are apt to deal irresponsibly with the metaphysical order. With one part of him Carlyle found the poet a kind of heroic figure belonging to all ages, a hero for whom it was 'a necessity of nature to live in the very facts of things'. But in his puritan preacher's voice he feared that the creative writer was liable to make things not found in nature, and so to parody the work of the divine creator. Thus, in the essay on 'Biography' (1833) he invoked another fictitious professor, Sauerteig, to remind us that 'Fiction, while the feigner of it knows that he is feigning, partakes more than we suspect of the nature of *lying*.' An emphasis falls on 'knows', since in Carlyle's creed (coloured as it is by his era's nostalgia for the naive at the expense of the sentimental) unconscious creation was blessed. Again, it 'is part of my creed that the only Poetry is History, could we tell it right'.[51] That belief, at least, is constant: more than thirty years later, in 'Shooting Niagara', he announced that 'the genuine "Art" in all times is a synonym for God Almighty's Facts – which come direct from Heaven, but in so abstruse condition, and cannot be read at all till the better intellect intepret them'.[52] 'Fact' allows pretty ample scope for changing definitions, of course, and often a value judgment about particular works (this is not about facts, therefore it's poetry, and bad) rather than about poetry as a whole is meant. (In the same essay, Carlyle talked about reading Shakespeare as history.) Nevertheless, there is a discernible shift of emphasis, even within the terms of an existing ambivalence, as he came to subordinate poetry within the sphere of letters. In the present age (a kind of mirror image Gradgrind comes to light) we must insist on fact.

There is, however, more to Carlyle's distrust of the creative writer than can be explained by reference to his inherent puritan distrust of 'feigning'. Sterling's visits to Italian art galleries were contemptuously dismissed as 'prescribed not by Nature and her verities, but by the Century expecting every man to do his duty'.[53] By exploring Carlyle's distrust of art further we may elicit something of central importance to our study. His theory of literary creation asserted not innovation, not modifying, but the interpretation of the truth obscured by the jumble of contingent circumstances. Between poetic creativity, and the realisation of the cosmos as manifestation of the eternal order we pass along the road of the seer or *vates*, the road by which the jester became the priest. His was what Kolakowski has called the 'nostalgia for revelation',[54] and his career illustrates the way in which the striving to take the chaotic back to uniform principle can be wedded to a social doctrine. The poet's role must converge with that of the seer; if it did not, so much the worse for the poet.

In his essay on Goethe's death, Carlyle had tried to preserve a major role for the poet in declaring that he was not just a singer of pleasant songs:

> The true Poet is ever, as of old, the Seer; whose eye has been gifted to discern the godlike Mystery of God's universe, and decipher some new lines of its celestial writing; we can still call him a *Vates* and Seer; for he sees into this greatest of secrets, 'the open secret'; hidden things become clear; how the Future (both resting on Eternity) is but another phasis of the Present: thereby are his words in very truth prophetic; what he has spoken shall be done.[55]

This might be a good defence of the poet against the Philistine, but in practice it implied severe limits on his creativity. Caird was to note – fairly, I think – that Carlyle tended only to approve of the kind of literature he was good at writing himself. Even when, early on, he looked forward to the fusion of poetry and philosophy, the former was to be submerged in the latter. In his essay on Novalis he anticipated the arrival of a third class of philosophers, those who would unite philosophy and poetry, for the 'division of Philosopher and Poet is only apparent and to the disadvantage of both'.[56] The *vates*, as channel between the phenomenal and noumenal worlds, occupied a crucial position in Carlyle's system. Any derogation of that high seriousness must indeed be irresponsible trifling. From creation to revelation lay a fatally easy road, and Carlyle's man-of-letters ideal rested on the identification of creation with perception:

> It is unexampled, I think, that calm creative perspicacity of Shakespeare. The thing he looks at reveals not this or that face of it, but its inmost heart, and generic secret: it dissolves itself as in light before him, so that he discerns the perfect structure of it. Creative, we said: poetic creation, what is this too but *seeing* the thing sufficiently? ... Goethe alone, since the days of Shakespeare, reminds me of it. Of him too you may say that he *saw* the object.[57]

Since the 'central principle is the same both in the philosopher and the poet', both become the mediators between the unseen world and the social, a 'perpetual priesthood, we might say'. We may infer that they do for society what society (whose eyes are glued to the actual) cannot do for itself. These last two quotations come from Carlyle's 1827 article on the 'State of German Literature', in which he rendered Fichte's *Gelehrter* as 'literary man'. It is time for us to examine the formulation of the idea of the literary man in whom the roles of poet, philosopher, and priest were combined.

Here, our main text must be the lecture from the 1840 series on 'The Hero as Man of Letters'. We have already noted that Carlyle was impressed by Fichte's Erlangen lectures 'On the Nature of a Scholar', which seem to have reinforced his own feeling of mission. Fichte's notion of the man of letters 'means, in its own form, precisely what we here mean', he announced in the hero lecture.[58] He left out the details, but warmly endorsed the general argument which he re-stated in his own terms. Historically, he argued, the writer of books came to replace the priest. The social medium on which his influence and the very form of his existence rested was the press. This required a definition of the church as 'the working recognised Union of our Priests or Prophets, of those who by wise teaching guide the souls of men'.[59] A definition which had the virtue of rendering priesthood, prophecy, and teaching interchangeable. Books had but altered the form of the church: 'He that can write a true Book, to persuade England, is not he the Bishop and Archbishop, the Primate of England and of all England? I many a time say, the writers of Newspapers, Pamphlets, Poems, Books these *are* the real working effective Church of a modern country.'[60] *Chartism* and *Past and Present* seem to constitute a very real claim for spiritual authority. In Carlyle as in Coleridge, the clerisy is seen in connection with the restoration of the organic nature of thought and of society. We have to see their proposals in the context of their strictures on the eighteenth century as a sterile age based on a false, mechanical philosophy. To Carlyle, the eighteenth century was the age against which the heroes, Johnson, Rousseau, and Burns (an unlikely triumvirate) had struggled with but indifferent success. He compared the organic with the mechanistic metaphor: 'The living TREE Igdrasil, with the melodious prophetic waving of its world-wide boughs, deep-rooted as Hela, has died into the clanking of a World-MACHINE.'[61] The result was the 'spiritual paralysis' of scepticism and the state of society diagnosed in 'Signs of the Times'. But it was possible to rout the mechanical philosophy, and at his most optimistic Carlyle was worthy of the optimism of the age. The man of letters remained an ideal hero for him as long as he felt capable of realising his own mission through letters. The literary class could not go on for ever 'unrecognised and unregulated like Ishmaelites among us'. In the hoped-for Literary Guild the outsider becomes the priest. Carlyle liked to think of himself as the outsider he in some ways was; Teufelsdröckh had been likened to the Wandering Jew, even to

Cain.[62] But the outsider was not in the end to prove such a stranger to his society's ways. All being well, the stone the builders rejected would become the cornerstone of the social edifice. Carlyle recognised that the organisation of the Literary Guild was a long way off, but insisted that a way out of chaos must be found:

> The result to individual Men of Letters is not the momentous one; they are but individuals, an infinitesimal fraction of the great body; they can struggle on, and live or else die, as they have been wont. But it deeply concerns the whole society, whether it will set its *light* in high places to walk thereby; or trample it under foot, and scatter it in all ways of wild waste (not without conflagration), as heretofore! Light is the one thing wanted for the world. Put wisdom in the head of the world, the world will fight its battle victoriously, and be the best world man can make it. I call this anomaly of a disorganic Literary Class the heart of all other anomalies, at once product and parent; some good arrangement for that would be as the *punctum saliens* of a new vitality and a just arrangement for all.[63]

About one detail, however, Carlyle was clear, 'That royal or parliamentary grants of money are by no means the chief thing wanted!'[64] Poverty was not good, but it could be a useful test of sincerity. The Literary Guild was a kind of church in exile, prepared to usher in the day when society should again admit its own rootedness in the eternal world. Johnson, Rousseau, and Burns, three examples of a limited sort of heroism, had lived as exiles in their own age. More could be hoped for. In Fichte's thought, as in the *Republic*, the philosopher is he whose vision is so far superior to that of ordinary mortals that he is alive to the supersensible essence of things. Thus – and there is undoubtedly a large compensatory element in the vision – he is more than a seer or a prophet: he is in some sense a ruler. Here the significance of Carlyle's identification with Fichte becomes clearer. He will claim the role of prophet for the man of letters, but in the new organic age the prophet will have become the priest. This was not just a comforting myth about a continually receding future; Carlyle continued to speak of the advent of the new organic age as just around the corner.[65] The order of the *Heroes* lectures is suggestive: in the early ones the procession of guises was acknowledgedly that followed in history: Divinity – Prophet – Poet – Man of Letters – King. 'All true Reformers . . . are by the nature of them Priests, and strive for a Theocracy.'[66] I can best clarify my argument by quoting Kolakowski's early essay on the 'Priest and the Jester', where he discusses the antagonism between the two types:

The priest is the guardian of the absolute; he sustains the cult of the final and the obvious as acknowledged by and contained in tradition. The jester is he who ... doubts all that appears self-evident. ... [Though] it is true that philosophers have amused monarchs, their antics have played a part in earthquakes – precisely when they were the gambols of jesters. Priests and jesters cannot be reconciled unless one of them is transformed into the other, as sometimes happens. (Most often the jester becomes a priest – as Socrates became Plato – and not vice-versa). In every era the jester's philosophy exposes as doubtful what seems most unshakable, reveals the contradictions in what appears obvious and incontrovertible, derides common sense and reads sense into the absurd. ... Depending on time and place, the jester's thinking can range through all the extremes of thought, for what is sacred today was paradoxical yesterday, and absolutes on the equator are often blasphemies at the poles. The jester's constant effort is to consider all the possible reasons for contradictory ideas. It is thus dialectical by nature.[67]

Carlyle's is the case of a jester who comes to feel himself the guardian of the absolute.

We are here dealing with a psychological movement akin to the one we found in Coleridge, and we should not be supercilious about the reasons for feeling that the world of early industrial England simply could not be the real world. At the same time, if we are to understand Carlyle, we must recognise the symptoms of retreat from particularity (*haecceitas* as Hopkins might have said) towards the rational world of spirit. To attempt to evade conditioning forces outside the rational self can be a costly enterprise. Of Schiller, Carlyle had early written with a marked admiration that the

Ideal Man that lay within him, the image of himself as he *should* be, was formed upon a strict and curious standard; and to reach this constantly approached and constantly receding emblem of perfection was the unwearied effort of his life.[68]

To continue this effort he kept apart from the temptations of the world:

he contrived to steer through life, unsullied by its meanness, unsubdued by any of its difficulties or allurements. With the world, in fact, he had not much to do.[69]

So as to overcome the divisiveness of the world of sense, Carlyle hypothesised a character type drawn to the security of the monistic world of spirit. Teufelsdröckh's way to the 'Everlasting Aye' – the recognition that the 'Universe is not dead and demonical, a charnel-house with spectres; but godlike, and my Father's!'[70] – was through renunciation, the idea of which had fascinated Carlyle in *Wilhelm*

Meisters' Wanderjahre, with its subtitle *Die Entsagenden* (the re-nunciants, as Carlyle had it). As Harrold has pointed out, Carlyle took *Entsagen* (renunciation) not as the withholding of elements that should be active at another time, but as a puritan giving-up of the wilful desires of the phenomenal self.[71] Hence he could identify it with the *Selbsttödtung* (literally, death of the self) he found in Novalis. Similarly, Fichte had argued that the life according to reason entailed forgetting oneself in the idea, and renouncing any enjoyment save that to be found in ideas. He, too, had attempted to have it both ways, claiming that everything 'great and good upon which our present existence rests ... has an existence only because noble and powerful men have resigned all the enjoyments of life for the sake of Ideas', but (having made this bid for heroism) also asserting that the sacrifice was of course easy, since once you had relinquished the lower life you did not have the base inclinations to be combatted.[72] Teufelsdröckh taught that the way to realise the Godlike in man was through the annihilation of self, thus taking advantage of the suffering of which the world was so liberal. 'Love not Pleasure; love God. This is the EVERLASTING YEA, wherein all contradiction is solved.'[73] He thus provided Carlyle with a mouth-piece for advocating a positive zest for martyrdom.

Unlike Coleridge, Carlyle did not attempt a philosophic appraisal of the world of spirit. It remained for him an oft-invoked possibility of a sphere 'wherein all contradiction is solved', yet a possibility with profound consequences for letters and the men of letters as mediators between the phenomenal and noumenal worlds. For it shuts out another possibility – that there might be conflict between genuine values, or discontinuities between the aspects of the Ideal. The best, Carlyle insists, is internally consistent. Therefore the shaping insight that was the seer's, that had been Goethe's, and that could be Carlyle's own, was the impress on the sensible world of an indissoluble order. It was entirely in keeping that he failed to grasp that Fichte's Divine Idea was an object of infinite activity, not a perfect and directing Being.[74] The unseen world rendered a legislative pattern.

TRUTH OR SHAM

Carlyle's mythopoeic powers and his ability to dramatise the tensions of his own life and role were considerable. He was, we know, fascinated by myth and legend and widely read in it. He endowed

English, French, and German history with a kind of mythic quality: the drama of the realisation of spiritual power was fundamentally the same in all ages and all cultures. Now in myth (as, in a rather different way, in imaginative literature) men have found ways to speak about problems that the law – or, in more advanced societies, the prevailing rationality – cannot cope with. They have made, so to speak, foraging raids on the realms of paradox and discordant meaning in an attempt to render it publicly comprehensible. Carlyle, however, wants to subordinate the myth to a prescriptive, legislative vision of the world. The lives of great men remind us of the ideal cosmos which it is our duty to realise on earth. The jester is banished, and with him goes the possibility of tragedy.

How can this be true of Carlyle, with his constant sense of suffering, and belief in its therapeutic powers? When Dante passed, he says, the people of Verona used to say:

'See, there is the man that was in Hell!' Ah, yes, he had been in Hell; – in Hell enough, in long severe sorrow and struggle; as the like of him is pretty sure to have been. Commedias that come out *divine* are not accomplished otherwise. Thought, true labour of any kind, highest virtue itself, is it not the daughter of Pain? Born as out of the black whirlwind; – true *effort*, in fact, as of a captive struggling, to free himself: that is Thought. In all ways we are 'to become perfect through *suffering*.'[75]

The answer is that Carlyle's belief in the virtues of suffering does not invalidate my argument. For in place of the potential conflict of one truth with another, one right action with another, he sets up the simple binary opposition of truth and sham. What he fears in the world of sense is not just conditioning by forces from outside the rational self, but also the divisiveness of drives and desires, the deep antagonisms that can emerge between one set of desires and another. Hence he asserts the singularity of the world of spirit, the myth without paradox. If we ground our duty on an unseen world of that sort, we are spared the confrontation of one value with another, and have merely to choose between fact and fiction, reality and semblance, truth and sham, heroism and valetism. The practical outcome of the uniformity of the spiritual world is that consistency of duty in which Carlyle desperately believed throughout his life. For the dread that you might be mistaken in your duty there was the simple injunction to do the job that was nearest. Teufelsdröckh gave a kind of hallmark to nineteenth-century England in insisting that 'Doubt of any sort cannot be removed except by Action. . . . *Do the*

Duty which lies nearest thee.'[76] This was indeed to preach earnestness to a nation that had plenty already, and it is a justified up-
dating of Arnold's criticism to remark, as has Goodheart, on the
irony of preaching the duty of work to a nation already in a frenzy
of economic growth.[77] Carlyle's world is an impoverished world
because it is one in which the absolute is in schematic opposition to
the world of sense. The only proper attitude is therefore submission
to immutable and inscrutable law. In such a world you either opt
for the good or you do not. Tragic suffering is either deserved, or
the suffering of the good trapped in an evil world, the captive
struggling to escape.

In identifying certain aspects of Carlyle's ideas of spiritual authority, I believe we can also discover more about his appeal to his
contemporaries, for which so many witnesses speak. Carlyle, following a beaten Romantic track, approached the abyss of the unconscious, but then fled back from the cave to the sunshine of rational
control and the cult of the authoritarian self projected as hero.
His historico-mythological dramas of heroism re-play over and over
again this emergence from the quasi-animal, conditioned life of the
mass to the freedom of leadership. In an early article, he quoted
Novalis's argument that nature was appalling, a kind of objective
correlative for the passions within man:

The waking man looks without fear at this offspring of his lawless Imagination; for he knows that they are but vain Spectres of his weakness. He feels
himself Lord of the world: his *Me* hovers victorious over the Abyss; and
will through Eternities hover aloft, above that endless Vicissitude. Harmony is what his spirit strives to promulgate, to extend. He will even to
infinitude grow more and more harmonious with himself and with his
Creation; and at every step behold the all-efficiency of a high moral Order
in the Universe, and what is purest of his *Me*, come forth into brighter and
brighter clearness.[78]

One source of Carlyle's appeal, I suggest, is just this: that in an age
of doubt concerning the functions of thought and the precarious
state of the rational ego, he appeared to have come to terms with the
volcanic forces within himself, and harnessed them for rational and
social ends. *Sartor Resartus* was the first instalment in the story of
this triumph over the forces of disintegration. We seem, not for the
first time, to be faced with an effort to socialise certain phenomena
which had been publicly adumbrated in the Romantic era. One
aspect of this accommodation of Romanticism to society has been

suggested by Goodheart: 'Out of an extraordinary insensitivity to
the claims of the poet – one might add to the claims of his own
raging imaginative energy – Carlyle prematurely committed the
poetic imagination to the social conscience.'[79] There was, however,
more than insensitivity at work. Determined opposition would, I
think, be nearer the mark. Spiritual authority, Carlyle proposed to
the Victorians, whether within the individual or in society, was normative. Building on elements he found in the German Romantics, he
had come to a recognition of the power of the unconscious within
the personality. This indeed was the germ of the 'Gospel of Silence',
and that it should become a Gospel is entirely characteristic of
Carlyle and his age. 'Unconsciousness belongs to pure unmixed life;
Consciousness to a diseased mixture and conflict of life and death;
Unconsciousness is the sign of Creation; Consciousness, at best, that
of manufacture. So deep, in this existence of Ours, is the significance
of Mystery. Well might the Ancients make Silence a God.'[80] In his
critique of the prevailing rationality as analysed in 'Signs of the
Times', and in his rejection of the usurpation within man of the
'mere argumentative region',[81] Carlyle had the makings of a devasta-
ting attack on the liberal rationality of his hated opponents. However, just at the point of leverage, he foreclosed on the attempt,
performing the manoeuvre that Nietzsche would have had no difficulty in diagnosing as that of the priest.

Let us go one stage further, for Carlyle was not Nietzsche, and
for him the moral view of man did not represent treason to the
potential of the self. The self was a whole, and it was no pre-
judgment of the issue to declare that it was a moral whole. The

thing a man does practically believe (and this is often enough *without*
asserting it even to himself much less to others); the thing a man does
practically lay to heart, and know for certain, concerning his vital relations
to this mysterious Universe, and his duty and destiny there, that is in all
cases the primary thing for him, and creatively determines all the rest.
That is his *religion*.[82]

We may applaud Carlyle for seeing religion as an act of the total
self, but the statement easily becomes tautologous. The account of
religion plainly springs from the same impulse as the view of society
resting upon a spiritual centre (for instance in 'Characteristics',
where the periphery of sensible history is epiphenomenal to the
centre: 'the Physical derangements of Society are but the image and
impress of its Spiritual').[83] The doctrine stands in healthy opposition

to unthinking pluralism. It asserts that man is '*one* ... and preaches the same Self abroad in all these ways'.[84] It asserts that all a man does 'is physiognomical of him'. Applied to society or to the universe, it asserts the interconnectedness of things.[85] The universe makes sense, and makes sense in historical terms. The doctrine is, in fact, a Romantic form of monism which Carlyle shares with Freud and, reinforced by the experience of writing novels (for it makes obvious sense to predicate the unity of a character with his situation in a work of fiction), with Lawrence. Now, this monistic drive is an essential moment of intellectual activity. But it needs to be corrected by another moment – that provided by the jester. If his philosophy is cancelled, the monistic drive hastens to assert that the meaning of the universe is not still-to-make, but immanent. The drive makes for a theodicy of the human psyche, deriving events from the nature of the beings who are subject to them. It is the jester's vision (or anti-vision) – that totality surpasses descriptions and is in itself merely a useful fiction – that tends to be confirmed by our experience of art: things are not discrete, 'forever in disconnection, dead and spiritless'. Nevertheless, the inscape, the configuration that the imagination grasps, is the work of the continued application of intelligence, not an all-embracing legislative order. For the jester, life, and man's interaction with the physical universe, is a process exhibiting tensions which may even be irreconcilable. Art can therefore register not only the conflict of values, but the drama of action and belief at points where moral certitude is inadequate or irrelevant. Carlyle's convergence with the ideology of his time is apparent in his postulating an absolute self to counteract divisive pressures. His tragedy was that he wanted to found spiritual power on unimpeachable authority.

The frustration of one whose ambition was authority – authority over the psyche, converting the lightning to light; authority over society, convincing it of its real needs – was bound to be terrible. Let us be fair to Carlyle: it is only with the arrogance of hindsight that we declare that his critique took a wrong turning and became a rationalisation for an authoritarian social mode. It is always easy to spot the shortcomings of other people's radicalism. His own road was no easy one. Through the pages of Froude, and in his own writings, we sense the mounting frustration, in the face of an iniquitous society, with the squandering of his own powers. Ruskin, who likewise formulated the idea of a spiritual order, felt a similar

resentment at the waste of his own potential: of Cruikshank he
wrote that it was 'no more his business to etch diagrams of drunken-
ness than it is mine at this moment to be writing these letters against
anarchy. . . . But in a sorely besieged town, every man must to the
ramparts, whatsoever business he leaves, so neither he nor I have had
any choice.'[86] I have already indicated what a direct route there was
for Carlyle from creativity to cosmos, from man of letters, through
seer, to avenging hero. The abstract condition of 'Hero', we should
remember, precedes any of the particular guises imposed by specific
historical situations, so there is an important similarity between
Johnson and Frederick the Great. Carlyle's ambivalence towards
letters was given an even more negative turn, not only by his growing
apprehension that the social world would not respond to writing in
the way he had hoped, but by disappointment in his fellow men of
letters, among whom he had, since coming to London, been marking
out possible followers.[87] Like a number of other powerful person-
alities in the annals of thought, he did not like his followers to show
too much independence; paradoxically, the prophet of the Literary
Guild remained alone.

The demands of the social crisis far outran the prescription of the
Literary Guild, and the implied nature of the great man and of the
measures Carlyle expected of him can be seen changing step by step
in the letters to Emerson, the *Latter Day Pamphlets* and 'Shooting
Niagara'. Even before he lost his faith in the capacity of literature
to effect social change, the nature of the theory is to be glimpsed in
his attitude to education. It is of course true that there is some
ambiguity in his thinking on this subject. As late as 1876 he wrote to
a young correspondent who had asked his advice on a choice of
career as follows:

On the whole there is nothing strikes me as likelier for one of your disposition than the profession of teacher, which is rising into higher request
every day, and has scope in it for the grandest endowments of human
faculties (could such hitherto be got to enter it), and of all useful and fruitful employments may be defined as the usefullest, fruitfullest, and also
indispensabilist in these days of ours.[88]

Carlyle clearly had in mind the Reform Act and Forster's Education
Act, and a reading of his most explicit writing on the Reform
question – 'Shooting Niagara' – must make us wonder about the
nature of the education under consideration. Here, for example, he
speculates on what a revived king and aristocracy might achieve:

Schools, for example, a schooling and training of [the kingdom's] young subjects *in the way that they should go, and in the things they should do*: what a boundless outlook that of schools, and of improvement in school methods and school purposes.

For Carlyle, even more explicitly than for Coleridge, or for Robert Lowe, education was a means of social control, a point confirmed by his rapid turning to the matter of military drill:

I always fancy there might much be done in the way of military Drill withal. Beyond all other schooling, and as a supplement or even succadaneum for all other, one often wishes the entire Population could be thoroughly drilled.... That of commanding and obeying ... is it not the basis of all human culture?[89]

We need not be surprised. Carlyle's hero had always had the job of commanding the mass of men who were incapable of far-reaching vision, and whose heroism could, at most, consist in the worship of the heroes who led them.

Carlyle's man of letters was a social organ on account of his spiritual leadership. Even through the educational prescriptions we seem to hear the mob of *Chartism* offering up its 'inarticulate prayers' – 'Guide me, govern me!', 'I am mad and miserable and cannot govern myself!' One final cross reference – this time to Carlyle's eclectic American disciple, Emerson – may be in order. For Emerson, when in 1837 he gave his Phi Beta Kappa address on 'The American Scholar', the American man of letters was to work towards what (in a curiously modern phrase) he called the 'gradual domestication of the idea of culture'. He was in fact to work on behalf of a socially dispersed process of education that would necessitate his own obsolescence, since the community of fully developed individuals would require neither him nor the state.[90] Carlyle, on the other hand, adhered to a dominative social model that required leaders and followers, and the composite figure of the man-of-letters hero testifies to his inability to dissociate importance as a writer from social power. He could not visualise a pre-eminence in letters that did not entail a general pre-eminence.[91] Boldly, he had refused to separate society's spiritual life (which includes what we call culture) from its political and social life. But as the hopeful intellectual had based his vision on the absolute, so the frustrated intellectual consoled himself with a fantasy of power. When the man of letters melted into the aristocracy of heroism, the tragedy was not Carlyle's alone.

4

THE MAJORITY AND THE REMNANT:
MATTHEW ARNOLD

[If] we are to derive comfort from the doctrine of *the remnant* (and there is great comfort to be derived from it), we must hold fast to the austere but true doctrine as to what really governs politics, overrides with an inexorable fatality the combinations of the so-called politicians, and saves or destroys States. Having in mind things true, things elevated, things just, things pure, things amiable, things of good report; having these in mind, studying and loving these, is what saves States.

Matthew Arnold, *Discourses in America*

Matthew Arnold, as has only recently been pointed out,[1] learned more from Carlyle than either he or most of his commentators have cared to admit. There are marked similarities in their theories of the moral nature of society, and of its cohesion and disintegration. Both represent developments from and reactions to aesthetic and political Romanticism. Both tended towards an absolutism of thought and style, and both, in advocating spiritual authority as an antidote to moral and cultural disintegration, created a place in their thought for a spiritual elite.

Arnold has an obvious place in any discussion of ideas of the *pouvoir spirituel* in nineteenth-century England. His works contain an analysis of the ills of society, seen as resulting from the defects of the inner life produced by a specific historical situation. By way of prescription, they contain an account of culture as a vivifying moral and intellectual force. Among the social implications of Arnold's theory of culture is one that justifies, in moral and social terms, the work of intellectuals or men of letters: 'The highly-instructed few, and not the scantily-instructed many, will ever be the organ to the human race of knowledge and truth. Knowledge and truth, in the full sense of the words, are not attainable by the great mass of the human race at all.'[2] It may be objected that it is unfair to portray Arnold as did Frederic Harrison,[3] as fastidious and out of touch.

Not only had he a very practical concern with education, but his social thought (it may be argued) was not intended as absolute statement, but rather as a corrective to the tendencies of his time: where Hebraism prevails, assert the claims of Hellenism; where fire and strength, the value of sweetness and light. The qualities and values he urges on the English, the argument continues, are complementary, not antagonistic, to the qualities and values they oppose. If Arnold is unfair, it is because he knows that there is no danger of the other side of the case going under. Thus he wrote in a letter from Italy in 1865 that 'a nation is really civilised by acquiring the qualities it by nature is wanting in; and the Italians are no more civilised by virtue of their refinement alone, than we are civilised by virtue of our energy alone'.[4] And there is more to the defence than an assertion of the dialectical nature of Arnold's thought. Is it fair, we might be asked, to take as philosophic formulations the writings of a man himself so deeply aware of the 'inadequateness of our speech'? Cannot we say of his writings – as he said of St Paul's – that they are a fatal rock to uninformed criticism 'because they are the products of a mind that was constantly growing, and because they affect the forms of logic and science which a complete notional system adopts, while their true character and force is that of an approximate experience'.[5] Should we not apply the very tact that Arnold sees as the fruit of much reading to his own use of concepts like 'righteousness', 'conduct', or even 'culture'?

The answers to questions such as these may be sought in a close study of Arnold's arguments and style. In brief, he does not live up to his own insights. The dialectic is too easily deserted in favour of the term of which he most approves. Again, the Arnold who wrote of the language of the Bible that it was 'language *thrown out* at an object of consciousness not fully grasped' coexisted with the Arnold of *Culture and Anarchy*.[6] The use of catchwords and repeated tags in a discussion of society tended to make his statements notional, even dogmatic. Recognition of his insights deepens our problems. The Arnold who, basing himself on the eternal truths of morality, longs for order and for an ideal state, is at the same time the historical relativist of *St Paul and Protestantism* or *Literature and Dogma*. We cannot help feeling, particularly in *Culture and Anarchy*, that the dogmatist lurks behind the apparently tentative formulations, behind the playfulness that purports merely to be having a little innocent fun with opponents. It is no answer to invoke

Arnold's own distinction between 'scientific' or 'notional' and 'experimental' or 'poetic' language; the argument of *Culture and Anarchy* is notional enough, and asks to be taken as such. In such an argument, the terms that were meant to adumbrate the fluid and the changing became absolute, while the repetition and the use of spiral logic create a mode of discourse that attempts to conceal its own notional claims. Arnold's habit of extracting nuggets from the masters – so amply evidenced in his Notebooks as well as in his published writings – is pertinent here, in that repeated quotation out of context forces complex works of literature to render up an oversimplified but readily assimilable lesson. Brought up in a climate of increasing historical relativism, and himself liking to regard things in a historical light, he persisted in taking certain texts as relevant to the present in a way not obviously connected with the circumstances of their origin. I would suggest here something to which we must return later – that Arnold's habit of setting up a timeless cultural canon is an important feature of his thought. The fact that something was said in a text regarded as classical could outweigh all merely historical considerations. To take one amusing example: Arnold's America was projected for the benefit of his English social criticism, and he therefore insisted on the United States' affinities with England. So, writing in 1882, he found forty years of massive non-English immigration irrelevant: 'I adhere to my old persuasion, the Americans of the United States are English people on the other side of the Atlantic. I learnt it from Burke.'[7] It was not the only thing he learnt, but, for anyone but Arnold, Burke would be a surprising source for the ethnic composition of American society in the 1880s.

DEMOCRACY AND AMERICA

Let us start by examining one of the lectures that Arnold took with him to the United States on his first visit in 1883, the lecture on 'Numbers, or the Majority and the Remnant', and by trying to see why Arnold considered this subject relevant for an American audience. This will introduce us to Arnold's vision of history and of the nature of the general crisis of his time. A prefatory word of warning is necessary: Arnold does not seek to endow a clerisy, and the non-institutional leaven in the lump on which he builds so much is at once a more secular and less highly-defined body than Coleridge's national church.[8]

Two of the three lectures that Arnold took to the United States in 1883 were written for the occasion. The other, 'Literature and Science' – representing an earlier phase of the 'two cultures' debate – was a version of his Rede Lecture given at Cambridge in the previous year. 'Emerson', the third lecture, described the effect of Emerson's writing on the young Arnold, and attempted an assessment of his status as a poet and philosopher. In 'Numbers' (first given in New York to an audience that included the ailing ex-President Grant), Arnold began by making clear that he was referring to his accustomed thesis about English culture and society: 'At home I have said so much of the characters of our society and the prospects of our civilisation that I can hardly escape the like topics elsewhere.'[9] After this opening, he picked up the subject of American society, praising it, with an irony that may well have been lost on his audience, for its scale and numbers that Bright (the liberal politician and publicist) was always talking about. But it was not size alone that offered grounds for satisfaction. Here the thesis emerged, and we must be struck by the simplistic, moral terms employed: 'Not that your great numbers, or indeed great numbers of men anywhere, are likely to be all good, or even to have the majority good.'[10]

Any doctrine of the elect or of the just remnant inevitably involves a projection of the nature of those who come outside the group of the saved, of those who are denied or who deny themselves the possibility of a larger life. Arnold helped to establish on English soil the idea of the Philistine, the type of man who was offered culture and cared not. Further, he proposed to his American audience that the choice before them was not merely between culture and Philistinism, but (as the Pauline and eschatological language insisted) between the salvation and the destruction of the state. Arnold's cultural thesis was, like that of so many of his contemporaries, rooted in the notion that culture and morality were in the last analysis the same. But within this general picture shifts of focus are observable. In 'Numbers' the question is in the first place one of morality (and morality in a deeply conventional sense) presented by those who aspire to firmness in their faith to those outside the fold. The severity of the priest and of the schoolmaster brood over the succeeding paragraph. For 'one of the wise men of Greece' said that the 'majority are bad'. The classical and Biblical canon provides the terms of the argument. Eternal truths shine mistily through the fog of the merely historical and factual. 'Much to the same effect . . . is the famous sentence of the New Testament: "Many are called, few chosen".'[11] Thus one of the central texts of predestinarian theology finds its way into the pages of the author of *Friendship's Garland*. With the sadness of his severity Arnold invokes Newman, thereby laying his own claim to the assurance that Newman himself arguably never quite attained, the sober wisdom springing from the secure possession of the know-ledge that men are essentially corrupt, and that genuine beauty and fundamental truth stem from outside the secular world. We have here one side of Arnold's dichotomy, a side prominently exposed in this lecture. On the other side, Arnold expects progress, and looks forward to radical improvement on earth. This side of Arnold remains in shadow in this lecture, though it is exposed in the slightly later essay 'Civilisation in the United States'. Yet the aim of the sectarian as of the Victorian optimist is perfection; at issue is the question whether that perfection will be found in another world, beyond the sufferings of sinful man, or whether all men may, even in this world, become partakers of it. Arnold is referring to 'Many Called, Few Chosen', cited years before in 'The Bishop and the Philosopher' as one of Newman's 'noblest sermons'. As it represents Newman at his most predestinarian, the significance of Arnold's having brooded over it is considerable. To read it is to find Arnold's 'austere, but true doctrine' in its religious setting. For in it Newman assembled quotations (some of which Arnold used) from Paul, Isaiah, Jeremiah, and Ezekiel in expounding the belief that

it is observable that Almighty God seems as if to rejoice, and deigns to delight Himself in this small company who adhere to Him, as if their fewness had in it something of excellence and preciousness.[12]

The identification with Newman is plainly significant. Arnold glosses the sentence quoted above:

This appears to be a hard saying; frequent are the endeavours to elude it, to attenuate its severity. But turn it as you will, manipulate it as you will, the few, as Cardinal Newman well says, can never mean the many.[13]

At this point one remembers with a certain longing the author of the explorations of figurative language in St Paul. The leaning towards Newman marks, I suggest, the attraction of the idea of the necessary corruption of man. At the same time, we must avoid the danger of laying too much stress on this point, of erecting a tendency into a declared dogma. The corruption of the majority is said at times to be a fact, 'the world being what it is' or, more explicitly, 'in the present state of the world'.[14] In all fairness we should also note that Arnold does not equate unsoundness with any one class, or use it as an argument against the extension of democracy:

It may be better, it is better, that the body of the people, with all its faults, should act for itself, and control its own affairs, than that it should be set aside as ignorant and incapable, and have its affairs managed for it by the so-called superior class, possessing property and intelligence. Property and intelligence cannot be trusted to show a sound majority themselves; the exercise of power by the people tends to educate the people.[15]

The unsoundness of the majority cuts across class boundaries. And in this lecture Arnold gives no clues to the sociological position of the remnant. They are merely those who recognise how things are, who see the object as in itself it really is.

The remnant as a concept was traced to Isaiah. To Isaiah rather than to Plato, since in the end all Plato could recommend the wise man to do was to lie low, 'as it were standing aside under a wall in a storm of dust and hurricane of driving wind'.[16] Isaiah's remnant, on the other hand, was to save the state:[17]

Though thy people Israel be as the sand of the sea, only a remnant of them shall return. This was Isaiah's point. The actual commonwealth of the 'drunkards' and the 'blind', as he calls them, in Israel and Judah, of the dissolute grandees and gross and foolish common people, of the great majority, must perish.[18]

The stylistic balance is nicely maintained as Arnold suggests a stance towards the present, giving as he does so a critique of the acceptance of politics as they are now:

No doubt, to most of us, if we had been there to see it, the kingdom of Ephraim or of Judah, the society of Samaria or Jerusalem, would have seemed to contain a great deal else besides dissolute grandees and foolish common people. No doubt we should have thought parts of their policy serious, and some of their alliances promising.[19]

But Isaiah was right, and so by implication was the critic of newspapers' editorial platitudes:

Let us read him again and again, until we fix in our minds this true conviction of his, to edify us whenever we see such a world existing: his indestructible conviction that such a world, with its prosperities, idolatries, oppression, luxury, pleasures, drunkards, careless women, governing classes, systems of policy, strong alliances, shall come to nought and pass away; that nothing can save it. Let us do homage likewise to his indestructible conviction that states are saved by their righteous remnant.[20]

Our hope in the present – this is the central argument of the lecture, and it represents an extension of the argument of *Culture and Anarchy* – is that the sheer numbers of modern society can provide us with a remnant large enough in absolute terms to save the state. That the world sketched in above really does exist around us now is the reason for urging the necessity of the remnant. In fact we have only earned the right to put our hope in the remnant when we 'are at one with the philosophers and the prophets in their conviction respecting the world which now is, the world of the unsound majority.'[21] How Plato or Isaiah held any convictions at all about 'the world which now is' is unclear. But behind Arnold's identification with the seers' vision lies a certain transcendentalism. His thought is not theistic in the sense in which Coleridge's is, yet in certain moods he hankers after the immutable laws of the eternal in accordance with which man should live, and deviation from which is incident to the fallen state. Next Arnold returns to Paul, with a passage from Philippians iv, 8. The importance of this passage for us is that it provides a link with the general cultural thesis, culture appearing conflated with the static, eternal body of truths, the yearning towards which is for Arnold the essence of morality. Culture and morality, it is implied, can be discussed in Pauline fashion: 'Whatsoever things are true, whatsoever things are elevated, whatsoever things are just, whatsoever things are pure, whatsoever things are of good report; if there be any virtue, and if there be any praise, have these in your mind, let your thoughts run upon these.'[22] This is adduced to show 'what it is that both Plato and the prophets mean when they tell us that we ought to love righteousness and to make our study in the law of the eternal, but that the unsound majority do nothing of the kind'. As far as the last clause is concerned, the passage does nothing of the sort. What it does demonstrate are the sources of communal life. In connection with Mill we must examine the 'intellectualist' idea of history, that is a theory of history which sees historical change and progress as caused by the progression of the human mind. Arnold's view sometimes appears similar. Certainly, he usually attributes change and progress to the world. But here approximation to the eternal law is sought. Such morality is to be the guide of national life, a life to which conventional politics and policies are mere epiphenomena. The matters just enumerated

do not come into the heads of most of us, I suppose, when we are thinking of politics. But the philosophers and prophets maintain that these matters, and not those of which the heads of politicians are full, do really govern politics and save or destroy states. They save or destroy them by a salient inexorable fatality; while the politicians are making believe, plausibly and noisily, with their American institutions, British Constitution, and civilising mission of France.[23]

The doctrine of the remnant is inextricably tied up with the contemplation of things elevated and things pure. In the passages where Arnold puts forward his doctrine we are constantly aware of the almost hypnotic effect of his technique. The repeated word or phrase, the positive and negative labelling insist on an argument that is never actually argued. 'A proposition whose validity we are resolved to maintain in the face of any experience' (in the words of A. J. Ayer) 'is not a hypothesis at all but a definition.' Whatever the reasons for Arnold's conclusions may be, they are concealed by the dexterous use of Plato and the prophets. Which is not to say that Arnold is guilty of deliberate evasion: his cultural thesis had become so plausible to him that he felt no need to argue it at length, and snapped up everything in the classics or Bible that seemed to support it. Here is the fruit of Arnold's regular method of argument, which works by asserting parallel propositions, and by the association of groups of words, so that the appearance of one tag immediately suggests another. The repeated phrase, indeed the whole associative technique, produces – or is intended to produce – a kind of conditioned response in the reader. One result of this axiomatic method is that it is often difficult to summarise Arnold's argument, because the conclusion is contained in the formulae through which the thesis is proposed. It is elicited by the repeated tags and familiar antitheses. 'Unsound majority', 'children of light', 'the study of perfection', 'sweetness and light', 'fire and strength', 'main current of national life', 'firm intelligible law of things', 'best that has been thought and said in the world', 'to make reason and the will of God prevail', have cumulatively an incantatory quality that incites the reader to suspend disbelief, or render himself liable to Arnold's mockery.[24]

The next part of the lecture was given over to the terrible results of not seeing things clearly and pursuing perfection. The two examples were English policy in Ireland (here Arnold was in a position

to state that the poverty of public life had resulted in a ghastly mess),
and the French worship of the goddess Lubricity (which would lead
to a ghastly mess before long). The argument then became tied up
with a confused discussion of the racial composition of the Gaul,
necessitating a racial interpretation of history which, taken literally,
would seem to make nonsense of the doctrine of the remnant.
Leaving aside the triumph of the Gallo-Latin over the German
quality in the Frenchman, we may note that there was a test of the
dangers of the worship of Lubricity. 'For this is the test of its being
against human nature, that for human societies it is ruin.'[25] Typically, however, Arnold neglected any empirical application of this
Burkean proposition, and went on to talk in an almost obsessive way
about the perils of dissoluteness. The fount of national life, it seems,
was not just morality, but morality conceived in a distinctly Victorian
way. Renan was taken to task for saying 'Nature cares nothing about
chastity'; 'What a slap in the face', Arnold replied, 'to the sticklers
for "whatsoever things are pure" '.

We have not lost sight of the remnant, for it was not to save the
state through elevation alone, but also through purity. The remnant
and the unsound majority were the poles of the same argument.
In case the Americans had missed the point, Arnold repeated it:
'If we are to enjoy the benefit ... of the comfortable doctrine of the
remnant, we must be capable of holding fast the hard doctrine of
the unsoundness of the majority, and of the certainty that the unsoundness of the majority, if it is not withstood and remedied, must
be their ruin.'[26] Democracy is inevitable; but so too – failing our
slight hope – is moral and social ruin. 'Hard' and 'austere' are our
tasks. If we are to pursue our liberalism to its bitter end, we must
not make the mistake of Lot's wife and look back to our benevolent
prejudices.

From the catalogue in Philippians iv, Arnold selected 'things pure'
and 'things elevated'. These the majority were incapable of contemplating, at least at the 'present stage of the world', and also, presumably, since the days of Plato and Isaiah. Since contemplation of
these things saved states, the remnant must of course do the job.
Arnold has interestingly extended the argument of Renan's *La
Réforme intéllectuelle et morale*. France

must recover through a powerful and profound renewal, a great inward
change, brought about by 'the remnant' among her people; and for this,
a remnant small in numbers would not suffice.[27]

If the disease raged unchecked

the life of that famous state will be more and more impaired until it perish. And this is that hard but true doctrine of the sages and prophets, of the inexorable fatality of operation, in moral failure of the unsound majority, to impair and destroy states.[28]

In France the task before the remnant was one of moral renewal. The task before the remnant in America was not so very different. The first question was, naturally, how the unsoundness of the majority would operate. We must examine the passage carefully.

I suppose that in a democratic community like this, with its newness, its magnitude, its strength, its life of business, its sheer freedom and equality, the danger is in the absence of the discipline of respect; in hardness and materialism, exaggeration and boastfulness; in a false smartness, a false audacity, a want of soul and delicacy. 'Whatsoever things are *elevated*', – whatsoever things are nobly serious, have true elevation, – that perhaps, in our catalogue of maxims ... is the maxim which points to where the failure of the unsound majority, in a great democracy like yours will probably lie.[29]

This points to the need for an agency to inculcate the 'discipline of respect', and in traditional societies such agencies were not far to be sought. In a letter of 1860, Arnold had written:

I see Bright goes on envying the Americans, but I cannot but think that the state of things with respect to their *national character*, which, after all, is the base of the only real grandeur or prosperity, becomes graver and graver. It seems as if few stocks could be trusted to grow up properly without having a priesthood and an aristocracy to act as their schoolmasters at some time or another of their national existence.[30]

We should not think that things elevated are different from things pure, since morality and culture are one:

the philosophers and the prophets, whom I at least am disposed to believe, and who say that moral causes govern the standing and falling of states, will tell us that the failure to mind whatsoever things are elevated must impair with inexorable fatality the life of a nation.[31]

But there is a hope, without which 'even the great United States must inevitably suffer and be impaired more and more until it perish'. ' "The remnant shall return"; shall "convert and be healed" itself first, and shall then recover the unsound majority.'[32] This lecture raises questions both about the relevance to a democracy of such an address, and about the nature of the remnant.

AN IMAGE FOR THE INTELLECTUALS

Bearings and influences

In talking about the idea of the remnant in Matthew Arnold's work, we are faced with several problems, of which the most outstanding is that as a social group it is never exactly defined, and its composition is not fully discussed. I nevertheless want to argue that Arnold was preoccupied with the social role of intellectuals – again, not a closely-defined group – and that awareness of this preoccupation can throw much light on his social writing.[33] We must be aware that in this country Arnold made a considerable contribution to the debate about the social role of the intellectual. His theory of culture as normative rather than exploratory, is intertwined with a theory of who represents culture in the community and what these representatives should do. His adumbration of a group identity for the intellectuals must in turn be seen in relation to his political theory. Not unnaturally, perhaps, he has not been discussed as a political theorist, since as such he is neither particularly original, nor particularly subtle. Yet, as the matrix of his cultural theory, it deserves closer attention than it has received. A study of it reinforces the impression of two modes of Arnold's thought: the progressivist, which sees the crisis of the present in a larger historical scheme, and the reactionary, which seeks the assurance of a static world of truths attainable by meditation on a 'classical' literary canon. Arnold's theory of culture fulfils a need created by his political diagnosis of the times. Tocqueville, the mentor of Arnold as of John Stuart Mill, should be allowed to sketch the terms of the discussion. The great social revolution proceeds on its inevitable way, but

the leaders of the state have never thought of making any preparation by anticipation for it. The progress has been against their will or without their knowledge. The most powerful, intelligent, and moral classes of the nation have never sought to gain control of it in order to direct it. Hence democracy has been left to its wild instincts; it has grown up *like those children deprived of parental care* who school themselves in our town streets and know nothing of society but its vices and wretchedness. Men would seem still unaware of its existence, when suddenly it has seized power. Then all submit like slaves to its least desires; it is worshipped as the idol of strength; thereafter, when it has been weakened by its own excesses, the law-givers conceive the imprudent project of abolishing it instead of trying to *educate and correct it*, and without any wish to teach it how to rule, they only strive to drive it out of government.[34]

Matthew Arnold was influenced by Burke as well as by Tocqueville, and without reference to their diagnoses, his historical vision loses part of its context of formulations and rationalisations. The questions he put to the present and to the putative future were ones which Burke and Tocqueville (representatives of different phases of the debate on the French Revolution) helped him to shape. His conception of the scope of the problem of equality and of the role of the spiritual power places his discussion within the contemporary argument about 'democracy'. Tendencies towards anarchy must be countered by assertions of the state as a community – above all an ethical and educational community. Equality and the trivialisation which was forecast to come with it must be countered by a social assertion of things elevated. My argument must necessarily be complicated: Arnold, for all his dislike of system, developed a coherent creed, and to show the relevance of his American argument to his general thesis will involve a discussion of his theory of classes, his relation to Tocqueville, and the historical nature of his thought. From the theory of classes stem questions about the 'elevated' and the 'noble' and what force in society is to represent those qualities. We shall have to touch on Arnold's notion of mental life. Arnold was no materialist, and for him the healthy society was in the first place a spiritually healthy society, in touch with the timeless body of moral truths to which great literature bore witness. Class was for him an historical conception, culture only partially so, and, since intellectual, moral and social health were ultimately the same, Arnold's approach to the history of society can be related to Mill's. Yet where Mill's intellectualism was dynamic, Arnold's conception of a timeless set of truths embedded in culture set up a curious tension with the historicism of his century of which Thomas Arnold had been a prophet. I shall suggest that the younger Arnold sets up a notion of culture as necessarily aristocratic, a notion in which culture and its social agents are normative and regulatory; even in his extremely valuable educational writings, culture is the light of an education whose aim is social control. I shall argue further that his insistence on 'totality' in art relates to his holistic vision of society, and to his advocacy of the national 'best self' as the only safeguard against 'anarchy'. 'Totality', the attack on 'provincialism', and the assertion of the educational state contain – even if latently – a rejection of diversity and of the possibility that innovation might have multitudinous origins. There emerges an idea of the remnant as proponents of a normative culture closely associated with 'manners'.

Undoubtedly the cause of social equality was advancing in Victorian England, and 'democracy' was generally held to be advancing at a very great rate. Society, it was widely believed, had to adjust rapidly if cultural and moral values as they had been known were to be preserved. As an optimist, Arnold believed that the great movement of society was in the right direction. As a man of culture, he had doubts on the score of Gadarene swine, and ended up with an entirely characteristic confusion between culture and righteousness. That culture *ought* to involve the maximum enrichment of people's lives in society is of course arguable. But Arnold is all too apt to set up a dialectic in which the term of which he approves is accorded ideal status, while that of which he disapproves remains merely empirical. He quite simply loads his argument in favour of one of his two postulates. Like Coleridge, he proposes an ideal cultural system, and then performs a dialectical conjuring trick by which the ideal is found to be latent in the *status quo*. As Henry Sidgwick put it in one of the first reviews of *Culture and Anarchy*, he drops 'from the prophet of an ideal culture into a more or less prejudiced advocate of the actual'.[35] Here again we are dealing with reactions to what were seen as mechanistic accounts of the human spirit, the most prevalent of which was liberal rationalism. That liberal rationalism was believed by Arnold to be more democratic and egalitarian than in the hands of the British middle class it actually was, does not concern us here. Arnold's reaction was to assert the primacy of the cultural community and to reject as inadequate the materialist criteria of social health. ('Socialistic and communistic schemes have generally . . . a fatal defect;' he noted in 1879, 'they are content with too low and material a standard of well-being.')[36] We must investigate the nature of the culture invoked against the liberalism of the day.

John Stuart Mill sometimes distinguished between the tendencies of democracy and the tendencies of capitalism, refusing to see them as necessarily working towards the same ends or as creating the same kind of society, but Arnold did not make this distinction. For him, commercialism, industrialism, all that he called machinery,

tended to ally with democracy. The danger to a commercial, democratic society like America lay in the absence of the elevated. We
shall have to ask how the elevated was supposed to counteract
the tendency of democracy to materialism. In doing so we shall see
where the 'discipline of respect'[37] comes into the picture.

Perhaps too much has been written about the 'revolt against the
eighteenth century'. The historians of that revolt have had to draw
up a projection of the 'eighteenth century' that matches that of the
sternest of its opponents. In any case, the revolt never became a
revolution, and there is no discontinuity in the intellectual tradition
of the enlightenment, a tradition which remained active in the
nineteenth century. Nevertheless (and restricting the discussion to
England alone), it is possible to see that Burke, and after him
Coleridge, advanced an idea of the community that was conceived
in opposition to threatened popular movements as a counter-assertion
to the 'politics of pure reason'. The politics of natural rights, and the
scientistic analysis of society, it was argued, were simply inadequate
to do justice to the richness of social life, and led in practice to the
dissolution of society. I have examined this stance in chapter 2.
Burke is a more direct influence on Arnold than on Coleridge.[38]
His account of the healthy society, of the importance of traditional
forms, of hierarchy, of the organic connections of social groups,
spoke directly to Arnold's imagination. It said so much to him, in
fact, that he attempted to combine Burke with his own 'liberalism
of the future'. Of this unlikely marriage the doctrine of the remnant
was one of the offspring. It was made possible by Burke's insistence
on the existence of the nation as an active entity, and on the state as
'the nation in its collective character'. For Arnold there was a continuity of national life that might well be invisible to most men, and
it resided in that 'best self' which stood for right reason and was
independent of all governments and governing classes as such.
According to Stanley, Thomas Arnold used to refer to his social
and educational microcosm at Rugby as 'our great self, the school'.[39]
Rousseau – or the aspect of that protean figure that lies closest to
Burke[40] – puts in a ghostly appearance. The 'rough', like the rest of
us, says Arnold, has no idea 'of a *State*, of the nation in its collective
and corporate character, controlling, as a government, the free swing
of this or that of its members in the name of the higher reason of
them all, his own as well as that of others'.[41] Like Coleridge, he
quotes Withers' lines:

> Let not your King and Parliament in one,
> Much less apart, mistake themselves for that
> Which is most worthy to be thought upon,
> Nor think they are essentially the State.
> But let them know there is *a deeper life*
> *Which they but represent;*
> *That there's on earth a yet auguster thing,*
> *Veil'd though it be, than Parliament and King.*[42]

We may well compare the higher reason with Rousseau's *volonté générale*. Like the *volonté générale* its embodiment in concrete institutions is an ambiguous affair. And similiarly, it has its counterpart, the mere *volonté de tous* in the 'everyday practice, deformed by stupidity and passions, of the common run of all of us'.[43] It will become the task of the saving remnant to teach the mass what their higher reason (their rational will, so to speak) really is.

History and the education of society

Arnold's statism is characteristically conceived in terms of the educational argument that the state exists to edify its members. We might go one step further than Arnold and supply the Coleridgean gloss that, without the educative process of which the state is an essential precondition, individuals cannot attain their full humanity. We must remember the argument about the nature of progress in which Arnold took part. In chapter 1, I gave a brief account of the new movement in historical studies which Thomas Arnold and others found in Vico and the German historians of the late eighteenth and early nineteenth centuries. This movement in historical studies implied a vision of social progress not as simply linear, but as proceeding through crises, and a vision of the character of a period as being based upon the configuration of power within society. Thus, in early nineteenth-century England, it was argued that the age of aristocracy was past, and the age of the middle class was coming in. One day the age of equality and the classless society might arrive. Further, the prevalent organic metaphor for the life of nations suggested that the unfolding process of history was a 'natural' progression. One possible conclusion was a Burkean reverence for institutions as the products of the diachronic communal wisdom, and an antipathy to the notion that they were merely artificial and readily manipulable expedients.[44] Yet in Thomas Arnold's thought, 'nature'

served a liberal conclusion, and his belief in the naturalness of progress is so widely evinced that it is hard to pick out examples.
It insists on a reading of the present that opposes conventional conservatism. Thus he wrote to J. T. Coleridge in 1830 that there

is nothing so revolutionary because there is nothing so unnatural and so
convulsive to society as the strain to keep things fixed, when all the world
is by the very law of its creation in eternal progress; and the cause of all the
evils of the world may be traced to that natural but most deadly error of
human indolence and corruption, that our business is to preserve and not
to improve.[45]

If you held such a belief, you might have to grit your teeth and
accept what was happening even though your prejudice was against
the emerging order. Tocqueville voices nineteenth-century progressivist commonplaces:

A great democratic revolution is taking place in our midst.
. . . the gradual progress of equality is something fated.
This whole book [*Democracy in America*] has been written under the
impulse of a kind of religious dread inspired by the contemplation of this
irresistible revolution advancing century by century over every obstacle and
even now going forward amid the ruins it had itself created.
God does not Himself need to speak for us to find some signs of his will; it
is enough to observe the customary progress of nature and the continuous
tendency of events.[46]

These commonplaces are relevant to Matthew Arnold. The whole
argument of the 1861 Preface to *The Popular Education of France*
('Democracy'), as of the much later lecture on 'Equality' is framed
within this historical thesis. Whatever our own leanings, says Arnold,
we must accept that society is moving towards equality and democracy. We can do nothing – even if we wanted to – to reverse this
trend: the growth of the 'modern spirit', critical and impatient, is
'natural and inevitable'.[47] The position is Tocqueville's.
   Thomas Arnold had not, however, been very explicit about the
decline of states. The decline of individual nations within the larger
scheme of progress was of course implicit in the Viconian model –
indeed in the very use of the organic metaphor – but it was a subject
on which Vico himself had been surprisingly reticent. Matthew
Arnold was not alone in feeling the need to fill out the historical
scheme. The link between immorality and social decay was made by
A. P. Stanley, who wrote a prize essay while at Oxford on *Whether*

States, like Individuals, after a certain period of maturity, inevitably tend to decay. In this essay the affinities between the Rugby movement and clerisy thinking are very apparent. Stanley argued that the organic metaphor could be misleading: decline was not inevitable, but moral, and could therefore be countered by a collective act of will. In morality, the analogy between the individual and the commonwealth held good: 'every consideration which justifies a belief in the moral corruption and probable deflection of individuals calls us to expect a similar corruption and deflection in nations'.[48] That was why we must have an antagonist principle in society to oppose the tendencies of materialist civilisation. For Stanley the highest 'antagonist power' was Christianity, but this should not be allowed to obscure the similarities of his ideas to those of Coleridge (who would, after all, have agreed), and to those of Carlyle and Mill. The point here, though, is that Matthew Arnold's identification of personal and social morality had a precedent within the Rugby movement. We have already noted his polemic on the subject of French 'lubricity': the Arnold of 'whatsoever things are pure', the Arnold who stated that the Renaissance died through obeying its lusts,[49] or who inveighed on behalf of the beleaguered seventh commandment,[50] was the same Arnold who garnered for his own edification such exhortations as Cicero's 'Turn away from sexual infatuations; for if you give yourself to them you will be able to think of nothing but the object of your love.' Or John Smith's 'While any inward lust is harboured in the minds of men, it will so weaken them, that they can never bring forth any generous or masculine knowledge.'[51] Dissipation is to be dreaded; energy is precious, and freedom exists only where we can curb the body's liability to lay waste its powers. The choice, reflecting a duality ubiquitous in the Victorian period, is one between thraldom and independence. Like Carlyle, Arnold holds out an ideal of restraint, of a free and ruling self taking charge of the instinctive impulses. For him, as Trilling pointed out, 'morality is essentially a check, a bridle, a renunciation'.[52] Personal affront merged into a vision of social decline, and the vision demanded a saving remnant. Expatiating, in *Literature and Dogma*, on the opposition between impulses and the 'real law' of man's being, Arnold quoted Aristotle: 'In all wholes made up of parts ... there is a ruler and a ruled; throughout nature this is so; we see even in things without life, they have their *harmony* or *law*. The living being is composed of soul and body, whereof the one is naturally ruler and the other ruled.'[53] Ironically, this passage comes from the argument in *Politics I* on behalf of slavery. Like Plato, and like Arnold, Aristotle went on to show that in the man in perfect condition the soul ruled over the body, 'although in bad and corrupted natures the body will often appear to rule over the soul'.[54] We have already noted how proponents of the clerisy tend to posit a 'higher' type of intellectual and moral health as the prerogative of the elite. Arnold was going to characterise the intellectual life by a striving towards the freedom of the noumenal self. Here, in *Literature and Dogma,* and calling upon Plato, Paul, and Bishop Wilson as well as Goethe as witnesses, he re-enacted Carlyle's transition from mastery to the 'joy of self-renouncement'. The 'best self' required a national superego.

The enormous responsibility towards society of those with a grasp of historical and moral principles is a corollary of the vision of history. Such a feeling of responsibility conditioned Tocqueville's whole sociological undertaking. It is a dimension of Thomas Arnold's famed earnestness. Stanley made the point when he said that we 'must remember how the Greek science, πολιτική, of which the English word "politics" or even political science, is so inadequate a translation – society in its connexion with the highest welfare of man – exhibited to him the great problem which every educated man was called upon to solve'.[55] The inner life of a nation, Thomas Arnold announced in his *Introductory Lectures in Modern History* soon after his appointment to the Regius Chair at Oxford, 'is determined by the nature of its ultimate end'.[56] And its end should be the 'setting forth God's glory by doing His appointed work. And that work for a nation seems to imply not only the greatest possible perfecting of the natures of its individual members, but also the perfecting of all those acts which are done, by the nation collectively.'[57] Matthew's was a weighty inheritance. We have already seen him copying into his Notebook a saying of Bunsen's about understanding the age (see page 9 above). Another saying is very relevant here: 'It is true that our class, the guild of the studious, does too little with the object of working upon the nation.'[58] Such was the mood in which the younger Arnold's enterprise was begun.

Two more aspects of Matthew Arnold's idea of history demand our attention. Both stem from Thomas Arnold. One is the idea of the 'modern' as it is to be found in 'The Modern Element in Literature' and elsewhere. This is a reference to his father's idea of

history, adapted in turn from Vico's *New Science*. Stanley wrote of
the elder Arnold's 'increasing sense of the value of ancient authors,
as belonging really to a period of modern civilisation like our own'.[59]
In 'The Social Progress of States' (which formed the first appendix
to his edition of Thucydides) he wrote of the 'ancient and modern
period in the history of every people'.[60] This theory gave some sort
of licence to his son's application of classical texts to modern conditions. The second aspect (linked to the conception of the recurrence of periods) is the recognition that in different periods of history
different social groups predominate. The 'popular party of an earlier
period becomes the antipopular party of a later'.[61] The critical transition (this, we should note, was written in 1830) had been from the
principle of aristocracy to that of wealth. The present stage was just
before the shift from the principle of wealth to that of numbers.
Most important, for our purposes, was the notion that each class
influenced the one that was to succeed it. This theory, suggestive of
a kind of primitive sociology of knowledge, led to a statement of the
necessity of educating the middle class as the class coming into
power, and with the working class under its tutelage. Thomas
Arnold's footsteps remained distinct for forty years after his pre-
mature death. 'It seems to me that the education of the middling
classes at this time, is a question of the greatest national importance.'
The commercial schools were inadequate, and in any case technical
and vocational training were not enough. Education should be for
the 'calling of a citizen and a man', it should give in fact not a
'professional' but a 'liberal' education. Thus Thomas Arnold wrote
in the Sheffield *Courant* in April 1832.[62] The historical frame of his
son's educational mission was already established, and it was to the
shared model that he appealed: 'Our present [social] organisation
has been an appointed stage in our growth; it has been of good use,
and enabled us to do great things. But the use is at an end and the
stage is over. . . . we are trying to live on with a social organisation of
which the day is over'.[63] Social equality and political democracy
were the necessary next steps in this progress, and any account of
Matthew Arnold's thought that failed to make this clear would be
inadequate. Nor should we overlook the degree of his self-identifica-
tion with the 'modern spirit':

Modern times find themselves with an immense system of institutions,
established facts, accredited dogmas, customs, rules, which have come from
times not modern. In this system their life was to be carried forward; yet

they have a sense that this system is not of their own creating, that it by no means corresponds with the wants of their actual life, that, for them, it is customary, not rational. The awakening of this sense is the awakening of the modern spirit. The modern spirit is now awake almost everywhere; the sense of a want of correspondence between the forms of modern Europe and its spirit. . . . Dissolvents of the old European system of dominant ideas and facts we must all be, all of us who have any power of working.[64]

Yet the assurance that a social stage is inevitable, even the assurance that for most people it will be a better stage, does not necessarily make the observer happy. 'The goal of humanity is not happiness', wrote Arnold's mentor Renan after witnessing the events of 1848, 'it is intellectual and moral perfection'.[65] We have already examined a pessimistic response in 'Numbers', and noted the importance of English discussions of American democracy. Rightly or wrongly, people looked to America as a test case for the operation of equality and democracy. If, Arnold wrote, we have to do without the state to fill the place of the aristocracy, 'the dangers of America will really be ours; the dangers which come from the multitude being in power, with no adequate ideal to elevate or guide the multitude'.[66]

Das Gemeine – *the poverty of democracy*

Arnold's cultural thesis sprang from the belief that democracy was the inevitable form of society in the future. Having sketched in the historical scheme within which he saw the advent of democracy, we must look in more detail at his analysis of its tendencies, and at his response to those tendencies. The central texts are the three essays on the United States that he contributed to the *Nineteenth Century* magazine, 'Democracy' (1861), 'Equality' (1879), and of course *Culture and Anarchy*. Arnold's concern here emerges as similar to Mill's anxiety over trivialisation, mediocrity, and the tyranny of public opinion. Clearly, we are dealing with a problem in the history of liberalism – the critique of liberalism by liberals in the interests of the maintenance of civilisation and culture. We may cite the doubts which Renan (in the guise of a 'bon esprit et un bon patriot') voiced in *La Réforme intellectuelle et morale*:

France is misleading herself about the form that the consciousness of the people can take. Her universal suffrage is a heap of sand, without cohesion or fixed relationship between the grains. No house could be built on that. The consciousness of a nation dwells in the enlightened part of the nation which leads and commands the rest. Civilisation was, in its origins, an aristocratic work, the work of a very small number (nobles and priests) who imposed it by what democrats call force and imposture; the preservation of civilisation is a task for an aristocracy too.[67]

What, in a classless society, was to represent the elevated, to stand for manners and civilisation? The question was pressing for Coleridge, for Mill, and for Arnold. Semantically, Arnold's use of 'vulgar' in antithesis to 'noble' is arresting. As a classicist, he was well aware of the word's basic meaning, and was equally sure that it was derogatory (a 'middle class vulgarised'). Into his general Notebook, under the heading 'Madame de Stael on Vulgarity', he copied a passage from Sainte-Beuve:

It was she who risked the word for the first time, and it became indispensable for describing the new characteristic of society. The word 'urbanity' was coined and entered the language in the early seventeenth century: it was only just that the word 'vulgarity' came on the scene at the end of the eighteenth.

We must insist on the urgent necessity, in the reign of democratic ideas, of maintaining or of building up the culture of the spirit as a counter-weight to the brutality and violence which is their natural bent.[68]

Like so many of his contemporaries, Arnold looked to America as an experiment in democracy and equality, a kind of gigantic laboratory for the predominant social tendencies of the age: 'To us ... the future of the United States is of incalculable importance. Already we feel their influence much and we shall feel it more. We have a great deal to learn from them, also, many things to beware of.[69] He had read Tocqueville's *Democracy in America* in the 1840s, and had come to know Emerson as one of the 'voices in the air' in his undergraduate days.[70] The three *Nineteenth Century* articles, two written before his 1882 visit, one after, simply extend his thesis about English society to America.

What is civilisation? It is the humanisation of man in society, the satisfaction for him in society, of the true law of human nature.[71]

What, he asked, was the attribute of a 'high and satisfying civilisation'? The answer was that it was interesting, a word he claimed to find in Carlyle:

There is our word launched – the word interesting. ... I take note, in the word interesting, of a requirement, a cry of aspiration, a cry not sounding in the imaginative Carlyle's breast only, but sure of a response in ... human nature.[72]

Material criteria for civilisation were rejected by a neat assimilation under the heading of 'comforts and conveniences of life', an argumentative move that largely ruled out all that material improvement might imply for the object of what Arnold contemptuously referred to as the 'cult of the average man'. In the light of this, the significance of offering the 'Numbers' lecture to an American audience becomes clearer. The theme of the leaven and the theme of American materialism had plainly been running through Arnold's head. It is there in 'A Word about America' which he published before he left England. '*Das Gemeine* is the American danger',[73] and he made play with a Boston newspaper's assertion that groups of cultivated people were to be found all over the States: 'all this must needs leaven American society, and must surely, if we can take example from it, enable us to leaven and transform our own'.[74] But he was quite sure that what he would find in the States would be Philistines – what was America but 'a colossal extension of the English middle class spirit'?

Arnold's prescription for America, as for England, was not the fostering of formal education merely, but the fostering of the 'discipline of awe and respect' through the action within the community of a cultivated group – the doctrine of the remnant in fact. Hence the importance in his argument of the absence of criticism of all the 'hollow stuff' to be found in the States: if Americans would but recognise their deficiency in the elevated and the beautiful, one 'would insist on no shortcoming'. England had much to learn from this failure of criticism: 'We may greatly require to keep, as if it were our life, the doctrine that we are failures after all, if we cannot eschew vain boastings, and vain imaginations, eschew what flatters us in the common or ignoble, and approve things that are truly excellent.'[75] Arnold could attempt to distance the debate about democracy by writing about America, but no such distancing was possible in his specifically English writings. Nothing could dissolve the great responsibility he felt for the re-creation of an enlarged intellectual life in the nation, the establishment of a climate in which genuine creative work could again be undertaken, or the establishment of a 'high, correct, standard in intellectual matters'.[76] America had never known the standards set in culture by an aristocracy, but England had, and should not squander her knowledge. Burke's idealised aristocracy ('without which there is no nation') was in many ways the model for the intellectual elite of later theorists.

The ideal aristocrat grew up regulated in his conduct by a sense that he was 'considered as an instructor of [his] fellow-citizens in their highest concerns', and he too was a necessary precondition of his society's true being. In the course of answering Rousseau, Burke had anticipated Coleridge's account of national integrity:

The state of civil society, which necessarily generates this aristocracy, is a state of nature; and much more truly so than a savage and incoherent mode of life. For man is by nature reasonable; and he is never perfectly in his natural state, but when he is placed where reason may be best cultivated, and most predominates. . . . Men, qualified in the manner I have just described, form in nature, as she operates in the common modification of society, the leading, guiding, and governing part. It is the soul to the body, without which the man does not exist.[77]

Arnold believed that some way had to be found of replacing this supposed civilising effect within the community. While his was no routine conservatism ('In the immense spiritual movement of our day, the English aristocracy . . . always reminds me of Pilate confronting the phenomenon of Christianity'),[78] he has a subdued longing for a state presided over by an ideal aristocracy. Aristocracies are 'in the grand style', he remarked. Reference to the 1853 Preface to his Poems, and to his Oxford Inaugural Lecture 'On Translating Homer', clarifies the social application of this literary critical concept. For the grand style is the style of those periods when man is most at one with himself, when doubts about the justice of social organisation do not arise, when the poet can rely on the organic surety of his being. Those periods in fact that were held to embody everything that was the opposite of the nineteenth century's self image. A habit of mind that connects heroic actions and the vivid, unselfconscious periods of the human spirit in an attack on materialism and Benthamite calculation is emerging, and there is a suggestion of Nietzsche or even Yeats about it. The present age, Arnold argued, was unsuitable for poetry. Writers

are told that it is an era of progress, an age commissioned to carry out the great ideas of industrial development and social amelioration. They reply that with all this they can do nothing: that the elements they need for the exercise of their art are great actions, calculated powerfully and delightfully to affect what is permanent in the human soul; that so far as the present age can supply such actions, they will gladly make use of them; but that an age wanting in moral grandeur can with difficulty supply such, and an age of spiritual discomfort with difficulty be powerfully and delightfully affected by them.[79]

The attitude may explain, among other things, Arnold's relative neglect of that flourishing verbal art form of his day, the realist novel. Presumably, its allegiance to the transitory, everyday world was too blatant to permit a claim to high seriousness. The poet's problem and the social problem were one, but where the poet could only deplore the inhospitality of the world to the homeless consciousness, the social critic chose the more extrovert course of fortifying the latter.

Let us take Arnold's diagnosis of the probable failings of democracy one stage further. His own career represents in a way a turning from poetry to prose. But his earliest formulations about society, and the questions he chose thereafter to put to contemporary societies, stemmed from his assessment of the poet's – specifically his own – relation to society. If we look back at 'Stanzas from the Grande Chartreuse', 'Palladium', 'Memorial Verses', 'The Scholar Gypsy', 'Thyrsis', or 'Empedocles', we find a recurrent lament over 'this strange disease of modern life,/With its sick hurry, its divided aims'. Here are both fear and resentment at the exhaustion of the powers of the sensitive man in such an age:

> For what wears out the life of mortal men?
> 'Tis that from change to change their being rolls;
> 'Tis that repeated shocks, again, again,
> Exhaust the energy of strongest souls,
> And numb the elastic powers.

The felt dissipation of energy in 'this iron time/Of doubts, distractions, fears' breeds a longing for 'The freshness of the early world', a world in which all was in harmony. Can it be that the recurrence to an idealised childhood, so characteristic of Romantic and Victorian literature, represents another form of response to accelerated social and symbolic change? The vision of an alternative world was carried over into Arnold's social criticism in which culture is visualised as a stabilising, integrating force, the channel between society and the realm of eternal law. There is a dual relevance here for Arnold's critique of democracy: first, the tendency to assert the eternal and unmoved represents a kind of agoraphobia induced by the historical relativism of the new history. If we do not want our own values to be examined in historical perspective, we must claim that they are in some way absolute, that they transcend the merely historical. Second, democracy comes to represent the apotheosis of the unstable, the mindless, the heedlessly diverse or the lower, animal self. Newman, in a passage whose bearing on Arnold's thought is obvious, had already illustrated the connection between the rejection of multifariousness, the longing for transcendent stability, and the righteousness of the few. There are

> numberless clouds which flit over the sky ... as many, as violent, as far-spreading, as fleeting, as uncertain, are the clouds and gales of human opinion; as suddenly, as impetuously, as fruitlessly do they assail those whose mind is stayed on God. They come and they go; they have no life in them or abidance.... They are the voice of the many; they have the strength of the world, and they are directed against the few.... On the other hand, divine truth is ever one and the same, it changes not, any more than its Author.[80]

Arnold, with no growing idea of the historical Catholic church to support him, proposed an equation between ordinariness and diversity, contrasting here sharply with Mill for whom one of democracy's chief dangers was that it led to social stasis. Our aim, Arnold wrote at the end of *Culture and Anarchy*, is to make 'the State more and more the expression ... of our best self, which is not manifold, and vulgar and unstable, and contentious, and ever-varying, but one, and noble, and secure, and peaceful and the same for all mankind'.[81] Nostalgia for an ideal aristocracy appears in the antithesis of 'noble-vulgar'. The part of Arnold that leans towards aristocracy and the grand style is the part that seeks a static harmonious world. For Arnold, the ideas of form and discipline go together with a longing for the security of hierarchic social values, and minister to a fear of the present, and of change foreseen as social disintegration. The English, he remarked in his Rede Lecture, wanted form, the 'sym-metria prisca' of the Greeks. This was where all our art failed. Elevation of character in a class of men

> may go along with a not very quick or open intelligence; but it cannot well go along with a conduct vulgar or ignoble. A governing class imbued with it may not be capable of intelligently leading the masses of the people to the highest pitch of welfare for them; but it sets them an invaluable example of qualities without which no really high welfare can exist.[82]

If this passage were merely defining an ideal governing class there would be less to argue with. But the reference is to the aristocracy-approximating English governing class which at that time, so Arnold thought, was passing away. If, he continued, the middle classes press on with their negative aims, the result would be

the decline of the aristocratical element, which in some sort supplied an ideal to ennoble the spirit of the nation and to keep it together.... [In this case] there will be no other element present to perform this service.[83]

The mantle of the aristocracy descended upon the remnant.

Arnold's cultured group was associated with the kind of values he attributed to an aristocracy at its best. Here the 1879 lecture to the British Institution ('Equality') is relevant. The subject is the necessity of social equality and our backwardness in England at providing it. The text is one attributed to Menander ('Choose equality and flee greed') and the argument ranks with Arnold's finest statements on behalf of democracy: 'The well-being of the many comes out more and more distinctly, in proportion as time goes on, as the object we must pursue.'[84] We are struck all the more forcibly, therefore, by the revivification of the notion of the gentleman, a notion which illuminates the debate on liberal education in the last century. The alternative to professional training is still liberal education, the education of the man who can look down upon professional training.[85] Senator Charles Summer, Arnold noted, had remarked during a recent visit on the number of 'gentlemen' in England. Arnold continued:

this large class of gentlemen in the professions, the services, literature, politics, – and a good contingent is now added from business also, – this large class, not of the nobility, but with the tastes of an upper class, is something peculiar to England.... It is aristocratic in this sense, that it has the tastes of a cultivated class, a certain high standard of civilisation.[86]

Arnold believed in the necessity of democracy, but dreaded its fissiparous tendencies. In consequence, he threw his weight on the side of whatever promised to be a stabilising and ennobling force.

Culture and morality

Into his discussion of democracy, Arnold introduced the ambiguous concept of manners. This term asserts a continuity with *mores/moeurs*, that is to say customs, the rules which govern men's social activities. It was used as a translation for both terms. But even *moeurs* is not neutral: as used by Tocqueville, it carries more than a hint of approval. *Moeurs* are the social customs that facilitate social intercourse. As soon as we ask whose social intercourse they facilitate and with whom, the concept becomes problematical.

European writers tended to note their absence in the United States, though Trollope, speaking of American public education, quoted the Ovidian 'emollit mores'.[87] But manners often carry a narrower sense in Arnold. They make people 'gentle' – the social resonances of the word are audible. 'Manners' can be propagated by a social group. Each class, we remember, was to educate the one that came after it, in a kind of nationwide monitorial system. But 'manners' are essentially normative, the symptoms of the social game among those who accept the rules of that game. The players of one game will not necessarily accept the rules promoted by the players of another. Yet Arnold sets up an ideal version of the manners of a particular period and stratum of society as a norm. A system of manners, he claims, promotes equality. 'It is by the humanity of their manners that men are made equal.'[88] However, the earlier argument and a quotation from Burke add something else: 'There ought to be a system of manners in every nation which a well-formed mind would be disposed to relish.' Once again, the marriage of hierarchic and democratic values is awkward. Among Burke's 'manners' would be deference towards social superiors. Arnold's gloss does not mitigate the problem: 'the power of social life and manners is truly, as we have seen, one of the great elements in our humanisation.... It brings men together, makes them feel the need of one another, be considerate of one another, understand one another.'[89] If there were any doubt that Arnold's thesis had an actual, historical point of reference his later account of the aristocracy should remove it. Although the English aristocracy's function was now gone, we should not forget that aristocracies have a sense for manners, and 'when the day of general humanisation comes, they will have fixed the standard for manners'.[90] The feeling is inescapable that the new class of gentlemen, the leaven in the lump of the middle class, were to carry on the good work. The modes of behaviour among the middle classes as a whole were not yet adequate for their historical mission. In Arnold's thought the things elevated which culture brought had an uncanny tendency to convege with the things elevated of a hierarchical social organisation. Both, at least, tended to instil the 'discipline of respect'.

'Manners' as a translation of *moeurs* sends us back to that culture for which the aristocracy had stood, and the state would come to stand. For *moeurs* are morals as well as manners. The identification of culture with morality – the merging of the objects of culture with those of morality – runs through Arnold's work. It must be seen in its context as a characteristic nineteenth-century conflation, as typical of Ruskin as of Arnold, and widely made in the period's writings on culture. Pater's doctrine of 'art for art's sake' was engendered to oppose it, and we might note here just how far Wilde's 'Critic as Artist', with its insistence that action 'is limited and relative', and its emphasis upon avoiding the 'tyranny of this dreadful social ideal' both springs from and is an answer to Arnold. Yet, ironically, Wilde too ends up appropriating a social role both for art and for criticism: the 'duty of imposing form upon chaos does not grow less as the world advances. There was never a time when Criticism was more needed than it is now. . . . It is Criticism, as Arnold points out, that creates the intellectual atmosphere of the age.'[91] But Arnold was less concerned than Wilde to preserve the autonomy of art or of criticism. That poetry or art in general could be exploring experience that was unassimilable to moral ideas or abstract categories of any sort, that genuine art might have pre-moral springs, or that there might be tragedy – or the least irony – in the assimilation of creativity to a didactic 'culture', seems never to have crossed Arnold's mind. The 'noble and profound application of ideas to life is the most essential feature of poetic greatness'.[92] Further still, a 'poetry of revolt against moral ideas is a poetry of revolt against *life*; a poetry of indifference towards moral ideas is a poetry of indifference towards *Life*'.[93] There is, of course, more than one way of reading such statements, but one does not need to make a dogma out of Blake's saying that 'the grandest Poetry is Immoral . . . Cunning & Morality are not Poetry but Philosophy; the Poet is Independent & Wicked; the Philosopher Dependent & Good',[94] in order to recognise that such a position as Arnold's, stated with such assurance, lends both itself and poetry to a vision of culture as authoritative. I have already suggested that Arnold's is a normative theory of culture.

'To habituate ourselves . . . to approve, as the Bible says, things that are really excellent, is of the highest importance.'[95] This is the keynote of Arnold's criticism, in the *Essays in Criticism* as in 'On Translating Homer'. True, he had perceptive things to say about some authors from outside his great tradition, but it is hard to resist the impression that anything outside that corpus was considered ephemeral. His judgment for poetry holds, one supposes, for the other arts:

constantly, in reading poetry, a sense for the best, the really excellent ...
should be present in our minds and should govern our estimate of what we
read. But this real estimate, the only true one, is liable to be superseded, if
we are not watchful, by two other kinds of estimate, the historic estimate
and the personal estimate, both of which are fallacious. A poet or a poem
may count to us historically, they may count to us on grounds personal to
ourselves, and they may count to us really.[96]

I have said before that Arnold is torn between allegiance to the
static world of truths and the dynamic, changing world. How significant, then, that when at the point of accounting for what poetry
does for us, he erects a timeless canon. 'Real' and 'really' can be
seen to undergo a semantic shift on several occasions in Arnold's
work. Thus he writes about 'fixing standards of perfection that are
real',[97] and in *Culture and Anarchy* he sometimes substitutes 'real'
for 'best'. Having adumbrated this distinction between evaluation in
historical and in real terms, Arnold engages in a mock debate with
Charles d'Hericault about the historicity of works of art, and ends
up in asserting their timelessness, defining a 'real classic' as belonging
to the 'class of the very best'. Now it would certainly be possible
to overemphasise the ahistorical nature of the culture defined by
Arnold's timeless canon. It was he, after all, who wrote of Jacobinism as leading to a static and abstract perfection: 'Jacobinism loves a
Rabbi ... it wants its Rabbi and his ideas to stand for perfection,
that they may with the more authority recast the world; and for
Jacobinism, therefore, culture, – eternally passing onward and seeking, – is an impertinence and an offence.'[98] Nevertheless, Arnold's
tendency to separate out the 'great', results in the assertion of a
canon that is normative in the sense that all other cultural activity is
measured against it. The nature of the demands made of culture
indicates that although it judges the historical world, it is not itself
rooted in that world. Arnold calls in culture to regulate the flux of
historical process. The establishment of 'classics', the use of 'touch-
stones' in poetry and maxims in philosophy for the assessment of the
poetry or thought of the present, has the effect of codification, of
creating a regulatory rather than an exploratory culture. 'Anarchy
and Authority' had been the title of the articles in which most of
Culture and Anarchy first appeared. Social and cultural criticism
face an identical task. The samples from the classics insist on set
standards for beauty (which, as Arnold reminded us in the Preface
to *Essays on Criticism*, 'is only truth seen from the other side')

and imply the need for critics as arbiters of the beautiful. Henry Sidgwick's contemporary criticism is powerful. At this time in history, he argued, we cannot afford to denigrate enthusiasm in the light of ideal harmony. Culture has, indeed, an enthusiasm of its own, but that is not sufficient for present needs. Secondly, culture will only appreciate enthusiasm when that enthusiasm is

picturesque, or thrilling, or sublime; upon some completed excellence of form culture will vigorously insist. May it not be that culture is short-sighted and pedantic in the rigour of these demands, and thus really defeats its own ends. . . ? If it had larger and healthier sympathies it might see beauty in stage of becoming . . . in much rough and violent work at which it now shudders. In pure art culture is always erring on the side of antiquity – much more in its sympathy with the actual life of men and society.

And Sidgwick ended:

Perhaps what is most disappointing in our culture is its want of appreciation of the 'sap of progress', the creative and active element of things.[99]

But for Arnold, culture was something out there, a source of criticism of the present while being itself securely rooted in the eternal. In it men are to seek purification of vision and turn back to the world to 'see the object as in itself it really is'. We must return to the critics who, educated in 'classical' literature, could see clearly what was happening around them and hold up a 'high, correct standard in intellectual matters'.

The function of criticism

The notion of the lettered class informed Arnold's thought about the state of the future. His Notebooks testify to this concern. For example, reading a review of a book on Humboldt in the *Revue germanique et française*, he noted that in 'Humboldt's eyes – after individual perfection the great thing to be aimed at de créer, par l'instruction, une aristocratie, la plus nombreuse possible, d'intelligence et de caractères'.[100] I shall argue further that the point of *Culture and Anarchy* becomes clearer if we see it as addressed to those whom its author variously calls the 'children of light', the 'aliens', and the 'lovers of culture'. Although 'Numbers' contained his clearest formulation of the idea of the remnant, the notion of the cultured group was always in Arnold's mind. That he was already thinking about it at the time when he began his work on the great educational commissions is proved by the 1861 article on 'The Bishop and the Philosopher' which I quoted on page 100. Here his stalking horse was John Colenso, the Anglican Bishop of Natal, who, in his attempt to reconcile the Old Testament with common sense, had already started down the path that was to lead to his excommunication for heresy. Arnold compared the bishop, to his disadvantage, with Spinoza, and found that the author of Ecclesiasticus, Christ, Pindar, Plato, Spinoza, and Newman 'in one of his noblest sermons' (the one used twenty years later in 'Numbers') were united in holding that the truth could only be entrusted to the few. His resentment stemmed more from his belief that Colenso's doctrines tended to unsettle the little instructed, than from the assessment that they did not tend to inform the highly instructed. In our times, he pointedly argued, we even had to let a translation of Spinoza pass, though ideally that philosopher's work should be left in Latin, the 'language of the instructed few'.

Times are changed since Spinoza wrote; the reserve which he recommended and practised is being repudiated by all the world. Speculation is to be made popular, all reticence is to be abandoned, every difficulty is to be canvassed publicly, every doubt is to be proclaimed; information which, to have any value at all, must have it as part of a series not yet complete, is to be flung broadcast, in the crudest shape, amidst the undisciplined, ignorant, passionate, captious multitude.

> 'Audax omnis perpeti
> Gens humana ruit per vetitum nefas:'

and in that adventurous march the English branch of the race of Japhet is, it seems, to be headed by its clergy in full canonicals.[101]

This argument is extended in Arnold's 1864 essay 'The Function of Criticism at the Present Time'. Its theme is well known: criticism is 'a disinterested endeavour to learn and propagate the best that is known and thought in the world', and its function in doing so is to 'establish a current of fresh and true ideas', thus creating the intellectual climate in which a genius could again write great literature. In his general Notebook, Arnold quoted Sainte-Beuve under the heading

CULTIVATED LITERARY OPINION

For literature to have a coherent and consistent life there must be a certain stability without stagnation. To foster emulation there must be a circle of competent, select judges; something or some one who organises, regularises, who orders and sets bounds, that the author can have in view and want to satisfy. Without that, he throws off all restraint, dissipates and wastes his powers.[102]

Criticism was not just the criticism of literature, and above all not just the criticism of English literature. Less clear is the kind of audience for whom the essay was intended; to real or potential critics, certainly, and it is apparent that the appeal was not directed towards those actually engaged in practical matters. The theme of the second part is that the critic must keep out of practical affairs: 'I say, the critic must keep out of the region of immediate practice in the political, social, humanitarian sphere, if he wants to make a beginning for that more free speculative treatment of things, which may perhaps one day make its benefits felt even in this sphere.'[103] In the principle of withdrawal from the practical sphere, a curious identity between the critics and the remnant of nearly twenty years later is emerging. Arnold states expressly that not everyone could learn to appreciate ideas:

The mass of mankind will never have any ardent zeal for seeing things as they are; very inadequate ideas will always satisfy them. On these inadequate ideas reposes and must repose the general practice of the world. That is as much as saying that whoever sets himself to see things as they really are will find himself one of a very small circle; but it is only by this small circle resolutely doing its work that adequate ideas will ever get current at all.[104]

Above all, the new dominant class needed its critics. In his American writings Arnold made much of the theme of 'national self-flattery'. There was no one to tell the American people the truth about themselves; instead there was a chorus telling them how wonderful they were. The theme appears in his English writings as well, notably in the third chapter of *Culture and Anarchy*. Here we find the link between the idea of the remnant and the touchstone theory of culture. Culture ministers to 'paramount authority', and points to the need for a 'sound centre of authority'.[105] This is at the centre of his discussion of democracy:

In other countries the governors, not depending so immediately on the favour of the governed, have everything to urge them, if they know anything of right reason (and it is at least supposed that governors should know more of this than the mass of the governed), to set it authoritatively before the community. But our whole scheme of government being representative, every one of our governors has all possible temptation, instead of setting up before the governed who elect him, and on whose favour he depends, a high standard of right reason, to accommodate himself as much as possible to their natural desire for bathos.[106]

A class basis for social dialogue was not enough. There was no one to criticise the shortcomings of each class except hostile classes whose criticisms could easily be discounted on the grounds of interest. 'In our political system everybody is comforted'; Arnold devoted several pages to showing how each class was flattered by its friends. We urgently needed a body to represent 'right reason' to the community. Arnold had in some ways a sociological bent: one remembers him at the Friedrich-Wilhelms Gymnasium at Köln asking the director to go through the admissions register with him, 'that I might see to what class in society the boys chiefly belonged'.[107] It is therefore surprising at first that he barely attempts a sociological account of the critics. All we learn is that 'within each of these classes [i.e. Barbarians, Philistines, Populace] there are a certain number of *aliens*, if we may so call them, – persons who are mainly led, not by their class spirit, but by a general *humane* spirit, by the love of human perfection'.[108] Yet we can, I think, read a kind of self-projection into Arnold's public utterances. At the present juncture, he notes at the end of *Culture and Anarchy*, the 'centre of movement is not in the House of Commons. It is in the fermenting mind of the nation; and his is for the next twenty years the real influence who can address himself to this.'[109] The ideal critic – this leads us to our final section – was to work together with the ideal State. Arnold's fear of social and moral disintegration resulted in an assertion of order in politics, of centrality in culture, and of the state as the organ of the collective best self.

THE BEST SELF

Thomas Arnold, we remember, had fired his pupils with a theory of the state as a moral and educational collective. His son fused this early lesson with his reading of Burke and Humboldt to produce an almost Napoleonic conception. We may suggest the connection between the political order and the moral or cultural role of the remnant by quoting Sainte-Beuve – the 'first of living critics', as Arnold called him in 1863.[110] Elsewhere he spoke of having soaked in Sainte-Beuve, and his admiration lasted; in 1887 he quoted Amiel's words on Sainte-Beuve's death: 'Infallibility of judgement is perhaps rarer than anything else, so fine a balance of qualities does it demand. . . . Like Plato's sage, it is only at fifty that the critic is risen to the true height of his literary priesthood, or, to put it less pompously, of his social function.'[111] The passage of Sainte-Beuve to which I wish to draw attention here comes from one of the *Causeries du lundi* of 1849–51, the essay entitled 'Literary Criticism under the Empire'. Obviously, we cannot legitimately claim that Arnold would have fully endorsed the argument. But the passage does suggest a mood which can be related to what Arnold has to say about epochs of dissolution and transformation in the Preface to *Essays in Criticism* and in 'The Function of Criticism'. Spiritual and cultural order appear as the other side of political order:

In 1800, we were at one of those epochs when the public mind tends to reform itself. The struggle was not yet over, but also, clearly, there was concert and harmony; there was opportunity for guidance. We were issuing from a long and frightful period of licence, eccentricity and confusion. A powerful man was re-establishing the social and political order on its bases. Whenever, after a long period of confusion, the political order recovers its ground and resumes its regular course, the literary order tends to fall in with it and to follow as best it can. Criticism . . . under the shelter of a tutelary power, accomplishes its work and places itself at the service of the common restoration. Under Henry IV . . . there was Malherbe; under Louis XIV, after the Fronde, there was Boileau. In 1800, after the Directory, and under the First Consul, we had in literary criticism the small change of Malherbe and Boileau, that is to say, men of intellect and sense, who formed groups and understood one another, who restored good order in the things of the mind, and acted as police in Letters. Some did this police duty very honestly, others less so; most of them brought to it a certain passion, but almost all, taking them at their starting point, acted usefully.[112]

'Men of intellect . . . , who formed groups and understood one another, who restored good order in the things of the mind' – the leaning is familiar, as is the identification with a 'classical' tradition (represented by Malherbe and Boileau) as opposed to diversitarianism or revolutionary romanticism. So, too, is the refusal or inability to ask whose was the order invoked in politics or literature. Sainte-Beuve, let us remember, accepted a university post from Louis Napoleon, from which, and in the face of student opposition, he defended the new government. Who for Arnold was to be the 'tutelary power'? The answer is the state, conceived of as the institutional version of the whole community's right reason. Our main texts must be *Schools and Universities on the Continent, A French Eton*, and, again, *Culture and Anarchy*, all products of the social and educational crisis of the 1860s.

We have already seen what Burke suggested to Arnold about the coherence of the nation, and that the latter's response to what he took to be social, cultural, and moral disintegration was to urge the setting up of the state as the representative of the collective best self. The role of 'intelligence' or 'light' was to recognise the choices open in the course of the great democratic revolution. One was disintegration. Negative liberalism was not enough. The Englishman's 'right to march where he likes, meet where he likes, enter where he likes, hoot as he likes, threaten as he likes, smash as he likes ... tends to anarchy.'[113] There is no point here in summarising the argument of *Culture and Anarchy*; we may merely note the obsessiveness of the polemic. The work has a status in Arnold's thought roughly comparable to that of *Church and State* in Coleridge's. Both represent responses to an alarming political situation hinging on a crisis over reform of the constitution. Arnold's response to the foreseen anarchy is crucial to my argument, and begins, notably, with a glance back to the politics of deference. It was evident, he felt, that

as feudalism, which with its ideas and habits of subordination was for many centuries silently behind the British Constitution, dies out, and we are left with our system of checks, and our notion of its being the great right and happiness of an Englishman to do as far as possible what he likes, we are in danger of drifting towards anarchy. We have not the notion, so familiar on the Continent and to antiquity, of *the State*, – the nation in its collective and corporate character, entrusted with stringent powers for the general advantage, and controlling individual wills in the name of an interest wider than that of individuals.[114]

Arnold's vision of the state was made possible by its identification with 'right reason'. Towards the end of his life Thomas Arnold had begun to have doubts about the theory of the moral personality of the state. 'In his latest lessons', Stanley notes, 'it was observed how, in reading Plato's Republic, he broke out into a solemn protest against the evil effects of an exaggerated craving after Unity.' In his studies of early Christian history he was struck by the thought that even the apostolic church had been corrupted 'not only by the Judaic spirit of priesthood, but even more by the Gentile spirit of government, stifling the sense of individual responsibility'. And Stanley quoted the Headmaster's own words:

I am myself so much inclined to the idea of a strong social bond, that I ought not to be suspected of any tendency to anarchy; yet I am beginning to think that the idea may be overstrained, and that this attempt to merge the soul and will of the individual man in the general body is, when fully developed, contrary to the very essence of Christianity.[115]

Yet Matthew Arnold believed firmly in the assertion of the state, though he left few clues as to how the state was to be organised. It was not, we know, to be in the hands of any one class.[116] Even the way in which the children of light were to suffuse the state with intelligence is unclear, though Arnold does remark that, though unlike in other things, Austria, Rome, and England 'are alike in this, that the civil organisation of each implies, at the present day, a denial or an ignorance of the right of mind or reason to rule human affairs'.[117] We can, however, see in *Schools and Universities on the Continent* another facet of Arnold's debt to Humboldt in the suggestion of an educational bureaucracy somewhat on the Prussian model, and we may, I think, suggest that Arnold envisages the men of culture acting as consultants to such an organisation. Thus he laments how easy it is for educated opinion not to be heard in the making of educational policy in England[118] (to be fair, in the era of Lowe's Revised Code, he had good reason to lament), and he asserts the importance in a modern state of having an education minister, with a non-political High Council of Education to help him.[119] The remnant made a brief appearance in the 1868 Preface:

These foreign Governments, which we think so offensively arbitrary, do at least take, when they administer education, the best educational opinion of the country into their counsels, and we do not.... The result is that while, on the Continent ... the best educational opinion of the country, – by which I mean the opinion of men like Sir James Shuttleworth, Mr Mill, Dr Temple, men who have established their right to be at least heard on these topics, – necessarily reaches the Government and influences its action, in this country there are no organised means for its ever reaching our Government at all.[120]

Our awareness of the educational reasons for Arnold's assertion of the need for the organised state should not blind us to some of the implications of his argument. I mean that beyond the healthy insistence of *A French Eton* on the inadequacy of *laissez-faire* methods of supplying education, and beyond the arguments of *Schools and Universities* for an augmented state, is the magnet of order and Napoleonic system. A historical reassessment was needed:

We in England, impressed with their faults because it was our lot to meet them as enemies, do not in general know the true merits either of the French Revolution or of the first Napoleon. Their faults are palpable and undeniable; their merits are equally undeniable. . . . The great merit of the French Revolution, the great service it rendered to Europe, was *to get rid of the Middle Age.* . . . The great merit of the first Napoleon, the great service he rendered to Europe, was *to found a civil organisation for modern society.*[121]

Our sense of the need for this insistence in the England of its time should not obscure its tendency.

The state and the intellectual health of society existed in reciprocal relationship. Italian statesmen understood, Arnold claimed, that a government's duty was not 'to fear and flatter ignorance, prejudice and obstructiveness' but to represent to the public that a good educational organisation and the intellectual grandeur of the nation were the surest foundations both of the power of the state and of the true and orderly liberty of the people.[122] In the drive towards the unification of Italy and Germany, Arnold found affirmed his own aims for a culture that was one and rested upon a centre. The best that had been thought and said in the world would inform the life of the new society, and for Arnold the best that had been thought and said in the world constituted a single stream. In the citing of Plato and the prophets, Christ and Paul, Shakespeare and Goethe, it is implied that all united in teaching complementary lessons. It would be easy to overlook what a vast assumption it is not only that we *could* know the best that has been thought and said in the world, but that the best that has been thought and said in the world (which it is the function of the critic not only to know but to propagate as well) should turn out not to be contradictory. 'Totality', another of Arnold's positives, is hinted at.

Totality was the attribute of culture that was harmonious and rested upon a centre. It, too, had its correlative in the world of institutions, and so its opposite, provinciality, came to include all that dissented from the establishment, all that threatened totality with disintegration. This resulted in an assertion, the remarkable nature of which is only explicable by an appreciation of how deeply Arnold yearned for the centre. 'The great works by which, not only in literature, art and science generally, but in religion itself, the human spirit has manifested its approaches to totality, and to a full, harmonious perfection, come, not from Nonconformists, but from men who either belong to Establishments or have been trained in them.'[123] Totality and harmonious perfection merge. Thomas Arnold had devoted much of his life to urging inclusiveness upon the Church of England. His son followed him in his aspiration after inclusiveness, but the nature of his feeling for establishments in general suggests that the tensions between them and those outside them were lost on him. This stands out in the 1864 essay 'Pagan and Mediaeval Religious Sentiment', or in the later essay on 'British Liberalism and Irish Catholicism'. His insistence that Englishmen should reassess the positives of Catholicism was undoubtedly valuable in its time. But the emotional drive in Arnold, as in T. S. Eliot, was towards the sanctioned imaginative repository of the centre. Migne's monumental collection of the writings of the church fathers, the *Patrologia*, stands as an image for the canon of truth. The totality for which establishments stood is central to the theory of culture. They stand for continuity. Establishments 'tend to give us a sense of the historical life of the human spirit, outside and beyond our own fancies and feelings; . . . they thus tend to suggest new sides and sympathies in us to cultivate.'[124] Let us recall the essay on 'The Literary Influence of Academies'. Academies could not of themselves further genius, but they could be, as Richelieu ('himself a man in the grand style') perceived, a 'potent instrument of the grand style'. They impose a 'high, correct standard in intellectual matters'. The standard should be set from the centre. Arnold can quote Renan approvingly: the French Academy has facilities for 'creating a form of intellectual culture *which shall impose itself on all around*'.[125] It stands for totality.

> Such an effort to set up a recognised authority, imposing on us a high standard in matters of intellect and taste, has many enemies in human nature. We all of us like to go our own way, and not to be forced out of the atmosphere of commonplace habitual to most of us; – '*was uns alle bändigt*', says Goethe, '*das Gemeine*'. We like to be suffered to lie comfortably on the old straw of our habits, especially of our intellectual habits, even though the straw may not be very clean and fine.[126]

It is quietly assumed that it will be our subjective, lower nature that opposes the imposition of authority, and Arnold's image adds an animal, even faintly scatological suggestion. The renewal of our intellectual habits comes not from the outsiders (by now identified with the degraded *volonté de tous* – the sum of unenlightened individual wills) who challenge the establishment and its standards, but

from the centre itself. Borrowing and adapting terms from Mannheim, we could say that for Arnold, ideology and utopia are one.

We have not left the children of light far behind. To reach a conclusion: Arnold's rejection of liberalism (tagged as 'doing as one
likes') was contemptuous and owes something to Newman. Diversity,
it is suggested, implies deviation from the truth: 'What a most awful
view does human society present to those who would survey it religi-
ously! [Newman had said] Go where you will, you will find persons
with their own standards of right and wrong, yet each different from
each.'[127] A later generation would dismiss Mill's pluralism as an
attempt to contain the genuine forces of change. That was not, however, Arnold's objection. His objection began (and here few of us
would, I think, wish to quarrel with him) with a challenge to what he
saw as the complacent *laissez-faire* of *The Times* and *The Daily News*.
Underneath, he wondered whether any good could come of people
doing what they liked, and he arrived at a contempt which tried to
identify experiment and variety with provincialism (in the pejorative
sense), as wrong-headed because ignorant of the standards of the
centre:

No doubt we have an infinite variety of experiments, and an ever-multiply-
ing multitude of explorers. Even in these few chapters I have enumerated
many: the *British Banner*, Judge Edmonds, Newman Weeks, Deborah
Butler, Brother Noyes, the Reverend W. Cattle, the Licensed Victuallers,
the Commercial Travellers, and I know not how many more; and the
numbers of the noble army are swelling every day.[128]

Aversion to the tone of a passage such as this should not blind us to
the cogency of the critique of liberalism to which Arnold contributed.
Renan, who had similarly urged the salvation of the mass through
the operation of an elite, speaks in the same vein: 'For what point is
there in freedom of assembly, if no one has anything worthwhile to
communicate? Or what point in freedom of speech if no one has
anything truthful or novel to say?'[129] Culture in Arnold's theory
may be infinite progress or becoming, but the national life is like a
pool with a fountain in the middle. The new life flows from the
centre outwards. And what the centre supplies, the centre can
regulate. It is possible for Arnold to believe that the intellectual, the
critic (he who should disclaim party in the name of a greater whole),
could work as a matter of course from the centre, under the aegis of
the state. The idea of the intellectual prevalent today as the outsider
or dissenter, is foreign to his thought. His work is relevant to this

study as a whole because he found a function for the remnant in the maintenance of an avowedly conservative culture. He formulated for future English practitioners the belief that culture could inform the national life through the organs of the centre.

In practice, this belief had a remarkable effect. It tended to assimilate the intellectual life to the processes of legitimation within society, claiming a higher reason on behalf even of the existing state. As Sidgwick noted, the shift from ideal to real was too easily accomplished. Forces in the national life which did not conform to the standards set from the centre were, by definition, anarchic, and made for disintegration. The Hyde Park episode of 1866 tells us much. Mill and Frederic Harrison worked for the Reform League, and petitioned the authorities for the use of Hyde Park for the demonstration. Arnold, on the other hand, faced with the symbolic collapse of the railings before the crowd of demonstrators, wrote that the task before the 'friends and lovers of culture was the suppression of anarchy and disorder: without order there can be no society, and without society there can be no human perfection'. Earlier, I suggested, a similarity between Arnold and Rousseau. We must not, however, take the similarity too far. It was, after all, Rousseau's theoretical achievement to separate sovereignty and government and to declare the government the servant of society.[130] Arnold, however, was apt to put sovereignty and government back together. We have seen that he was torn between visions of man as corrupt and as perfectible. Perhaps one could go a step further, and say that when pressed, he opted not for Rousseau, but for Hobbes: 'Thus, in our eyes, the very framework and exterior order of the State, *whoever may administer the State*, is sacred; and culture is the most resolute enemy of anarchy, because of the great designs for the State which culture teaches us to nourish.'[131] Arnold's political and cultural theory as a whole was not inconsistent with this reaction.

THE RECONSTRUCTION OF OPINION:
JOHN STUART MILL

It has often struck me that one of the many causes which prevent those who cultivate moral and political truth from occupying the place and possessing the influence which properly belong to them as the instructors and leaders of mankind, is that they never consider themselves as other labourers do, to constitute a *guild* or fraternity, combining their exertions for certain common ends, and freely communicating to each other everything they possess which can be used to promote these ends.

Mill to J. P. Nichol, 16 January 1833

I do not find my enjoyment of speculation at all abated though I see less and less prospect of drawing together any body of persons to associate in the name & behalf of any set of fixed principles. Still, no good seed is lost: it takes root & springs up somewhere, & will help in time towards the general reconstruction of the opinion of the civilized world, for which ours is only a period of preparation.

Mill to Gustave d'Eichthal, 14 September 1839

The writings of John Stuart Mill clearly invite consideration in a study of the idea of the clerisy. At first sight it might seem surprising that the author of *On Liberty* should be found prescribing explicitly or by implication for the existence of a spiritual power. Yet it has long been recognised that, although he stands in a different tradition from that represented by Coleridge, Carlyle, and, to some extent, Arnold, his speculative ambit overlapped with theirs. To be able to include him in our study is an important argument for the breadth of the appeal made by the clerisy argument. For he was a child of eighteenth-century materialism and empiricism, an agnostic and a utilitarian. His strategy could not involve postulating a higher level of reality or a noumenal self by means of which to evade the limitations of the phenomenal level. And he was attracted to the positivism of Auguste Comte whose *pouvoir spirituel* (intellectual elite) was, at first sight, a very different affair from that of Coleridge. Yet in recent years, Mill has been attacked not only for his narrowness and self-righteousness as the propagator of a 'debased secular puritanism', but also (and more radically) as the exponent of a clerisy made in his own image. Maurice Cowling finding Mill to be the godfather of the 'improving intelligentsia', argues that his 'proselytizing liberal-ism' was a 'narrow and intolerant creed', and that his aim, even in *On Liberty* was not to free men from the impositions of all doctrine, but merely from the impositions of doctrines opposed to liberalism; in fact to make the world safe for 'rational education', 'rational thinking', and the 'assured leadership of the rational clerisy' – yet all based on an illegitimate claim to rationality.[1] Now, we do not have to share Cowling's animosity against the 'improving intelli-gentsia' to see that his conservatism has exposed an aspect of Mill of which we ought to be aware. We must ask how far Mill lays himself open to Cowling's criticism, and how far the clerisy ideal enters into or provides the stimulus for his work. The search throws light both on Mill and on the argument for a clerisy.

TOWARDS A NEW ORTHODOXY

Education and the utilitarian dilemma

Mill escaped from the confines of philosophic radicalism with the aid of Wordsworth, Goethe, Coleridge, Carlyle, and the Saint-Simonians. He received so many influences and drew on so many schools in educating himself in that many-sidedness that attracted him in Goethe, that to enter his thought is like being dropped into the deep end of nineteenth-century intellectual history.[2] An assess-ment of his thought in general is not, however, my object. I am concerned with what he did with the idea of the clerisy. Now, in developing the idea and drawing on those authors who, like Coleridge, Saint-Simon, and Comte, endorsed for him the idea of spiritual power as wielded by intellectuals, Mill was exploring a territory to which he attained access through a dilemma in his inherited liberalism. From his father he inherited the view that the great organ of social change at the present time was education. There is a great deal of eighteenth-century optimism behind this thesis – an Helvetian state of mind which believes in the formation of the individual through appropriate conditioning. This stream descended from Helvétius through James Mill (see, for example, the latter's famous essay on 'Education') to his son, who wrote in his

Autobiography of the appeal exercised by the 'unlimited possibility of improving the moral and intellectual condition of mankind through education'.[3] A serious drawback is indicated by Marx:

> The materialist doctrine that men are products of circumstances and up-bringing, and that, therefore, changed men are products of other circum-stances and changed upbringing, forgets that it is men that change cir-cumstances and that the educator himself needs educating. Hence, this doctrine necessarily arrives at dividing society into two parts, of which one is superior to society.[4]

Education was to go hand in hand with the extension of democracy and equality. Yet implicit in James Mill's 'Education', as in *An Essay on Government*, was the guaranteed enlightenment of the educators.

But there was a further and related problem. The doctrine that society, once rid of sinister interests, would automatically achieve the optimum conditions for individual development, assumed a solution to one of the central problems of philosophic radicalism – the tension between the natural and artificial fusion of interests.[5] We have here a practical consequence of the central utilitarian doctrine. Is the principle of utility descriptive or prescriptive? If the former, why has it ever been abandoned, and why are efforts necessary to achieve its social recognition? If the latter, what be-comes of its claim to rest on existing human nature? An uneasy consciousness of the need to look beyond the pleasure principle characterises the younger Mill's work. The principle of utility, Bentham had written, 'approves or disapproves of every action whatsoever, according to the tendency which it appears to have to augment or diminish the happiness of the party whose interest is in question'.[6] It became Mill's concern to ensure that the party was the community and not just the individual. The first condition of a healthy society, he proclaimed in his essay on Coleridge, was a 'system of *education*, beginning with infancy and continued through-out life, of which, whatever else it might include, one main and incessant ingredient was *restraining discipline*'.[7] In the absence of such discipline, personal impulse would triumph and the 'natural tendency of mankind to anarchy' reassert itself. The recognition of the dilemma necessitated making explicit the role of the spiritual power which would urge men towards 'that entireness of sympathy with all others, which would make any real discordance in the general direction of their conduct impossible'.[8] Until men at large realised that there was a hierarchy of pleasures, of which the highest were the intellectual and moral (and therefore social), there would be need of those 'best furnished with the means of comparison' to play Socrates to society's pig. The self-sufficiency of intellectual pleasure is not questioned: the education of society, as of self, requires the supervision and regulation supplied by the moral reason. Mill frequently reminds one of Schiller's warning: 'I call a man tense when he is under the compulsion of thought, no less than when he is under the compulsion of feeling. Exclusive domination by either of his two basic drives is for him a state of constraint and violence.'[9] By this standard Mill was – perhaps even more aspired to be – a very tense man indeed. A characteristic note is sounded in his account (in the original draft of the *Autobiography*) of his relationship with Harriet Taylor: 'we disdained, as every person not a slave of his animal appetites must do, the abject notion that the strongest & tenderest friendship cannot exist between a man & a woman without a sensual relation'.[10] The lesson – as Mill made quite clear in *Utilitarianism* – was that liberalism, too, could profess renunciation. An altruistic morality requires the suppression of emotional needs which Mill believes to be inevitably selfish. His preoccupation implied a consciousness of the potentially fissiparous nature of society – that was why Coleridge's emphasis on the principles of cohesion was to be welcomed. It led him to the investigation of nature as non-ethical.[11] But it also led not to the integration of intellect and passion, but to the assertion of their irreconcilable opposition, and the awarding of a governing place to intellect. In social thought this dichotomy (with which, within the liberal tradition, we can see Forster trying to cope after the turn of the century) meant the victory of the artificial over the natural fusion of interests. Coleridge's message fell upon good ground. Philosophic Toryism, Mill wrote to his friend Sterling in 1831, was aware that it was good for man

to submit both his body and mind to the guidance of a higher intelligence and virtue. It is therefore the direct antithesis of Liberalism, which is for making every man his own guide and sovereign master. . . . It is difficult to conceive a more thorough ignorance of man's nature, and of what is necessary for his happiness, or what degree of happiness and virtue he is capable of attaining than this system implies.[12]

Here, Mill's idealist and positivist acquisitions merge. For it was on precisely this basis – the sterile individualism of an age of transition, and the tendency of the most energetic impulses of human

nature to oppose the harmony of the whole – that Comte established
the need for the *pouvoir spirituel*, the *force morale* which was alone
'capable of surmounting or rather of sufficiently counterbalancing
the power of the anti-social tendencies which are naturally preponderant in the constitution of man'.[13] Mill adopted this argument,
and we see that individual and social education are parallel. In the
words of the *System of Logic*,

> as the strongest propensities of uncultivated or half-cultivated human
> nature (being the purely selfish ones, and those of a sympathetic character
> which partake most of the nature of selfishness) evidently tend in them-
> selves to disunite mankind, not to unite them, – to make them rivals, not
> confederates; social existence is only possible by a disciplining of those
> more powerful propensities, which consists in subordinating them to a
> common system of opinions. The degree of this subordination is the measure
> of the completeness of the social union, and the nature of the common
> opinions determines its kind. But in order that mankind should conform
> their actions to any set of opinions, those opinions must exist, must be
> believed by them. And thus, the state of speculative faculties, the character
> of the propositions assented to by the intellect, essentially determines the
> moral and political state of the community.[14]

An excellent justification for writing a system of logic. Mill's determination to expose himself to various and irreconcilable opinions
and arguments reminds one often of the intellectual adventures of
German intellectuals like his own mentor von Humboldt, pursuing
the salvation of his soul through multifarious self-cultivation.[15] But in
a curious way, Mill's education and his relationship with his father
had prepared him for the road he was to take. To court exposure to
different schools and beliefs, to search for strength in being contra-
dicted, remained the wistfully self-conscious 'mental progress' upon
which the *Autobiography* insists. And the common factor of the new
doctrines which Mill attempted to reconcile during the 1830s was
their concern with the intellectual precondition for a revivified
society, and consequently with the role of people like himself as the
guardians and guides of their fellows.

The nature of progress

In his reaction from 'the dogmatic disputatiousness of my former
narrow and mechanical state', Mill entered on paths which looked
strange to his more doctrinaire friends.[16] He was moved by poetry,
talked about the cultivation of feelings, discovered Coleridge,

Carlyle, Maurice and Sterling, Goethe, Saint-Simon, the latent royalism of the French reaction, and last but not least, Tocqueville. The relevance of these heterogeneous attractions to his educational and cultural creed will, I hope, become clear in due course. For the present, I want to say that Mill's awareness of Saint-Simonism and of Comte following his meeting with Gustave d'Eichthal in 1828 led him to a view of the history of the western nations that was foreign to the Benthamite tradition. In common with positivism, however, philosophic radicalism had its eschatological fervour. Mill's transition was perhaps eased by this shared sense of the crucial importance of the present age – the age, for one, of the sweeping away of sinister interests, and, for both, of the transition to a rational society. Mill was excited by the zeal of *Le Producteur* (the Saint-Simonian periodical) and of Comte's early *Système de Politique Positive*. True, he remained critical of Saint-Simon and of Comte, and repulsed d'Eichthal's attempts to enrol him in the Saint-Simonian sect, but he gained a vision of history for which, odd as it may seem, his acquaintance with the Coleridgeans of the London Debating Society was simultaneously preparing him. Society, he learned, passes through 'organic' and 'critical' stages. The one sees hierarchy, social contentment, the maintenance of orthodoxy; the other questioning of traditional institutions, and the assertion of the individual right to think. Both stages are essential to development, and the function of a critical period is to usher in a new organic period. As 'natural' and 'transitional' periods, these concepts were basic to some articles that Mill wrote for Leigh Hunt's *Examiner* in 1831, and which were later published together as *The Spirit of the Age*.

As we go deeper into Mill's concept of the educational elite, we shall find that at different stages in his thought the elite performs either of two social functions which seem, at first sight, incompatible: it either maintains orthodoxy, or it supports 'antagonism' – that is to say opposition to the prevailing orthodoxy. Only in the context of his social thought as a whole can it be seen that the two are not incompatible if visualised in operation in different states of society. This is, however, to anticipate my argument. In 1831 Mill put forward in the *Examiner* articles his most explicit statement of the natural–transitional dialectic:

Society may be said to be in its *natural* state, when worldly power and moral influence are habitually and indisputably exercised by the fittest persons whom the existing state of society affords.

Society may be said to be in its *transitional* state when it contains other persons fitter for worldly power and influence than those who have hitherto enjoyed them: when worldly power and the greatest existing capacity for worldly affairs, are no longer united but severed; and when the authority which sets the opinions and forms the feelings of those who are not accustomed to think for themselves, does not exist at all, or, existing, resides anywhere but in the most cultivated intellects, and the most exalted characters of the age.[17]

Mill thus helped to popularise a self-image of the age which was becoming acceptable in these years.[18] Transitional periods were necessary to progress, for without them the hardened carapace of the old order would stifle all innovation and that which, years later, Mill was to call the 'disposition to aim at something better than customary, which is called, according to circumstances, the spirit of liberty, or that of progress or improvement'.[19] Here, in articles contributed to a vital debate in a year of political crisis, we sense the young intellectual's excitement at the vision of the positive future. The articles have a twofold relevance to Mill's argument for an elite: in them are contained his criteria for a healthy state of society towards which the present age was bound. And within that account is a prescription for an intellectual elite. Let us examine the argument.

Mill begins from the proposition – regarded as self-evident – that the present age was one of transition, where discussion had penetrated deep into society. Yet society had not yet got beyond the stage of negative criticism, and negative criticism itself knows nothing of the future. Hence the only way out of this blind alley was through the activity of those who were not bound by their own time:

The wisest men in every age generally surpass in wisdom the wisest of any preceding age, because the wisest men possess and profit by the constantly increasing accumulation of the ideas of all ages: but the multitude (by which I mean the majority of all ranks) have the ideas of their own age and no others: and if the multitude of one age are nearer the truth than the multitude of another, it is only in so far as they are guided and influenced by the authority of the wisest among them.[20]

The wisest and best ought to guide and influence the rest of the population by an authority gained from going beyond the frontiers of the age. The heart of the argument is contained in the next essay, and may be summarised thus. In an age of transition, private judgment is substituted for the old guides. Yet private judgment is not in itself a good. Essential as it is for seeing through decayed orthodoxy, it is inadequate to map the road ahead. How can society proceed? Mill's answer to this question indicates how far the notion of an aristocracy of spirit had already permeated his consciousness:

Those persons to whom the circumstances of society and their own positions in it, permit to dedicate themselves to the investigation of physical, moral and social truths, as their peculiar calling, can alone be expected to make the evidences of such truths a subject of profound meditation, and to make themselves thorough masters of the philosophical grounds of those of which it is desirable that all should be firmly *persuaded*, but which they alone can entirely and philosophically *know*. The remainder of mankind must, and except in periods of transition like the present, always do, take the far greater part of their opinions on all extensive subjects upon the authority of those who have studied them.[21]

Mill thus refloats the Platonic distinction between knowledge (which pertains to the elite) and opinion (which pertains to the mass) upon positivist waters. He is dealing with one of the outstanding problems of an advanced society – the sheer volume of knowledge relevant to any situation in which society finds itself – but his solution runs perilously close to the devaluation of any but philosophic knowledge. Common sense and the judgment of the half-instructed are dangerous: 'It is therefore, one of the necessary conditions of humanity, that the majority must either have wrong opinions, or no fixed opinions, or must place the degree of reliance warranted by reason, in the authority of those who have made moral and social philosophy their particular study.'[22] It is clear that Mill has an idea of specialism and of the role of the specialist in society that was new in his time. The criterion for authority in intellectual matters (upon which social matters rest) is not heredity, nor experience in political practice, but prolonged and profound speculative study.

As we might expect, the analogy is taken from the physical sciences. Echoing a Comtean commonplace, Mill writes that we 'never hear of the right of private judgment in physical science'.[23] But, unfortunately, social science has not yet achieved positive status. At present, in the social sciences 'this imposing unanimity among all who have studied the subject does not exist; and every dabbler, consequently thinks his opinion as good as another's'.[24] In attempting to form social and hence political science upon an outsider's image of natural science, the young Mill thus stands near the headwaters of the British positivist tradition. And we must stress the heavily fictional and hopeful nature of the image of science upon which the analogy rests: the history of geology in Mill's own time furnishes an amusing gloss on 'imposing unanimity'. At all events, and with a highly innocent view of natural science behind it, social science began life asserting the need for an elite of social scientists. The fact that philosophy was on the verge of attaining positive status had been Comte's burden from 1822, and Mill learned from him to what extent the natural sciences provided a model. The early draft of the *Autobiography* shows how the philosophic radical was converted to positivism:

Hitherto it had not occurred to me that the case would be the same in the moral, social, & political branches of speculation if they were equally advanced with the physical. I had always identified deference to authority with mental slavery & the repression of individual thought. I now perceived that these indeed are the means by which adherence is enforced to opinions from which at least a minority of thinking & instructed persons dissent; but that when all such persons are as nearly unanimous, as they are in the more advanced of the physical sciences, their authority will have an ascendancy which will be increased, not diminished, by the intellectual & scientific cultivation of the multitude, who, after learning all which their circumstances permit, can do nothing wiser than rely for all beyond on the authority of the more instructed.... From this time my hopes of improvement rested less on the reason of the multitude, than on the possibility of effecting such an improvement in the methods of political & social philosophy, as should enable all thinking and instructed persons who have no sinister interest to be so nearly of one mind on these subjects, as to carry the multitude with them by their united authority.[25]

When the elite are united, the multitude will willingly defer to their authority. Note, too, that Mill's ideal philosophic elite has no 'sinister interest'. Their disinterestedness in relation to society is as much taken for granted as their scientific objectivity. The theory outlined above had a real meaning for Mill in terms of his own activity. Thus he later wrote to Comte about his *Logic*: 'I am beginning to hope that the book will become a true philosophic rallying point for that group of the scientific English young who do not set much store by religious ideas.'[26]

The discomfort of ages of transition was only tolerable since it was historically essential. It behoved Mill to look to the outcome. Towards this end – the rise of the new orthodoxy as yet concealed in the womb of history – all disinterested efforts must be directed.

He therefore turned to consider 'moral influence, or power over the minds of mankind'. There were three sources of moral influence: 'eminent wisdom and virtue, real or supposed; the power of addressing mankind in the name of religion; and finally, worldly power'.[27] When an opinion is sanctioned by all three of these authorities, it becomes the 'received opinion', and, in a natural state of society, the received opinion reigns supreme. A natural state of society is one in which 'the opinions and feelings of the people are, with their voluntary acquiescence, formed *for* them, by the most cultivated minds which the intelligence and morality of their times call into existence'.[28] Mill has conjured up some serious problems in political theory: granted that he wants to avoid coercive authority, it is still difficult to see in what sense the people can be said *voluntarily* to accept the formation of their opinions and feelings by the elite. And, in any case, *quis custodet ipsos custodes?* We have here another example of the convergence, or rather of the similarity between the idealist and positivist traditions. As Coleridge had sought to provide a social base for his clerisy in the context of his attempt to advance the dynamic philosophy, so Mill urges the importance of the intellectual elite in the context of the propagation of the positive philosophy, and looks forward to an age in which the problems of politics and society will at last be seen as problems which can be solved in the terms of natural science. We may not doubt that, at this stage in his career at least, Mill yearned for the advent of the natural age. We would not, he said in speaking of the medieval clergy and their temporal supporters, want any one to be burned for doubt, but 'the deep earnest feeling of firm and unwavering conviction which [such condemnation] presupposes, we may, without being unreasonable, lament that it was impossible, and could not *but* be impossible, in the intellectual anarchy of a general revolution in opinion, to transfer unimpaired to the truth'.[29] The truth, of course, was positive philosophy. That was the task ahead: the adherents of the true philosophy must work towards the natural age. In this, the last essay, there is some doubt about the order of action, and in particular about the relations between worldly and moral power. Clear, however, is the notion that the traditional governing classes had had their day: the 'superior capacity of the higher ranks for the exercise of worldly power is now a broken spell'. Into the vacuum created by their supposedly imminent displacement, the intellectuals will step. The governing classes must 'be divested of their monopoly of worldly

power, ere the most virtuous and best-instructed of the nation will
acquire that ascendancy over the opinions and feelings of the rest,
by which alone England can emerge from the crisis of transition, and
enter once more into a natural state of society'.[30]

Mill did not explicitly say who were the 'virtuous and best instructed of the nation'. But he was writing in a political paper at
the height of the reform crisis, and it is reasonable therefore to
assume that he had something more substantial than a mere hope
in mind. My own candidate for the post of national intellectual
elite would be the philosophic radical group – his father, Roebuck,
Molesworth, Hume, Place, and himself.[31] That they formed the only
existing group to which Mill's aspirations could apply is apparent
from the early correspondence with d'Eichthal. He could not, he
explained, go so far as being a Saint-Simonian himself, but 'je tiens
bureau de St. Simonisme chez moi', and he advised his friend on
the distribution of copies of the *Globe* in England. (The list of
recipients included Dr Arnold, James Stephen, and Dr Whateley.)[32]
The feeling of belonging to a kind of intellectual advance-guard was
irresistible. He approved highly, he told d'Eichthal of the concept of
the *pouvoir spirituel*, and in his letters he sketched the natural state
in much the same way as he was to do in the *Examiner* articles.
Yet he was not attracted to becoming a member of the sect. 'Saint-
Simonism is all in all to you', he remarked calmly to d'Eichthal in
1832, 'but to me it is only *one* of a variety of interesting and important features in the world we live in'.[33] The claim seems to be
true, but, in this formative period, when he was drawing so much
from so many systems of thought, Saint-Simonism (and particularly
its development by Comte) exercised a particularly profound influence over him. One of its effects was to cause a modification of his
Helvétianism in suggesting an orientation of the educational effort.
There is a curious confluence of Helvétius and Coleridge in the
statement in his 1836 article on 'Civilization' of the need for the
'regeneration of individual character among our lettered and opulent
classes, by the adaptation to that purpose of our institutions, and,
above all, of our educational institutions'.[34] All the influences which
Mill absorbed in this period of his life suggested the crucial importance of speculative and scientific thought and thinkers.

We have now examined the use Mill made of Saint-Simonian
thought in *The Spirit of the Age*, and noted certain common ground
between the various theories which appealed to him. We have now

to explore another common factor among these theories, and in doing so, a recurrent aspect of his thought. That is what, using Cowling's word, I will call his 'intellectualism' – the belief that human progress is dictated by the progress of the speculative intellect, a belief which has as its corollary the fact that the history of mankind can be identified with the history of ideas. I have already suggested that Mill's intellectualism represents a kind of surrogate idealism, and we need not be surprised that this is so. Positivism and idealism, as (from the standpoint of competitive liberalism) Hayek has argued in his provocative book *The Counter-Revolution of Science*, have much more in common than has always been acknowledged. For many eighteenth-century thinkers, intellectual constellations replaced providence in human history, and the notion was carried on and developed by the heirs of the enlightenment. Comte, like Saint-Simon, held that the way in which man knows the universe determines his history. But he also held that the attainment of perfect knowledge is feasible. Such intellectualism is deeply relevant to our study, since the predominance of ideas in human history – the supremacy of the communal intellect – implies the hegemony of that group which devotes itself to the life of the mind. The theory fulfils some of the functions of idealism in bolstering the self-image of the intellectual. For it shows (or purports to show) that the life of society is not only accessible to, but is actually in some sense the material embodiment of, the life of thought. Significantly, it is a doctrine that Mill never retracted, and that we may therefore assume was still held by him even in the years of *On Liberty* and *Representative Government*. The formulation that appeared in the first edition of the *Logic* in 1843 was retained in the succeeding editions. In Book VI, Mill spoke of the difficulty of establishing the laws of social change from multifold empirical observation. So

it would evidently be a great assistance if it should happen to be the fact, that some one element in the complex existence of social man is preeminent over all others as the prime agent of the social movement. For we could then take the progress of that one element as the central chain, to each successive link of which, the corresponding links of all the other progressions being appended, the succession of the facts would by this alone be presented in a kind of spontaneous order, far more really approaching to the real order of their filiation than could be obtained by any other merely empirical process.

Now, the evidence of history and that of human nature combine, by a striking instance of consilience, to show that there really is one social element which is thus predominant, and almost paramount, among the agents of the social progression. This is, the state of the speculative faculties of mankind.[35]

What intellectual could fail to feel at home in such a world? The argument is, of course, pure Comte, and the ground of Mill's partnership with him in the preparation of the forthcoming 'réorganisation intellectuelle'. The thesis was embedded in the vision of human history and the law of the three stages, as Mill would have discovered when, in 1828, he read Comte's early *Système*.[36] It was elaborated at formidable length in the historical sections of the *Cours de Philosophie Positive* – the fourth, fifth, and sixth volumes, which Mill read as they came out. In Leçon 51 Comte stated that 'one would not hesitate to grant the first importance to intellectual evolution, as the necessarily preponderating principle of the whole of human evolution'.[37] And the consequence, which Mill was to explore in the relationship of 'art' (i.e., practice) and science at the end of the *Logic*, was of course that 'intellectual and subsequently moral reorganisation must necessarily precede and direct political reorganisation properly so-called'.[38] The relevance of this orientation of thought to our subject is clear.

A tendency to see history – and thus given historicist premises, the future as well – in terms of the development of speculative thought entailed an emphasis on the historical role of the pioneers and guardians of thought (in a phrase, the *pouvoir spirituel*) – an implication which Comte had early followed up.[39] Intellectualism was a feature of the eighteenth-century tradition from which Saint-Simon and his disciple Comte emerged. The nearer Condorcet's *Ésquisse d'un tableau historique des progrès de l'esprit humain* (1795) comes to his own time, the less weight attributed to social and economic factors, and the more to the courses of intellectual history. Thus he attributes the French Revolution to the 'propagation des lumières'. By this time we are becoming too familiar with the hopes entertained for positivist science (itself so closely bound up with the intellectualist theory of history) to be much taken aback by Condorcet's claim that the division in society between the group 'destined to teach' and that 'made to believe' was found 'too frequently in all periods of civilisation for it not to be founded in nature itself'.[40] One more example of early positivist optimism comes from Madame de Staël's *De la littérature considérée dans ses rapports avec les institutions sociales* (1800), the earliest instance known to me of studies on 'literature and society', and in itself a plea for the *littérateurs* to stand out against repression. Why, she asked rhetorically, 'might we not one day achieve the drawing up of tables which would contain the solution to all political questions according to statistical information, and according to the positive facts which will be collected on each country?'[41] A configuration of ideas linking history, positive science, and the putative role of the *pouvoir spirituel* was becoming commonplace in French positivist thought.

Mill, like his French co-seekers, was exploring paths left open by the enlightenment. But with our modern division between arts and natural science we should not make the mistake of reading such a compartmentalisation into the philosophers with whom we have to deal. For them, positive science and philosophy not only marched hand in hand in the present, but would actually converge in the future. Comte looked forward to the day when the separation between morals, politics, and science would end, and positivism reign supreme. It is therefore important to examine what for Mill were the innovating forces in society, the forces which (within the general scope suggested by his intellectualism) would shape the future. We have to conclude that by 1842 the positive philosophers constituted such a force: it 'is becoming more & more clearly evident to me that the mental regeneration of Europe must precede its social regeneration & also that none of the ways in which that mental regeneration is sought, Bible Societies, Tract Societies, Puseyism, Socialism, Chartism, Benthamism, &c. will *do*'.[42] We would expect to find Mill rejecting religion and religious bodies. But we should also recognise that he does not include imaginative writers among the innovators. For all his own vivid awareness of Wordsworth and Vigny, for all Abrams' attempts to argue Mill's sympathy (based on the essays he wrote for the *Monthly Repository*) for an appreciation of expressivist theories of poetry, Mill entertained an ambivalence towards poetry and fiction that reminds one at times of the later Carlyle.[43] In his experimental diary for 1854 we read:

The Germans and Carlyle have perverted both thought and phraseology when they made Artist the term for expressing the highest order of moral and intellectual greatness. The older idea is the truer – that Art, in relation to Truth, is but a language. Philosophy is the proper name for that exercise of the intellect which enunciated the truth to be expressed. The Artist is not the Seer; not he who can detect the truth, but he who can clothe a given truth in the most expressive and impressive symbols.[44]

This subordination of the creative writer stems, I suggest, not just from Mill's positivism (in the broadest sense), but from the habits of mind to which positivism appealed, that eschatological sense that leads so easily to a humourless earnestness felt to be required by the historical crisis. He wrote a little earlier in the same Diary (and presumably unwittingly echoing Kant) that verse, like other art, is of course eternal, but it should not be indulged in at the present time: the 'regeneration of the world in its present stage is a matter of business, and it would be as rational to keep accounts or write invoices in verse as to attempt to do the work of human improvement in it'.[45] Serious, prosaic, immensely aware of the age of transition and its demands, Mill put his stamp on the character of intellect. Positivism rationalised a distrust of poetry that we have found elsewhere. In Comte's theory, imagination had, in the course of human history, to be subordinated to reason and observation.[46] To the role of sovereign rationality Mill was to devote much thought.

THE AUTHORITY OF THE INSTRUCTED

Clerisy and pouvoir spirituel

We noted earlier that in different places in Mill's writings we can find the force of institutionalised intellect occupying apparently incompatible positions – those of orthodoxy and antagonism. We must now examine more closely Mill's arguments on the subject of the functions of the intellectual elite. Chronologically, the first that he defined in the wake of his acquaintance with the thought of Coleridge and the Saint-Simonians was the function of promoting orthodoxy and social cohesion. A force making for social cohesion was necessary, and at the present time religion still supplied such a force. Thus we find in an early letter to Sterling:

An infidel who attempts to subvert or weaken the belief of mankind in Christianity ought not, in my opinion, to form a part of the national clerisy; not because he may not be performing a conscientious duty in so doing, but because it is to me a proof that he misunderstands the wants and tendencies of his age, and that the effect of his exertions would probably be to make men worse instead of better by shaking the only firm convictions and feelings of duty which they have, without having even a remote chance of furnishing them with an effective substitute.[47]

Christianity, as many intellectuals would later have agreed, may be useful as a social and moral force. And the need for an orthodoxy is taken for granted – Christianity must not be attacked until an 'effective substitute' is ready. We can relate this to the *Examiner* articles of the same year, with their longing for the assurance of a natural age in the midst of the doubts and conflicts of an age of transition. But Mill was confident that a natural age would arise from the chaos, and with it would come a new orthodoxy. The Saint-Simonian, he wrote to d'Eichthal, was the 'greatest enterprise now in progress for the regeneration of society', and he was inclined to think that some form of Saint-Simonian organisation would be the 'final and permanent condition of the human race', even if that condition took longer to achieve than the disciples expected.[48] Here Mill wrote of the future in much the same way as he was to do in the *Examiner* articles. The uninstructed

shall entertain the same feelings of deference & submission to the authority of the instructed, in morals and politics, as they at present do in the physical sciences. This, I am persuaded, is the only wholesome state of the human mind; and the knowledge that we ought to look to it as the ultimate end, has a great tendency to protect us from the many errors which the philosophers of the 18th. century fell into, & which all will be liable to who suppose that the diffusion of knowledge among the labouring classes & the consequent improvement of their intellects is to be the grand instrument of the regeneration of mankind.[49]

In such an age of transition, the few who were conscious of the problem of their times were to work for the new state of society. Mill has drawn out the elitist implications of utilitarianism at the expense of egalitarianism.

This, then, together with a reading of Coleridge's recent *Church and State*, was the background to Mill's most explicit statement on the subject of the clerisy – the article in the *Jurist* for February 1833 entitled 'The Right and Wrong of State Interference with Corporation and Church Property', his contribution to the vigorous debate on the reform and status of the Church of England.[50] Here, within the framework of the Saint-Simonian diagnosis of the times, Mill presented a Coleridgean argument. That we cannot merely regard the argument as a facet of his early thought is suggested by the fact that he reprinted it in *Dissertations and Discussions* in 1859. Together with a letter to Sterling of 20–2 October 1831, and the Coleridge article of 1840, it constitutes his most explicit restatement

of Coleridge's case, and lends much weight to his own remark to
J. P. Nichol on the subject of *Church and State*: 'Few persons have
exercised more influence over my thoughts and character than
Coleridge has; not much by personal knowledge of him, though
I have seen and conversed with him several times, but by his works,
and by the fact that several persons with whom I have been very
intimate were completely trained in his school.'[51] We must examine
the argument of the *Jurist* article.

There were many publicists in and around 1833 to substantiate
Mill's claim that no one 'can help seeing that one of the most
pressing of the duties which Parliamentary reform has devolved upon
our public men, is that of deciding what honestly *may*, and, supposing
this determined, what *should*, be done with the property of the
Church, and of the various public corporations'.[52] Mill turns first to
what *may* be done. Endowments, he argues, may be diverted, using
two main criteria: first, that the legislature should employ land thus
diverted usefully; second, that it should depart as little as possible
from the founder's intentions without sacrifice of 'substantial utility'.
The argument then takes a Coleridgean turn. Mill has recourse, in
effect, to the 'idea of the institution', and discovers that in its idea
the church is an educational and moral institution, its property 'held
in trust for the spiritual culture of the people of England'.[53] Mill, we
discover, is turning against the idea of minimum government in the
field of education. The 'primary and perennial sources of all social
evil, are ignorance and want of culture'.[54] Not even the best-
developed balance of political powers can eradicate this evil. The
process by which people are made aware of their ignorance and want
of culture operates on a wide front. For the removal of these evils
the mass depends upon

the unremitting exertions of the more instructed and cultivated whether in
the position of the government or in a private station.... The instruments
of this work are not merely schools and colleges, but every means by which
the people can be reached, either through their intellects or their sensi-
bilities: from preaching and popular writing, to national galleries, theatres
and public games.[55]

Education is envisaged not as merely the domain of schools, but as
a process involving the whole community. Yet Mill does not trust
to unaided social forces to furnish such education. Free enterprise is
not enough:

Let us do what we may, it will be the study of the merely trading school-master to teach down to the level of the parents, be that level low or high; as it is of the trading author, to write down to the level of his readers. And in the one shape as in the other, it is in all times and all places indispens-able, that enlightened individuals and enlightened governments should, from other motives than that of pecuniary gain, bestir themselves to provide (though by no means forcibly to impose) that good and wholesome food for the wants of the mind, for which the competition of the mere trading market affords in general so indifferent a substitute.[56]

The first breach in the wall of Mill's *laissez-faire* occurred, it is interesting to note, in connection with education. The clerisy had its cue:

A national *clerisy* or clergy, as Mr. Coleridge conceives it, would be a grand institution for the education of the whole people: not their school education merely, though that would be included in the scheme; but for training and rearing them, by systematic culture continued through life, to the highest perfection of their mental and spiritual nature.[57]

The argument was repeated in the Coleridge article of 1840, where Coleridge was praised for insisting on the importance of certain things that had been deficiently treated by the eighteenth-century tradition in which Mill himself was raised. Thus, he had

vindicated against Bentham and Adam Smith and the whole eighteenth century, the principle of an endowed class, for the cultivation of learning, and for diffusing its results among the community. That such a class is likely to be behind instead of before the progress of knowledge, is an induc-tion erroneously drawn from the peculiar circumstances of the last two centuries, and in contradiction to all the rest of modern history. If we have seen much of the abuses of endowments, we have not seen what this country might be made by a proper administration of them, as we trust we shall not see what it would be without them.[58]

Philosophic radicalism – perhaps in some ways contrary to its reputation – so far from being totally antipathetic towards a theory of intellectual establishment, could indeed provide a starting place for such a theory. It is hard to resist the impression that the estimate rose as it came to look more possible that philosophic radicalism could have an audible say in national affairs; its exponents thus became candidates for the role of national elite. James Mill wrote, two years after his son, in the second number of the *London Review* an article on 'The Church and its Reform', which provides evidence for my case that the seed contained in philosophic radicalism only needed a favourable climate to spring up. 'The time is come', began the agnostic author of the *Britannica* articles on 'Education' and 'Government', 'when a service of unspeakable importance could be rendered to the community, by a full and detailed exposition of the good which *might* be done by a well-ordered and well-conducted clergy.'[59] From here he went on to argue that the Church of England did not represent a meaningful religion: tests of utility showed that its ministers and services were socially harmful. Religion he assumed to be an entirely social exercise, to be justified in social terms. In place of the Church of England, James Mill sketched a secular church with the object of promoting adult and communal education. There would be a clergyman in each 'conveniently-sized district, called a parish', with a bishop or 'inspector' over groups of such clergy. Common rejoicings together were suggested, of 'a gentle character; harmonizing rather with the moderate than with the violent emotions; promoting cheerfulness, not profuse merriment'.[60] On Sundays there would be common meals, for which *Agapai* would be a suitable name, with tea or coffee to drink. In this light, the younger Mill's absorption of Coleridge seems less of an aberration. The nature of intellectual authority, and its institutional basis were subjects profoundly linked to his own role and that of people whom he admired.

The debilitating influences of the age

The social function of the intellectual force to which he strove to give institutional form presented Mill with a dilemma. As we have seen, he was at first inclined to the view that its function was to promote continuity and social stability. But it was also to promote progress, and serve as an opposition to all that is established and ordinary. At first sight, these views appear to be radically opposed, yet I shall argue that they can in fact be reconciled. In doing so it will, I hope, be possible to shed light on some of Mill's characteristic preoccupations. Left to its own devices, society fragments under the pressure of selfish forces, and such fragmentation is essentially unprogressive. Progress is, for Mill, a force making for cohesion, for the subordination of the egoistic propensities to an altruistic and social morality. In exploring the apparent paradox pertaining to the role of Mill's elite we should start with three articles: that on 'Civilization' which appeared in the *London and Westminster Review* for October 1836, and the two reviews of the first and second volumes of Tocqueville's *Democracy in America* (1835 and 1840). Here we glimpse the modification of Mill's political theory under the influence of Tocqueville, the 'Montesquieu of our times'.[61] Democracy is inevitable, Tocqueville and the philosophic radical agree. But what Mill came to believe during the 1830s (and Tocqueville was at least partly responsible) was that the movement towards democracy was not in itself enough, and that – given the tendencies of a commercial civilisation – the characteristic of the achieved democracy would not be the continuation of healthful change, but social stasis. Democracy, if allowed to set in as the rule of appetite, would turn out to be a profoundly conservative force. We can thus, I believe, explain the link between *The Spirit of the Age* and *On Liberty*. 'You have changed the face of political philosophy', Mill wrote to Tocqueville in May 1840, and it is apparent that the crucial change consisted in furnishing a more sophisticated account of democracy than was available in the utilitarian tradition – an account which tallied with the direction in which Mill's own thought on the subject was moving. Thus he went on to speak of his pleasure in finding that one of Tocqueville's conclusions was one that 'almost alone' he himself had been asserting in England, namely 'that the real danger in democracy, the real evil to be struggled against, and which all human resources employed while it is not yet too late are not more than sufficient to fence off – is not anarchy or love of change, but Chinese stagnation and immobility'.[62] Like Arnold, Mill believed that society, unirradiated by the intellectual or cultural force, tends to mediocrity. But where Arnold envisaged the ordinary condition of society as being characterised by futile agitation, and restless hunting after novelty, Mill envisaged it as characterised by reactionary conformity. His attitude towards intellectual forces was drawn from a reading of the future, since no one – least of all Mill – would dream that liberal democracy was achieved in 1832. Hence the significance for our argument of his article on 'Civilization', in which he extended the argument of the review of the first part of Tocqueville's *Democracy*. Civilisation, Mill argues, is good, but we need to develop new rules in accordance with its development. There are tendencies in the face of which we must establish 'counter-tendencies, which may combine with these tendencies, and modify them'.[63] There, in brief, is Mill's later political and cultural theory. The argument continues with an analysis of the tendencies of civilisation, demonstrating the passage of power from smaller to larger groups. The necessary effect of this levelling down is the enervation of the individual, his feeling of helplessness in the face of the larger forces at work. Mill's response is Coleridgean: we must re-educate our 'lettered and opulent classes'. Here, then, is our counter-tendency, and the rest of the essay is devoted to the means available for re-education, an attack on educational traditionalism that looks back to the essay 'On Genius' (1832), and forward to the Inaugural Address at St Andrew's (1867), with its prescription for an 'enlightened public: a body of cultivated intellects, each taught by its attainments in its own province what real knowledge is, and knowing enough of other subjects to be able to discern who are those that know them better'.[64]

In view of the job crying out to be done, Mill belabours the universities. His estimation of their potential value gives edge to his attack. Are these, he asks, 'the places of education which are to send forth minds capable of maintaining a victorious struggle with the debilitating influences of the age, and strengthening the weaker side of Civilization by the support of a high Cultivation?'[65] Mill has assimilated the Coleridgean distinction between cultivation and civilisation, and adapted it for his own purposes. 'Where no vision is the people perisheth': the universities are not living up to the part they should play. In 1835, he reviewed Adam Sedgwick's *A Discourse on the Studies of the University*, in the course of which he remarked that the function of the university was to 'keep alive philosophy'. Here again, the counter-tendency theme was prominent:

there is an education of which it cannot be pretended that the public are competent judges; the education by which great minds are formed. To rear up minds with aspirations and faculties above the herd, capable of leading on their countrymen to greater achievements in virtue, intelligence, and social well-being; to do this, and likewise so to educate the leisured classes generally, that they may participate as far as possible in the qualities of these superior spirits, and be prepared to appreciate them, and follow in their steps – these are purposes requiring institutions of education placed above dependence on the immediate pleasure of that very multitude whom they are designed to elevate.[66]

Society forms, as it were, in concentric rings around the 'superior spirits'. Tocqueville's work confirmed Mill in his belief that the advance of democracy brought with it the danger of stagnation, and that consequently, counter-tendencies must be established. But democracy was not in itself the only danger. It also tended to allow the predominance of a single class. Mill criticised Tocqueville for inadequate discrimination, for 'confounding the effects of democracy with the effects of Civilization. He bound up in one abstract idea the whole of the tendencies of modern commercial society, and gave them one name – Democracy.'[67] See what happens to literature, says Mill, when it becomes popular – it too is afflicted by the 'dogmatism of common sense': 'There needs no Democracy to account for this – there needs only the habit of energetic action, without a proportional development of the taste for speculation.'[68] Cultural and social mediocrity is in fact the result of the predominance of a single class, in the absence of other classes or groups to stimulate it. To counteract the tendencies of a society in which a single class will predominate, Mill prepares what will become the liberal creed of pluralism. His means of doing so is our concern here. For, he says, we must organise a 'great social support for opinions and sentiments different from those of the mass'. Quite consciously (as the essay on Bentham shows), he was modifying the Benthamite theory of numerical democracy in the direction of a sociologically more sophisticated model. His social model was committed, like Coleridge's, to the interaction of forces, but, unlike Coleridge, he was worried about the ways in which progress might be halted, and his intellectual elite is therefore visualised as a stimulant to dissatisfaction.

It may seem that we have lost sight of the function of inculcating orthodoxy. In fact, we have not. What has happened is that, by the mid-1830s, the argument has been projected into the future. Mill has not lost sight of the stage of his development represented by *The Spirit of the Age*. The positive truths to be attained by the philosophic class will one day constitute the orthodoxy to which a new natural age will subscribe. But tomorrow's orthodoxy is today's opposition, and during the intellectual (and consequently social) crisis portrayed in *The Spirit of the Age* the role of philosophy is bound to be as counter-tendency. As society enters its positive stage this antagonism will cease to be necessary. As Saint-Simon's codifiers put it, in the context of the medieval separation of the temporal and spiritual powers, antagonism, 'in making straight the ways of a greater cohesion, and hastening the day of universal society, consumes itself little by little, and moves towards its final disappearance'.[69] But there was obviously room for doubt about the timing of the positive future, and around 1840 we sense the overlapping of the

Mill of *On Liberty* with the Saint-Simonian Mill. Not that he had ever been a blind adherent. We have noted the reservations he mentioned to d'Eichthal. Even more relevant here is a letter he wrote to d'Eichthal a few months after writing the *Examiner* articles. The Saint-Simonian, he wrote, was the 'greatest enterprise now in progress for the regeneration of society', and he was inclined to see in some form of their organisation the 'final and permanent condition of the human race'. But he then proceeded to take issue with the disciples, in suggesting that the final condition would take longer to reach than they supposed.[70] Unlike Saint-Simon (and later Comte), he did not believe that Western man stood on the very brink of the new age. The tendency to postpone the advent of the positive age was to have important consequences in terms of Mill's thought. But we cannot discuss his later thought on the subject of the intellectual forces in society without examining his dialogue with and subsequent deviation from Auguste Comte.

Comte and the function of antagonism

Mill had no doubt in the 1830s that the positive age would come. What was in doubt was the schedule, and consequently the question of how long the counter-tendencies and the tendencies would continue their dialectical struggle. The dialectical model of progress is implied in the very theme of the articles on Bentham and Coleridge: unlikely as it must seem to the doctrinaire followers of Bentham, the two are allies, and the 'powers they wield are opposite poles of one great force of progression'.[71] But – and this is crucial – Mill looks forward to the day when progress by opposition will no longer be necessary, that is when positive truth in matters of morals and politics will have been attained. The positivist, like the classical Marxist, believes in the relativity of all forms of thought except the ultimate one. Among

the truths long recognised by Continental philosophers, but which very few Englishmen have yet arrived at, one is, the importance, *in the present imperfect state of mental and social science*, of antagonistic modes of thought: which it will one day be felt, are as necessary to one another in speculation, as mutually checking powers are in a political constitution.[72]

The 'present imperfect state of mental and social science' carries the implied comparison with the final state into which some natural sciences are now entering, and where, consequently, debate is no longer necessary. Conflict will not continue for ever. Thus Mill speaks of what he will call the 'Germano-Coleridgean' reaction to the eighteenth century, and argues that it was less violent than earlier reactions to earlier theses. In this it was faithful to the 'general law of improvement', that 'oscillation, each time, departs rather less widely from the centre, and an ever-increasing tendency is manifested to settle finally on it'.[73] The dialectical process is only leading up to the stability of truth which will be achieved in the glorious sun of positivism. Mill described this stage of his thought in the *Autobiography*:

[The] chief service which I received ... from the trains of thought suggested by the St Simonians and by Comte, was that I obtained a much clearer conception than before of the peculiarities of an age of transition in opinion, and ceased to mistake the moral and intellectual characteristics of such an age, for the normal attributes of humanity. I looked forward, through the present age of loud disputes but generally weak convictions, to a future which will unite the best qualities of the critical with the best of the organic periods; unchecked liberty of thought, perfect freedom of action in things not harmful to others; but along with this, firm convictions as to right and wrong, useful and pernicious, deeply engraven on the feelings by early education and general unanimity of sentiment, and so well grounded in reason and in real exigencies of life that they shall not, like all former and present creeds, religious, ethical and political, require to be periodically thrown off and replaced by others.[74]

The imputed stability of the coming age fulfilled some of the same functions for Mill as did the unity of the ideal world for Coleridge. And so great was his longing for it, that he apparently did not see any incompatibility between 'unchecked liberty of thought' and the 'firm convictions as to right and wrong', maintained by 'general unanimity of opinion' and in no need of periodic renewal. Quite what area was left for the operation of unchecked liberty of thought it was left for us (to whom the benefits of consensus appear more dubious) to speculate.

Such was Mill's position in 1840, shortly before his first letter to Comte. Progress arose from opposition. Ultimately, however, truth would be reached, and, as its advent approached, the oscillation between opposed opinions would diminish. Until such time, the intellectual force had the job of maintaining the alternatives – of insisting on just those things that society, left to itself, was most liable to overlook. Why did Mill pursue the connection with Comte further? He had, after all, disagreed from the start with some aspects of the *pouvoir spirituel.* Two letters written over thirty years apart are relevant. The first is the letter to d'Eichthal of 7 November 1829 (quoted on page 150). In it Mill expressed his enthusiasm for the idea of the *pouvoir spirituel* and for the idea that one day the uninstructed would defer to the opinion of the instructed in morals and politics as they now did in the physical sciences. However, the letter continued,

> I object altogether to the means which the St. Simonists propose for organizing the *pouvoir spirituel*. It appears to me that you cannot organize it at all. What is the *pouvoir spirituel* but the insensible influence of mind over mind? The instruments of this are private communication, the pulpit, & the press. If you attempt to collect together the instructed you must have somebody to chuse them, & determine who they are; in what respect, then, will this differ from an elective national assembly with a qualification for eligibility, not a qualification of property, but of education.[75]

This appears to undermine Saint-Simon's final hierarchy, headed by the inventors and industrialists and supported by the artists and *savants*. The second letter was written more than thirty years later to Comte's follower Celestin de Blignières.

> See now in what I believe myself to be in disagreement with you. I am strongly disposed to believe ... that the very nature of a legitimate *pouvoir spirituel* does not allow of actual organization. Where there is no fundamental agreement on doctrines among the spiritual leaders, any attempt at organization (even supposing it practicable), would be clearly harmful. If, on the other hand, such agreement existed, organization into a corporation would seem to me unnecessary.[76]

The phrase from the earlier letter, 'the insensible influence of mind over mind' sticks in the memory. For it suggests that even in the heyday of Saint-Simonian influence over him, Mill had something of the same sense of the role of the *pouvoir spirituel* that was implicit years later in *On Liberty* and *Representative Government*. In this scheme, the organised clerisy of the *Jurist* article was no monopolistic corporation, but a sub-division of the greater and unorganised force constituted by the eminent and instructed minds whose influence was to combat the forces of mediocrity. And while in 1862 Mill still believes in the possibility of substantial agreement among the enlightened on all serious subjects, he believes that agreement arises from assent, not from coercion. Given this important element of continuity in his thought, we might well ask what Comte's account of the *pouvoir spirituel*, with all its tendencies towards tyranny, could say to Mill? The answer lies in his letters to Comte, and in the fifth and sixth volumes of the latter's *Cours de Philosophie Positive*, which contain the historical part of the positive philosophy.

Comte's account of the history of Western man is a masterpiece of intellectualism. The obdurate details of history do not bother him in the least. If, as Jerome Buckley has argued, Mill was relatively indifferent to history, then Comte was even more so.[77] What mattered in human history was the development of intellect, and thus the stages of man's cognition of himself and of the universe. The heart of Comte's historical thesis was the rehabilitation of medieval Catholicism, blackened and misunderstood by eighteenth-century historians (Leçon 54). What is important here is not Comte's idiosyncratic reading of medieval political and social theory, but his warm applause for the social and political wisdom of Catholicism, and consequent rabid distrust of Protestantism, the religion of individualism and insubordination. His claim that to the positive school 'it belongs exclusively to pronounce a just and definitive judgement on Catholicism' is not totally unfounded.[78] Comte admired the 'profound wisdom of Catholicism in subordinating the whole of human life to morality so as to direct and control it thereby',[79] and for 'restricting more and more the right of supernatural inspiration'. Thus the tendency of Protestantism was 'to cause a regression (on this score as on so many others) in the gradual development of humanity . . . since its supposed reformation consisted entirely . . . in little by little vulgarising and finally individualising that mystic faculty – a proceeding which could not fail to generate immense disorders, intellectual at first, and subsequently social.'[80] Catholicism also discovered the most fundamental principle of social life, a principle which relentlessly pursues the reader of the *Cours*, to wit, the separation of spiritual and temporal powers. The speculative class arrived on the scene in the polytheistic period, the second of the three sub-periods (fetishistic – polytheistic – monotheistic) of the theological era, and, although the confusion of powers was characteristic of that period, 'the regular existence of the class of speculative men among the principal Greek nations, must be regarded as the first true germ of that grand social separation'.[81] Out of polytheism arose monotheism, a revolution comparable to that of our own times, and in due course medieval Catholicism achieved its great work, the separation of powers: 'Such was, at bottom, the great intellectual function (in itself transitory) pertaining to Catholicism: to prepare, under the theological regime, the elements of the positive polity.'[82]

What Mill found to his purpose in Comte should now, I think, be becoming clear. He read the fifth volume shortly after it was published in 1841, and on 25 February 1842 wrote to the author: 'I can at least indicate what has been for me so far the most positive and certain result of reading the fifth volume: a complete conviction of the validity of the great principle which you alone among contemporary philosophers have enunciated: the complete separation of the two powers, temporal and spiritual.' Mill goes on to say that Comte had finally cured him of the confusion of the temporal and spiritual powers that arose from claiming temporal primacy for the philosophers. In other words, Mill found in Comte a confirmation of his theory of antagonism, an apparently masterly (because of springing from a systematic account of Western intellectual history) endorsement for the theory of counter-tendencies advanced in his article on 'Civilization'. The succeeding passage is crucial, for it shows how it was possible for Mill to find an ally in Comte.

What I owe ... to your book is your formulation in terms of the principle of the separation of the temporal and spiritual powers, and of the organization of each on the foundation proper to them, of a more vague doctrine that I myself drew from history, and launched into the discussions of the day as a decisive rebuttal of democratic or Benthamite political systems. Here is that doctrine: that in all human societies where the existence of true conditions for progress continues to be witnessed *a posteriori* by their history, there has been – at least in effect – an organized antagonism. I have always found a serious difficulty in conceiving the form in which this principle which is necessary to progress could be applied to modern politics. But in the separation of power which you have proposed I see the solution to the problem.[83]

The passage is rich with subjects for comment. Mill is still consciously concerned to supplement orthodox liberal theory. He has made explicit the theory of antagonism, and finds confirmation in Comte for the association of the poles of progress with the temporal and spiritual powers. We should not leap too rapidly to the conclusion that he misunderstood Comte's essentially monist position. In the fifth book of the *Cours*, describing the emergence of the separation of powers, Comte had written of them each seeking 'above all the ascendancy or maintenance of its own exclusive domination: so that the solution naturally depended upon their necessary antagonism'.[84] Progress emerges (by a kind of cunning of reason) from the struggle to predominate. Again, on the subject of the modern work of 'réorganisation spirituelle' in Europe, Comte wrote that the two powers must not be allowed to wage a 'lutte déplorable', but then qualified his statement by adding that we must organise a 'happy and permanent conciliation between them, which can convert this vicious antagonism into a useful rivalry'.[85] There were, then, on the strength of the fifth book, good grounds for seeing in Comte a proponent, if not of antagonism, at least of 'utile rivalité'. On 4 March Comte replied in a guarded way that in Mill's letter, he had well stated the necessity of continued antagonism.[86] To judge by the space given, the point did not interest him very much. This was, however, enough for Mill, and when he in turn replied, he spoke of Comte's 'philosophic sanction for the principle of continued antagonism as the pre-condition of human progress'.[87] Within the greater field of positivism, their concordance was limited to agreement over the value of the conflict of the two powers. Once this agreement was jeopardised, or the dialectical model for progress cast into doubt, the concord would be at an end. We come now to the parting of their ways, and the implications of this parting for Mill's theory of spiritual power.

Comte thoroughly approved of Mill's *magnum opus*, the *Logic* when it was published in 1843, but the convergence of opinion for which both had hoped failed to arrive, and their correspondence down to 1847 when they ceased to write to each other demonstrates the widening of their disagreements. Ten years later Comte died, having carried his system and plans for the religion of humanity to Napoleonic lengths, and in 1865 Mill published his two critical articles on Comte in the *Westminster Review*. Mill had all along been too independent to enter into the master-disciple relationship which seems to have been the only form of intellectual partnership of which Comte was capable, and his independence found expression in the recognition that the positivist system was too all-pervasive, too inflexible, too totalitarian even, to allow room for other thinkers. And this philosophic monomania characterised Comte's conclusions as well: systematisation was the 'fons errorum' of his speculations.

The reasons for their divergence have been discussed by Mueller, and by Simon.[88] We are not here concerned with their differences over political economy, psychology, or the role of women in society, but with their debate on the *pouvoir spirituel*. Their difference was not, let us be clear, over the intellectualist interpretation of history. Against Herbert Spencer's assertion that ideas 'do not govern and

overthrow the world; the world is governed or overthrown by feelings, to which ideas serve only as guides', or his contention that
practically 'the popular character and the social state determine
what ideas shall be current', Mill still argued in 1865 that 'the
history of opinions, and of the speculative faculty, has always been
the leading element in the history of mankind'.[89] Secondly, Mill was
not quarrelling with the notion that there ought to be a spiritual
power in society. In the first of the 1865 articles, Mill commended
Comte for his 'revival of the Catholic idea of a Spiritual Power',
and added later 'That education should be practically directed by
the philosophic class, when there is a philosophic class who have
made good their claim to the place in opinion hitherto held by the
clergy, would be natural and indispensable.'[90] The dispute was on
two main grounds. The first was that of the degree of organisation,
an old source of disagreement between Mill and the positivists, and
one that we have seen expressed to d'Eichthal and Blignières. The
second was more fundamental and concerned the social function of
the spiritual power, and, by implication, the nature and limits of
social progress. Mill formulated his disagreement with the Comtean
notion of establishment in the first of the *Westminster Review*
articles. The constitution of the spiritual power presupposed the
unanimity of opinion in matters of morals and politics which there
was among astronomers about astronomy. (In Comte's favour, it
should be said that the population to whom the members of the
spiritual power were to act as mentors would by no means be
ignorant; rigorous courses of study were laid down for them.) So far,
Mill agreed, but then applied the same argument as we have seen
him express before: if such unanimity existed, then organisation
would be unnecessary. If it did not, then organisation would be
impossible, and pernicious even if it were possible. Moral tutelage
may be useful when exercised by individual members of the speculative class,

> but if entrusted to any organized body, would involve nothing less than a
> spiritual despotism. This however is what M. Comte really contemplated,
> though it would practically nullify that peremptory separation of the
> spiritual from the temporal power, which he justly deemed essential to a
> wholesome state of society.[91]

This leads us to the second, and more fundamental ground for
disagreement – the role of the spiritual power in social dynamics.

It became clear to Mill, in fact, that Comte had no intention that the antagonism between the spiritual and temporal powers should extend beyond the historical period in which they were then living. He recognised what Fitzjames Stephen, from the conservative side, would later recognise, that – despite the doctrine of the separation of powers – the only logical conclusion for Comte's spiritual power was ultramontanism.[92] In the course of Mill's dialogue with Comte, he became aware of dangers in the doctrines to which (eager to extend and supplement his inherited liberalism) he had so readily assented. While their correspondence continued he was struck by the danger of something for which he coined the term 'pédanto-cratie', and, in his review of Guizot's *Essays* and *Lectures on History* (1845), pointed to the danger that the predominance of one element in society would stifle the 'perpetual antagonism which has kept the human mind alive':

Education, for example – mental culture – would seem to have a better title than could be derived from anything else, to rule the world with exclusive authority; yet if the lettered and cultivated class, embodied and disciplined under a central organ, could become in Europe, what it is in China, the Government . . . the result would probably be a darker despot-ism, one more opposed to improvement, than even the military monarchies and aristocracies have in fact proved.[93]

Mill had been enough of a positivist to look forward to the attain-ment of positive truth as the final goal of society. We have noted some of his statements to this effect. As late as *On Liberty*, he sees progress as leading to the cessation of serious controversy with the once-for-all establishment of positive truths. But the point is that by this time – the mid-1850s – he had pushed such a future to a very great distance, and used it merely as a source of occasional reference – 'in an imperfect state of the human mind the interests of truth require a diversity of opinions'.[94] We have already noted Mill's tendency to postpone the advent of the positive age. As he got older, he relegated it to the status of a truism beyond the bounds of his ordinary thought. While I agree with Graeme Duncan's statement, in his recent book *Marx and Mill*, that 'it seems clear that Mill did not regard significant intellectual conflict as a permanent feature of human society', for he 'was not, in the long term, a pluralist in relation to either the political or the intellectual worlds', I would want to add that the long term was, by the time he wrote *On Liberty*, a very long term indeed.[95] To all intents and purposes, his thought now centred on the model of progress through debate which underlies the book. For Comte, on the other hand – as for Saint-Simon before and Marx after him – the dialectic was to cease with the attainment of the awaited age. The dialectical model for progress informs Mill's critique of the Comtean *pouvoir spirituel*, and his rejection of what he believed to be spiritual despotism. That all

education should be in the hands of a centralized authority, whether composed of clergy or of philosophers, and be consequently all framed on the same model, and directed to the perpetuation of the same type, is a state of things which instead of becoming more acceptable, will assuredly become more repugnant to mankind, with every step of their progress in the unfettered exercise of their highest faculties.[96]

The progress of the speculative intellect brings about the progress of society, but no one in this age can set a term to its advance. The intellectualist who also believed in the finite nature of knowledge must therefore believe that at some point progress will cease because no longer necessary. For Comte, the antagonism, about which he appeared to agree with Mill (indeed, up to a point, did agree) in 1842 was merely a feature of the metaphysical and critical age whose historic role was to cast out the relics of the theological age, and, by its purely negative function, to prepare for the positive future. Mill, by contrast, became increasingly an agnostic where the positive future was concerned: one might, for the sake of the imperative, assume it would come about, but could not predict its timing or nature in any detail. Doubtless, Mill appeared to Comte to have frozen intellectually at just that very critical stage which positivist theory showed to be but a transitory and ephemeral stage of the human spirit. Ultimately, the debate about the role of the opposition was a debate about the nature of progress, and hence also the cumulative nature of knowledge. Mill had already modified the episodic theory of progress. In 1865 he attacked Comte's relegation to a transitory phase of the free development of human intellectual powers. Of course he agreed (he would not have been Mill if he had not) that 'no respect is due to any employment of the intellect which does not tend to the good of mankind', but he defused this proposition by observing that we cannot say here and now what branch of knowledge will not, at some time, be of value to humanity. There is little point here in detailing the rest of the attack on Comte's prescriptions for repressing 'intellectual anarchy' by subordinating the intellect to the *coeur* represented by the High Priest.

While Mill held that Comte 'was justified in the attempt to develop his philosophy into a religion ... [and] that all religions are made better in proportion as, in their practical result, they are brought to coincide with that which he aimed at constructing',[97] he found the cult, with its observances, saints, and hierarchy utterly ridiculous. Comte had, in fact, very little to say to Mill by this time. In the course of their dialogue Mill had grown away and his idea of the intellectual or spiritual power had developed pragmatically so as to be scarcely recognisable to the positivist looking down from his eminence on those who preferred to stay behind in that metaphysical desert where discussion and debate were still necessary. Our final task in this part is to examine what remains of the spiritual power in Mill's late works.

REPRESENTATIVE GOVERNMENT

There is no need here to give a detailed account of *On Liberty* (published in 1859, but written in 1854), which in turn underlies *Representative Government* (1861). It is well enough known that the argument is the liberal creed that the object of society is the maximum development, compatible with the claims of society, of the individual potential. Individual development is both function and cause of social progress. Pluralism is the hallmark of the theory. 'No community has ever long continued progressive, but while a conflict was going on between the strongest power in the community and some rival power'.[98] I think we can accept Mueller's argument that *On Liberty* is not an exposition of economic, political, and social *laissez-faire*, but rather that Mill 'consciously linked his defence of liberty to the single area of speculation', and that the attack was directed against uniformitarians like Comte rather than socialists like Louis Blanc and Fourier.[99] The argument that the book was primarily concerned with intellectual freedom is corroborated by a letter from Mill to Pasquale Villari, explaining why he had not sent him a copy. It 'has no validity whatsoever except for England. It discusses moral and intellectual liberty, in which the Continental nations are as much above England as they are beneath us in political liberty'.[100] And we must remember that for Mill, speculation is not a peripheral area, but central to social health, being concerned with 'the mental well-being of mankind (on which all their other well-being depends)'.[101] To speculation, and consequently to progress, opposition and debate were integral. No more than Milton could Mill 'praise a fugitive and cloistered virtue'. Truth requires advocates: 'truth has no chance but in proportion as every side of it, every opinion which embodies any fraction of the truth, not only finds advocates, but is so advocated as to be listened to'.[102] The point is not merely the elimination of falsehood, but the assertion of complementary truths. Mill has applied to a whole society the imperative of many-sidedness which he desired to obey in his own life. Like Thomas Mann, he provides one of those relatively rare spectacles of a man who grows less authoritarian and more open-minded as he grows older. And this broadening is apparent when he writes of the advocates of novelty.

In Mill's last major writings the intellectuals have not passed out of sight altogether. But the front of opposition to custom and the tyranny of public opinion has broadened: none has the right to claim for his group a monopoly of innovation. Custom and progress do not divide neatly between the temporal and spiritual powers, and in place of the Saint-Simonian *pouvoir spirituel* Mill offers only an informal solidarity between the members of the lettered class. The shift in emphasis can be documented from the third chapter of *On Liberty*, 'Of individuality, as one of the elements of well-being'. The only antidote to social stagnation is the prevalence of individuals who have maximised their potential. That is why it is 'desirable ... that in all things, which do not primarily concern others, individuality should assert itself'. Such is the reason for the quotations from Humboldt, or the description of the book in the *Autobiography* as 'a text-book of a single truth ... the importance, to man and society, of a large variety in types of character, and of giving full freedom to human nature to expand itself in innumerable and conflicting directions'.[103] It is, however, hard to resist the impression that this maximisation is expected to take place at the level of verbal and conceptual skill alone. Mill, I suspect, envisaged a community whose health could be ascertained by the number of doctrines held and seriously argued, and whose members would express themselves in the elaborated code.

The theory of the *pouvoir spirituel* cannot be divorced from larger issues of social theory. Comte, we have seen, praised the Catholic Church for withdrawing the right to be supernaturally inspired from individuals, and investing it in a corporation. This prefigured the intellectual monopoly of the positivist regime. But Mill revolted, and declared that he 'who lets the world, or his own portion of it, choose his plan of life for him, has no need of any other faculty than the ape-like one of imitation'.[104] Although at certain stages of society it might be necessary for popes (Comte cannot have been far from his mind) to assert powers over the whole man, now 'the danger which threatens human nature is not the excess, but the deficiency of personal impulses and preferences'.[105] The problem now was to guarantee personal liberty and sponaneity in a society believed to be adverse to outstanding qualities. If we are to see how the prescriptions of *Representative Government* tally with the liberal individualism of *On Liberty*, we shall have to recognise that Mill is extending and continuing the argument of 'Civilization' from a quarter of a century before. In 1836, unchecked commercialism, allied with democracy threatened distinction in individuals and groups. By the time of *On Liberty*, it is democratic society which tends, by giving predominance to a single class, to make individuals mere examples of man *en masse*.[106]

Into this framework fits the argument of *Representative Government*.

The natural tendency of a representative government, as of modern civilization, is towards collective mediocrity: and this tendency is increased by all reductions and extensions of the franchise, their effect being to place the principal power in the hands of classes more and more below the highest level of instruction in the community.[107]

The argument we have been following through this chapter explains sufficiently, I think, the equation implied here between mediocrity and lack of instruction, resting, as it does, on an equation between high instruction and the capacity both to evade prostration before the ordinary, and to challenge one's society. We know by now the essential function of antagonism in social progress, but also that the tendency of democratic society is to erode distinctive forces.

The great difficulty of democratic government has hitherto seemed to be, how to provide, in a democratic society, what circumstances have provided hitherto in all the societies which have maintained themselves ahead of others – a social support, a *point d'appui*, for individual resistance to the tendencies of the ruling power; a protection, a rallying point, for opinions and interests which the ascendant public opinion views with disfavour.[108]

What circumstances provided, was of course, an aristocracy, and social groups which acted to challenge the ascendant power in society. But the aristocracy was no longer capable of fulfilling this role, even if it were still desirable that it should, and society was not so constituted as to allow for a class of prophets. Rather, the only 'quarter in which to look for a supplement, or completing corrective, to the instincts of a democratic majority, is the instructed minority'.[109]

By a different route, Mill has reached a position curiously similar to Arnold's. But more institutionally-minded than Arnold, he set out to propose that classic of liberal opposition – Hare's proportional voting scheme – to which he added the provision that the educated should have more votes than the rest. The details of this scheme (*Representative Government*, chapter 7) do not now concern us, but two points come to our attention. One is that Mill's discussion of the role of the educated elite in a supposedly democratic society finds a number of affinities in the debates on the second Reform Bill, and indeed converges with the more general theory of representative government. In his *English Constitution*, whose starting place was an objection to the theorising of *Representative Government*, Walter Bagehot argued the need for the few to act in the name of the many and to temper the ignorance of those whom they represent. Bagehot expressed as a sociological fact what Mill hoped would turn out to be the case:

It has been thought strange, but there *are* nations in which the numerous unwiser part wishes to be ruled by the less numerous wiser part. The numerical majority ... is ready, is eager to delegate its power of choosing its rulers to a certain select minority. It abdicates in favour of its *élite*, and consents to obey whoever the *élite* may confide in.[110]

The second point is that considerable special pleading was required to press the right of the intellectuals to plural voting. What, we might ask, becomes of Mill's famous doctrine of the 'spirit of an institution' when one portion of the community is allowed more votes proportionally than another? Mill's answer is remarkable. He begins by saying 'I do not regard equal voting as among those things which are good in themselves' – a curious statement in view of his admirable advocacy of votes for women. Furthermore, equal voting implies a 'wrong standard'.[111] In fact the spirit of the institution is a better one if the highly educated are seen to have more weight than ordinary citizens, since it is for the citizen's good 'that he should think that every one is entitled to some influence, but the better and wiser to more than others, it is important that this conviction should be preferred by the state and embodied in the national institutions.[112] The dispositions whose course we have charted, work to permit the uncomplicated identification of the 'better and wiser' with the highly educated minority. It is not as easy as it may seem to write off this position as inconsistent. Within the limitations of his starting place, Mill has remained faithful to the theory of the spirit of the institution. A fruitful line of criticism might be that which seeks to know why the intellectuals – however selected – should be supposed to be the innovators, the radicals, the wise, and the good. There seems to be a term of the argument missing, and this term can be supplied only by recourse to the argument (now become an assumption) that the *pouvoir spirituel* is necessarily a challenging and innovating force. The rest of the argument has evaporated, leaving this residue behind it. This, then, is the ghost of Mill's earlier infatuation with an ideal clerisy. He might have recalled the objection he stated to d'Eichthal years before over the Saint-Simonian intention of placing the

pouvoir spirituel in the *savans* and *artistes*: I do not know how it is in France, but I know that in England these . . . are the very classes of persons you would pick out as the most remarkable for a narrow & bigotted understanding, & a sordid and contracted disposition as respects all things wider than their business or families.[113]

But let us note that even here he objects not to the idea of the *pouvoir spirituel*, but, on empirical grounds, to the choice of groups in whom it is to be invested. He could envisage an ideal spiritual power, and it has been my suggestion that the ideal was based on the group surrounding him when his adulthood of missionary zeal began. That ideal lives on, in attenuated form, in the wise and good of *Representative Government*. Such a class will not be composed of any old intellectuals, but of disinterested people of Mill's stamp. It is, in fact, an ideal group. But while he has idealised the intellectual power, he has not done the same for the rest of the population on whose existing imperfections the need for an intellectual class rests. In these circumstances, the educational argument for democratic institutions (usually characteristic of Mill), begins to look a little wilted. Normally, he can be expected to argue the educational value of administering one's own affairs, and of participation in public life. What becomes of this argument if one group in society is seen to carry more weight than your own? The answer comes back in terms so often used to justify a competitive economic system: the 'position which gives the strongest stimulus to the growth of intelligence is that of rising into power, not that of having achieved it'.[114] We cannot escape the dichotomy between the ideal intelligentsia (uncorrupted, apparently, even by having achieved power), and the actual state of the rest of the population with its need for intellectual improvement. This is what is left of the theory of the *pouvoir spirituel*.

We should, however, be wrong merely to insist on the limiting aspects of Mill's mature thought about the role of the intellectuals. He remembered that the goal was the ennoblement of all, and erected no barrier to prevent entry into the educated ranks. But his was an ambiguous theory. Shortly after the publication of *On Liberty*, he wrote to his friend Alexander Bain:

The 'Liberty' has produced an effect on you which it was never intended to produce, if it has made you think that we ought not to attempt to convert the world. I meant nothing of the kind, and hold that we ought to convert all we can. We must be satisfied with keeping alive the sacred fire in a few minds when we are unable to do more – but the notion of an intellectual aristocracy of *lumières* while the rest of the world remains in darkness fulfills none of my aspirations – and the effort I aim at by the book is, on the contrary to make the many more accessible to all truth by making them more open-minded.[115]

While Mill does not want a rigid hierarchy, he longs for an assured base from which to convert the world. His was not in the end – as the history of his relationship with Comte shows – the intolerance of a proselytising creed. The Religion of Humanity that we find in 'The Utility of Religion' or in *Utilitarianism* is an attenuated affair, the symptom of a longing for a community of unselfish endeavour, rather than a dogmatic religion. Nevertheless, the impulse towards authoritative oversight of society's affairs is not irrelevant to Mill's liberalism. His endeavour overlaps with that of other proponents of the clerisy. He did not, it is true, propose a noumenal self either for himself or for society. 'Manysidedness' was the motto of development. But diversity had to be regulated by the purifying intellect which could alone maintain unselfishness and social cohesion. And, reassuringly, a surrogate idealism proposed that the intellect really did play a preponderant part in the making of human history. Of the ambiguity of the principle of utility Mill had achieved his own resolution. His empiricism would perpetually hanker after rationalism. But it was a resolution (as Fitzjames Stephen was well aware) that was to be haunted by the paradoxical notion of spiritual authority. From that spectre Mill, for one reason and another, showed no eagerness to escape.

6

THE IDEA OF
A UNIVERSITY

We are beginning to see, that science and letters are a vocation, that they have a value in themselves, and are not merely useful as teachable material. ... That universities have other functions than that of educating youth. That liberal and scientific culture, intelligence, and the whole domain of mind, is a national interest, as much as agriculture, commerce, banking, or water supply.

Mark Pattison, 'Review of the Situation'

Although he circumscribed government interference in social life, Mill believed that there were some areas in which government intervention was not only justifiable but actually necessary. Thus he spoke of provision for the 'maintenance of what has been called a learned class':

The cultivation of speculative knowledge, though one of the most useful of all employments, is a service rendered collectively, not individually, and one for which it is, *prima facie*, reasonable that the community should pay.... It is highly desirable ... that there should be a mode of insuring to the public the services of scientific discoverers, and perhaps of some other classes of savants, by affording them the means of support consistently with devoting a sufficient portion of time to their peculiar pursuits. The fellowships of the Universities are an institution excellently adapted for such a purpose; but are hardly ever applied to it, being bestowed, at the best, as a reward for past proficiency, in committing to memory what has been done by others, and not as the salary of future labours in the advancement of knowledge.[1]

In chapter 6 I want to follow the idea of the clerisy into the rather more dispersed field of the debates on the nature and functions of the university. I shall show that theories of the intellectual elite were active in the thinking of at least some of the university reformers, and I shall attempt to document the manner in which the university came to be seen as the primary institutional base for that elite. In doing so, I hope to suggest indirectly some of the ways in which this idea bears upon the development of the modern university. The available sources are extensive, and I can only deal with what I take to be a representative fraction of them. Even from such a survey we can form some estimate of the currency of ideas on how the academy could in principle be reformed for ends that were at once intellectual and social. T. H. Huxley, for instance, whose training, interests, and frame of reference might be supposed to have set him outside the ambit of proponents of the clerisy, envisaged an ideal university. Speaking at the opening of Johns Hopkins University in Baltimore, he remarked that

it is of vital importance to the welfare of the community that those who are relieved from the need of making a livelihood, and still more, those who are stirred by the divine impulses of intellectual thirst or artistic genius, should be enabled to devote themselves to the higher service of their kind, as centres of intelligence, interpreters of Nature, or creators of new forms of beauty. And it is the function of a university to furnish such with the means of becoming that which it is their privilege and duty to be.

He concluded his address by proclaiming that

the universities ought to be, and may be, the fortresses of the higher life of the nation.[2]

But this was an ideal which the English universities were not yet fulfilling. The regret with which Huxley described the imperviousness of the English universities testifies to his high hopes of what they could become. English intellectual eminence, he noted in 1868, was maintained by the Grotes, Mills, Faradays, Lyells, or Darwins, but such men were usually left to attain their eminence through unaided intellectual power:

They are not trained in the courts of the Temple of Science, but storm the walls of the edifice in all sorts of irregular ways, and with much loss of time and power, in order to attain their legitimate positions. Our universities do not encourage such men; do not offer the positions, in which it should be their highest duty to do, thoroughly, that which they are most capable of doing.[3]

That so many of the nation's intellectuals were trained or carried on their work outside the universities was coming to be a subject for comment. That it was seen as an anomaly is evidence of the germination of a new and demanding conception of the function of the academy.

In connection with this development we must consider further a subject which has already occupied us with Coleridge and Arnold. That is the idea of 'liberal education', vividly alive in the period of the great educational commissions of the 1860s, and related to ideas of spiritual power and intellectual leaven. We shall be concerned with a form of education, which, while it was to be offered to a relatively dispersed elite, took as its model and its highest achievement, the philosopher whose virtues were recapitulated by Jowett, the reforming Master of Balliol. The ideal of modern times no longer retained the simplicity of the classical period; knowledge was fragmented and the affair of specialists. But

> there may be a use in translating the conception of Plato into the language of our own age. The philosopher in modern times is one who fixes his mind on the laws of nature in their sequence and connexion, not on fragments or pictures of nature; on history, not on controversy; on the truths which are acknowledged by the few, not on the opinions of the many.... Like the ancient philosopher he sees the world pervaded by analogies, but he can also tell 'why in some cases a single instance is sufficient for an induction' (Mill's Logic 3,3,3) while in other cases a thousand examples would prove nothing. He inquires into a portion of knowledge only, because the whole has grown too vast to be encompassed by a single mind or life.... Like Plato, he has a vision of the unity of knowledge, not as the beginning of philosophy to be attained by a study of elementary mathematics, but as the far-off result of the working of many minds in many ages.[4]

Liberal education – which, Jowett urged, it was the task of the university to provide – was founded on such a conception of the philosopher and of philosophy. We shall come to note, not for the first time, the appropriation of an active theory of mind and education by the theorists of an elite. We are here dealing with the propagation in the context of far-reaching educational reform of a class system of knowledge described in our own time by Basil Bernstein: only the few

> *experience* in their bones the notion that knowledge is permeable, that its orderings are provisional, that the dialectic of knowledge is closure and openness. For the many, socialization into knowledge is socialization into order, the existing order, into the experience that the world's educational knowledge is impermeable.[5]

In forging theories of the early modern university the thinkers with whom we shall be concerned proposed to legitimate such a state of affairs in the name of sound learning and the best interest of society.

I wish to question the adequacy of a type of idealisation of the university which may still be heard today. Thus Northrop Frye, in an article on spiritual authority, finished by identifying with the tradition he found represented by Arnold:

A century later, we seem to be living our lives on two levels. One is the level of ordinary society, which is in so constant a state of revolution and metamorphosis that it cannot be accepted as the real form of human society at all, but only as the transient appearance of real society. Real society itself can only be the world revealed to us through the study of the arts and sciences, the total body of human achievement out of which the forces come that change ordinary society so rapidly. Of this world the universities are the social embodiment, and they represent what seems to me today the only visible direction in which our higher loyalties and obligations can go.[6]

That there is a 'real society' beyond the transient phenomena of 'ordinary society', that the universities are, in their idea, the guardians of the true vision – these are just the arguments that we are trying to locate in the nineteenth century.

THE UNIVERSITIES AND THE NATION

It is highly significant that claims that the universities should be the home of the spiritual power begin to be heard in a period of serious social disturbance and fears of civil war – the late 1830s and early 1840s. It is of further significance that they should be heard from educated persons at the very time when the Tractarian controversy was casting into doubt the capacity of the church to act as social moderator. Shortly after 1840, James Heywood, then Registrary of the University of Cambridge, had the idea of producing an English edition of a recent book on the English universities by V. A. Huber, Professor of Western Literature at Marburg. This work's message was that the English universities were better than was believed by the people in Germany (or, for that matter, in England), and that they had been of inestimable social value in forming the English gentleman. To Huber it was still in doubt whether 'democratic inundation will swamp the old Universities, with the rest of Old England, in industrial barbarism!'[7] Heywood's enterprise would be of little interest had the job of translating and editing it not been left to Francis Newman (John Henry's younger brother).[8] Since Francis Newman disagreed with Huber, who was, he felt, too conservative, he explained his own position in a long preface where he asserted that he was a radical in the matter of university reform just because he had a 'high conception of the dignity and vocation of a University':

In my apprehension, England needs her Universities to assume a place of intellectual, moral and spiritual authority, such as shall place them above the dense clouds of party. They should move in a higher, serener atmosphere, unaffected by its storms. Reverenced by all, they should restrain all, and unite all.[9]

This, we should note, was written in 1843 when England's most articulate ecclesiastical leaders were embroiled in the struggle for Oxford. The image of reconciliation was crucial – authority presupposed equilibrium. Newman, who knew well enough how things were at Oxford, had more to say –

The *political* importance of our Universities appears to me in a widely different light from that which Professor Huber describes and seems to defend. In the progress of society, the rule of the sword and of blind veneration gives way to that of intelligence; for which reason the Monarchical and Ecclesiastical powers become less and less able to unite, by virtue of mere external pretensions, the parts of a great nation. As yet, happily, the Crown stands quite above the conflicts of party: and it is difficult to limit the reconciling influence which might be exerted by a sovereign of mature and unblemished wisdom. But such personal qualifications cannot be secured by any institutions; and I need not prove, that no permanent union for England can be expected from this quarter. As for the organs of the National Church, they have unhappily long and long since thrown themselves into the scale of party, with a unanimity surpassing that of the Universities. The mass of the nation is learning ... to hope much from the fears, and little from the justice and wisdom of those in power: and there is no umpire left between rich and poor, 'to lay his hand upon us both'. If it is too early for thoughtful men to ask, what is to save our children from Civil War, it at least is not too early to inquire, whither we are to look for that profound, tranquil, unbiassed Political Wisdom, which becomes the more essential for our welfare, the more our population increases in density, our social relations in complexity, and our whole civil state in advancement. *Such* wisdom must rest upon a broad surface of History, and be deeply grounded on a knowledge of the moral, social, and spiritual nature of Man. It can be no fruit of the genius of the individual, but the net result of the experience of ages and of the experience of ten thousand intellects: and, as such, it would diffuse itself not as a set of propositions based on the authority of a few eminent professors, but as a spirit breathing through the whole minds of those who have access to its abode. Now this is the political side of the ideal which I form of the Universities; this is, I think, the part the Nation needs them to play. Such a function is essential for the permanent welfare of the Body corporate; and it seems impossible to point out any other national Organ, by which the function could be executed. At present, unhappily, the greatest questions of Politics are decided among us by voting, not by knowledge. Measures intended for popular benefit can hardly be carried without the help of popular fanaticism; and leave behind them unreasonable expectations, certain to issue in disappointment and in a craving for greater changes.[10]

There is much for our attention here. Let us note first the assertion of a reconciling function at a time of social and political unrest. This was a time when many of the articulate were implicitly or explicitly asserting the role of a spiritual power in saving society. It was the period of the 'Condition of England question', and of the first wave of 'social purpose novels', novels which appeal to the educated reader to take cognisance of the state of society and use their influence on behalf of the weak. The movement which sought a spiritual role for the universities shared a common dynamic with other social movements, including the 'Broad Church' exponents of the missionary function of the educated, among whose writings we from time to time find passages that parallel or overlap with the university theorists.[11] Then we should note in Newman's argument that the national church is no longer capable of performing the function of reconciliation. The nation should be at one with itself: in the next year Disraeli was to publish his description of Egremont, walking (significantly) in the grounds of a ruined abbey, and learning to his astonishment that there was not one nation but two. That there were two nations, and even that rival parties existed, was a symptom of spiritual malaise to which a spiritual power should address itself. Most people can hope little from the justice of those in power: there 'is no umpire left between rich and poor, to lay his hand upon us both'. England needs, it seems, blessing, rather than economic reorganisation. The passage represents a stage in the process of secularisation, a stage when the concepts of the spiritual, cultural and moral life of the nation were not dissociated. Once again we find that the intellectual and the moral life of the nation are identified as one. If no institutional basis for wisdom is found, all we can look forward to is worse and worse division, leading even to civil war. The permanent welfare of the 'Body corporate' and its continued progress towards the rule of 'intelligence' requires the university to be the abode of wisdom, for there is no other institution left to play this part. We are back to a recurrent theme of this study – the assumed antithesis between democracy and wisdom, expressed with varying degrees of hostility, towards a democracy that is divisive and the promoter of 'opinion' rather than 'truth'. Thus Newman contrasts 'voting' and 'knowledge' and leaves us with the impression that ideal universities will educate the populace in the folly of 'unreasonable expectations'. An element of social control was openly acknowledged.

Although, as will become clear, the clerisy argument was by no means limited to the reformers of the older universities, the structure of Oxford and Cambridge was more apt to give rise to such hopes. In the following pages I shall therefore concentrate more on the reform of Oxford and Cambridge rather than on the concurrent process of founding new university colleges. Changing opinion within combined with powerful pressure from without to bring about the formation of an Oxbridge whose institutions were in essence those we know today. The process was a slow one, and at the end of the century it could still be reasonably maintained that the older universities were the playground for the sons of the upper and to some extent professional classes, and grievously self-absorbed as well. Nevertheless, there is a great difference between the Cambridge of Romilly's Diary and the Cambridge of Sidgwick's later years, or between the Oxford of Mark Pattison's undergraduate days and that of his rectorship of Lincoln. Even if their social make-up and governing class image had changed little, they were more highly organised, more professional, more dedicated to educational ideals. Above all, their dons were more conscious of themselves as an intellectual community with high responsibilities towards their society.[12] From around 1830, and the awakened educational fervour which had seen the foundation of University College London, the universities had been the subject of astringent criticism. Their advocates – as the possibility of founding new universities became clear – were not the least astringent. If, like Francis Newman (who became Professor of Latin at University College London in 1846), you had a 'high conception of the dignity and vocation of a university', unreformed Oxbridge was likely to affect you as a depressing sight. Clough remarked to the commissioners of 1850 that the English universities were 'simply finishing schools for the higher classes in general',[13] and Matthew Arnold a few years later that they were 'at best, but the continuation of the sixth form of Eton, Harrow or Rugby'.[14] By this time, however, reforms were being made, and were to some extent taking the direction that academic liberals wanted them to take. Figures like Jowett, Pattison, and Whewell become prominent. We can see a growing interest in German universities which would long remain an example to the reformers.[15] More important perhaps, is the emergence of a new style, a new tone among some undergraduates. From the late 1820s we can sense new ideals of intellectual and social commitment growing up among the sort of undergraduates who formed the proliferating student debating and paper-reading societies, and of which the Cambridge 'Apostles' is merely the most famous.[16] At the end of the 1830s and during the 1840s there were some who – while not necessarily throwing in their lot with the Tractarians – felt deeply committed to the reform of spiritual institutions, and carried on a conscientious search for work that would benefit society. At Oxford one senses the influence of Thomas Arnold; indeed, the influence of Rugby and the Arnoldian ideals at Oxford deserves to be properly studied. From our point of view its importance is in providing a set of ideals for middle-class young men, troubled by religious doubt, but desirous of influencing society. They started to become conscious of themselves as a group, as a kind of clergy even when they did not in fact enter the church. Reading the memoirs and essays, one comes to recognise a tone. A Rugby master, once briefly a pupil of Thomas Arnold's at his school at Laleham in Surrey, wrote to Stanley after Arnold's death:

Every pupil was made to feel that there was a work for him to do, that his happiness as well as his duty lay in doing that work well. Hence an indescribable zest was communicated to a young man's feeling about life; a strange joy came over him on discovering that he had a means of being useful, and thus of being happy; and a deep respect and ardent attachment sprang up towards him who had taught him thus to value life and his own self, and his work and mission in the world.[17]

The sense of mission is crucial. Shudder as we may at the self-consciousness of the thing, there is something symptomatic about a letter that Clough, then still a sixth former at Rugby, wrote to a friend who had gone up to Cambridge. One suspects that this kind of talk, redolent of a more general middle-class sense of mission (we call it Victorian now), was common among one kind of Dr Arnold's pupils.

It is that very thing with which you uphold Cambridge that makes me prefer Oxford. I mean the αὐταρκεῖα of the Rugby set. At Oxford we only form part of a larger set, and there is more hope there that a little leaven will leaven the whole lump.[18]

If we recognise the prevalence of this kind of thinking among some, at least, of those who went up to university in the late 1830s and 1840s, we may understand more of the dynamics of the inchoate and minority academic liberalism of the next decades. When about to go up to Balliol, Clough compared Oxford to Cambridge again, and noted that Oxford's

> place in relation to the Commonwealth is far higher, for good or evil. Suppose Oxford became truly good and truly wise, would it not be far more important and a far greater blessing than Cambridge in the same condition?

And he went on to speak of the 'Oxford public and political and national feeling'.[19] What is important for us is not Clough's reasons for preferring Oxford to Cambridge, but his vocabulary. With undergraduates who spoke this language, the Jowetts and Pattisons could set about renovation. A very brief sketch of the processes of reform will indicate under what conditions and with what hopes the reformers worked.

A convenient date to start with is 1850, the year in which the two Royal Commissions on Oxford and Cambridge were set up. These reported two years later, and the consequent reforms, arrived at with much haggling and compromise, were looked back to by many in the later nineteenth century as representing the decisive change from the eighteenth- to the nineteenth-century university. Changes continued after 1854, and, after the recommendations of the Commissions of 1877, culminated in the statutes of 1881. During these years, the examination system was extended and made coterminous with the honours system. The Church of England monopoly was broken by the abolition of subscription to the Thirty-Nine Articles for matriculation, and by the repeal in 1871 of the Universities Test Act, enabling non-conformists to take degrees. The general rule that fellows of colleges must be in holy orders was gradually relaxed, as was the celibacy requirement. Henry Sidgwick and others pioneered higher education for women. These changes and the forces behind them are relevant to our present subject in that they affected the role of the academic body. For whatever stand one took during these years, the very fact of debate made the universities conscious of themselves as scholarly and educational institutions, and as needing to justify their position, even their existence, in social terms. Arguments or rationalisations on their behalf imply a consciousness that justification is expected. Perhaps most important for our purposes is the growing professionalisation of the universities. In part this was the result of increased detachment from the church. We see a group emerging which consists of teachers or scholars rather than clergymen. We have the refurbishing of the Renaissance institution of professorships, so that they offer a goal for academic advancement other than a college headship or preferment to a college living, and so that their holders form a teaching and re-searching body. During the debate on the 1850 Commission, academic liberals, led by Henry Halford Vaughan, the Regius Professor of Modern History at Oxford, argued for the professorial as opposed to the tutorial system, an argument in which they had Mill's backing, though Pattison at the time dissented.[20] We have the beginnings of the faculties as an active and co-ordinating force, and of the groupings of colleges for the purposes of joint lecturing. In 1881 university lecturers arrived, as also did the modern adminis-trative and financial organs of the university. The same years show an increasing selfconsciousness on the part of the academic body, as the power of the heads of houses and of the masters of arts at large was reduced in favour of the democracy of the 'resident senior members' – Congregation at Oxford and the Regent House at Cambridge. At Oxford, where, up to the time of the first Com-mission, the majority of fellowships had been closed, the closed fellowships were abolished in 1854.[21] In the debate on university reform two main ways of thinking are evident among those who consider the question of what a university exists for. I want to con-sider these in the light of the above.

Broadly speaking, there were those who believed that the univer-sity's main task, its main mode of influencing the community at large, was the education of young men, preparing them for a life in the world by training them to go behind surface appearances. Its object, as John Henry Newman put it in the preface to *The Idea of a University*, 'is the diffusion and extension of knowledge rather than the advancement'.[22] 'Perhaps it is one of the first-fruits of university reform', wrote T. H. Green in 1877, and with the nascent university extension movement in mind, 'that men are now forth-coming from Cambridge and Oxford who will enter, without any of the caste-spirit of the conventional university man, but with unabated zeal for the knowledge which "does not pay", into the educational life of cities.'[23] Then there were those who believed that education in the direct sense ought to be a secondary consideration, and that the university was, in its essence, a community of scholars which served society best by pursuing its own scholarly concerns. Needless to say, these are ideal types, and few if any could hold either view unmixed with the other. Both in any case have in common the belief that the university needs justifying in terms of social value, however indirect. It is nevertheless meaningful to say that Whewell, Jowett, John Henry Newman, and T. H. Green are examples of the first type, and Pattison of the second. I want to discuss next these two ideal roles for the university, and I shall take first the argument which sees the university as producing a spiritual power distributed in society.

LIBERAL EDUCATION

In a collection of essays on the subject of liberal education published in 1867, the year of the Reform Act and the Report of the Clarendon Commission on the Public Schools, it was noted that the universities had 'before them no less a problem than to organize National Liberal Education'.[24] The argument, put forward by Newman, Jowett, or Green, for sending out into the world young men who have been specially trained to serve society, is inseparable from the concept of liberal education. The intention of the advocates of education was not to send out specialists or professionals – historians, classicists, economists, or theologians. Professional specialisation was growing during this period, as the diversification of the curriculum witnesses, but it was not yet the norm. The educationalists shared with the authors of the Northcote–Trevelyan Report on the civil service the idea that society needed educated men, capable of finding their way among the specialisms, or of taking up politics or administration, but in the first place educated to see further than the mass of citizens, to see the whole where they saw but the part. Unlike the ordinary man, the highly educated man was not the passive recipient of knowledge but had, by his own activity, gained a grasp of its underlying principles. The concept of liberal education and its cognate, classical education, meets us at every turn in the nineteenth century. It represented an aspiration which Huxley could voice as readily as Arnold, Pattison as readily as Newman.[25] It is worth examining closely since, with its assumed aims, it will be found within the argument for education as well as for the community of scholars.

The concept, as we have already seen, lies very closely to the central concerns of this book.

What, then, is liberal education? It is, of course non-vocational, but more than that it is the education suitable for a free man. But the free man is also the virtuous man of Aristotle's *Ethics*; he who has recognised that the highest good lies in minimising dependence upon the material world. The perennial attraction of the supposedly higher form of intellectual health reappears, and with it the corollary that for the ordinary man there is but the compromise between the demands of the higher and lower faculties. One mode of freedom is of course to be free from pressing economic need, and we should recognise how far claims for a clerisy emanate from a group which, while it comprised many hard-working and socially aware persons, still took for granted the cushioning of cheap domestic labour and the advantages of safe investment in the railways and other great industrial enterprises of the day. Liberal education presents itself as the education of those free from the tyranny of sense, and from enslavement to phenomena. 'In a word', remarked Pattison, 'liberal education is philosophical.'[26] We should not use the nineteenth-century concept of liberal education without some explanation, for it was the product of a specific though prolonged intellectual and social crisis, in the course of which the old structures of thought and belief appeared to be giving way. In retrospect, we can see the seeds of disintegration in any historical period, however coherent its structures, and however self-confident its spokesmen. Nevertheless, it is impossible to do justice to any aspect of nineteenth-century intellectual history without recognising to what extent men saw history as the alternation of organic and critical periods, and their own period as a critical period of unprecedented fragmentation. There has until recently been a custom of regarding the Victorian age as one of optimism. But even the confidence in social, moral, and technological progress that we find proclaimed by the liberal politicians, the leader writers or the occasional Macaulay or Bright, depended upon the familiar historical paradigm of the age, and consequently upon the expectation of change. Out of the chaos of society and of speculative opinion there might emerge either a new organic period or – and anxiety about the alternative was widespread – anarchy. Many doubted the capacity of any existing class in society to offer a firmness of moral, spiritual, or political authority. All the more pressing, therefore, was the need to foster a class of men who could understand what was going on, whose mental activity would be some guarantee of unity in a disintegrating world. In connection with Arnold we noted the overlap between idealised conceptions of aristocracy and those of spiritual authority. I pointed to the significance of the use of words like 'nobility', 'noble', 'manly', or 'vulgar' in a cultural context. I would add to that list 'liberal' as used in 'liberal education'; 'liberal knowledge' was glossed by Newman as 'gentleman's knowledge'. The universities, it came to be believed, were to create the new 'free man'.

I have said that nineteenth-century intellectuals were conscious of a fragmentation of the intellectual universe, a fragmentation that could not but be noticed to have its parallels in the social sphere. Specialism versus general comprehension was one of the perennial arguments in the educational thought of the period. People were conscious, from very early in the century, of an increasing heterogeneity of the world of mind and extended discourse. George Eliot was not alone in the feeling (however original was her choice of words) when she remarked that addressing the nineteenth-century public could be like speaking from a camp-stool in a parrot-house (*Middlemarch*, Book II, chapter xv). The consciousness of the dissipation of the secular mind, I have argued, provided an incentive to the development of the transcendentalist epistemology of the turn of the nineteenth century. The fragmented and evanescent world of the ordinary became the object of the lower faculty of cognition – in Coleridgean terms, the understanding – and the infinite world of truths and principles became the object of the higher faculty – the reason. But even within the empirical tradition, the consciousness of intellectual division of labour grew. Let us take an exceptionally clear formulation of the objects of liberal education from the beginning of the century. In 1809 the *Edinburgh Review* published a review of Edgeworth's *Professional Education* by Sydney Smith, the regular *Edinburgh Review* contributor and friend of Jeffrey, Playfair, and Brougham.[27] In the article he attacked the current curriculum of the University of Oxford as being utterly unrelated to the needs of the modern world. Not that he was adverse to classical education as such, but classical education was a partial form of education, and classics were badly taught anyway. The English were apparently afraid of letting their young men discuss important, contemporary questions. He himself was in favour of liberal education, but one in which all sciences had a place: 'what ought the term

University to mean, but a place where every science is taught which is liberal and at the same time useful to mankind?'[28] Edward Copleston, Provost of Oriel and one of the first of the new Oxford philosophers, the so-called 'Oriel Noetics', had saved up several attacks on Oxford by the *Edinburgh Review*. In 1810 he published 'A Reply to the Calumnies of the Edinburgh Review against Oxford'. Much of this lengthy pamphlet was devoted to contesting earlier statements on the state of physical science and classical learning at Oxford. But in the last part Copleston took Smith to task, and in doing so put forward a persuasive defence of liberal education, and, more than that, of classical education as *the* liberal education. Sydney Smith and his like, Copleston was sure, boded no good to liberal education. The last part of his reply deserves careful attention for the way in which it proclaims the value of liberal education, and the value to society of those who have had such an education.

Copleston begins by distinguishing between education in the interests of the individual and that in the interests of the public. Locke, he found, described well the 'true principles of educating a gentleman', but he, too

> like most other writers on education, occasionally confounds two things which ought to be kept perfectly distinct, viz. that mode of education which would be most beneficial, as a system, to society at large, with that which would contribute most to the advantage and prosperity of an individual. These things are often at variance with each other. The former is that alone which deserves the attention of the philosopher; the latter is narrow, selfish, and mercenary.[29]

There are two things to notice here, and we can best get at one through the other. Copleston's statement is in fact opposing the available liberal ideology of the day in which the working out of enlightened self-interest would automatically prove to be to the best advantage of society. It is an irony, and a deeply revealing irony, of the theory of 'liberal education' that its theorists came to oppose materialist liberalism precisely over the question of what constitutes the full development of the individual – Mill's dilemmas are highly articulated versions of the dilemmas which faced liberals with a belief in education. Secondly, what Copleston sets against the professional (i.e. self-interested) education is the ideal of 'gentlemen's' education. He was not to be the last to invoke the ideal of the disinterested 'gentleman'. We should expect that Copleston opposes the doctrines of political economy, and this he proceeds to do. Strikingly, he attacks the theory of the advantageousness of the division of labour in a tone and with arguments that we recognise in many other and later opponents of the 'dismal science'. Concentration on a single employment does indeed improve skill and speed in performances,

> But while [the man] thus contributes more effectually to the accumulation of national wealth, he becomes himself more and more degraded as a rational being. In proportion as his sphere of action is narrowed, his mental power and habits become contracted; and he resembles a subordinate part of some powerful machinery, useful in its place, but insignificant and worthless out of it.[30]

It is amusing to imagine this eighteenth-century Oxford don in the company of Wordsworth, Southey, Carlyle, and Marx. One could not trust, with Adam Smith, that the spread of enlightenment would counteract the tendencies of the division of labour. Society requires other contributions from the individual besides the particular duties of his profession. Without an enforced consciousness of social duties society becomes as fragmented as industry:

> if no such liberal intercourse be established, it is the common failing of human nature, to be engrossed with petty views and interests, to under-rate the importance of all in which we are not concerned, to carry our partial notions into cases where they are inapplicable, to act, in short, as so many unconnected units, displacing and repelling one another.[31]

Now Copleston is not discussing the mental cultivation or lack of it of factory operatives. He is discussing, as he put it a page later, 'those liberal pursuits, which in a refined state of society engage the attention of the higher orders'. If we ask how the division of labour affected the higher orders, the answer would seem to be in the intellectual fragmentation which threatened the educated classes. Hence the importance of his remedy, which, as it reminds us of Coleridge, looks forward to all theories of liberal education as the cultivation of the intellectual faculty, the antithesis of the system of importing facts into the mind. The passage quoted above continues:

> In the cultivation of literature is found that common link, which, among the higher and middling departments of life, unites the jarring sects and subdivisions in one interest, which supplies common topics, and kindles common feelings, unmixed with those narrow prejudices with which all professions are more or less infected. The knowledge too, which is thus acquired, expands and enlarges the mind, excites its faculties, and calls those limbs and muscles into freer exercise, which, by too constant use in one direction, not only acquire an illiberal air, but are apt also to lose

somewhat of their native play and energy. And thus, without directly qualifying a man for any of the employments of life, it enriches and ennobles all.[32]

The study of literature, that is to say letters, *literae humaniores* (Latin and Greek, ancient history, and philosophy), is thus both a socially and intellectually harmonising and reconciling activity. So Copleston came back to his defence of Oxford as a centre for the diffusion of liberal awareness in society:

> If such be the advantages of a system founded in the study of ancient literature, it cannot be an object of indifference with the nation, to see it firmly established and well endowed. To preserve and uphold with due care this venerable edifice, a large appropriation both of the men and of the property of the country may well be made. Many there certainly ought to be, whose peculiar office should lead them to examine diligently all its parts, to bring together such materials as are necessary to counteract decay, to maintain its solidity, to cleanse, to improve and embellish it. But it is the free communication of its use to the public, which is their leading purpose; and according as that is well or ill performed, the judgment of the public should be pronounced.[33]

I have devoted this much space to Copleston's pamphlet because in it appear most of the arguments used later in favour of liberal education. It was to this controversy that Newman returned when explaining what he meant by liberal education.[34] From Newman to Mill – and it is not perhaps sufficiently noticed how significant it is that they could both be proponents of liberal education – the argument is basically the same. 'Liberal' is contrasted with 'useful', for that which warrants the description 'useful' is too partial, too closely allied to the narrow criteria of the professional. Liberal education is the extension and formation of the mind through philosophy (in the broadest sense), or the embracing of ideas in relation to each other. The doctrine of liberal education depends upon the doctrine of the active mind. Claims for the operation of the intellect in society naturally rest on claims for the active powers of the intellect itself. Education, said Newman, evincing the side of himself that was closest to Coleridge, was not the communication of knowledge, important though that communication was:

> The enlargement consists, not merely in the passive reception into the mind of a number of ideas hitherto unknown to it, but in the mind's energetic and simultaneous action upon and towards and among those new ideas, which are rushing in upon it. It is the action of a formative power, reducing

to order and meaning the matter of our acquirements; it is a making the objects of our knowledge subjectively our own, or, to use a more familiar word, it is a digestion of what we receive, into the substance of our previous state of thought; and without this no enlargement is said to follow. There is no enlargement, unless there be a comparison of ideas one with another, as they come before the mind, and a systematizing of them. We feel our minds to be growing and expanding *then*, when we not only learn, but refer what we learn to what we know already. It is not the mere addition to our knowledge that is the illumination; but the locomotion, the movement onwards, of that mental centre, to which both what we know, and what we are learning, the accumulating mass of our acquirements, gravitates. And therefore a truly great intellect, and recognized to be such by the common opinion of mankind, such as the intellect of Aristotle, or of St. Thomas, or of Newton, or of Goethe . . . is one which takes a connected view of old and new, past and present, far and near, and which has an insight into the influence of all these on one another; and without which there is no whole, and no centre. It possesses the knowledge, not only of things, but also of their mutual and true relations; knowledge, not merely considered as acquirement, but as philosophy.[35]

But the paradox we noted when talking of Coleridge stands: an epistemology (and hence by implication, or, as in this case, explicitly, an educational theory) is advanced which appears to be applicable to all. Yet the highest mental activity, the forming and creative process, turns out to be the attribute of an elite.

Now, I have already remarked on the paradox that Newman, an arch-opponent of liberalism, was one of the century's prime spokesmen on behalf of liberal education. The problem is this: there was a growing tendency, in the period under discussion, to see knowledge as progressive and cumulative, to acknowledge differences in mental attitudes from era to era, and to project the growth of knowledge and hence of human understanding into the future as a continuing process. Yet, for Newman, the knowledge that really matters is objectively independent of the march of mind. The presupposition of liberal education is the primacy of the intellect and its power over the subjects of its knowledge. Now it is true that Newman insists on the wholeness of the human being, on the impossibility of divorcing spirit and intellect; nevertheless, there is no understanding without belief, and the cultivated intellect was, as Newman had occasion to note, liable to revolt, to operate 'under the notion . . . that the human intellect, self-educated and self-supporting, is more true and perfect in its ideas and judgments than that of Prophets and Apostles, to whom the sights and sounds of Heaven were immediately conveyed'.[36] Now, G. H. Bantock has argued that it was precisely his theology that enabled Newman to give a due place to the objective content of education and to insist on a hierarchy of educational values that should not require justification in merely social or psychological terms.[37] Because he identifies himself with the educational tradition he believes Newman to represent, Bantock has put his finger on the problem. The affinity between Newman and the other spokesmen for liberal education lies in the fact that they, too, were attracted towards a world of transcendent (and hence unarguable, uncontaminated) values; thus they defended education against the prevailing ideology of utility and materialist liberalism, and against the democratic subjectivism which they believed to be allied to that ideology.

In the 1852 lectures, which, augmented, became *The Idea of a University*, Newman's recourse was, of course, to the church. In his witty attack on Peel and Brougham of 1841 he had attacked secular knowledge as sole content of education and disposed of the theory that studying physical science could be morally improving.[38] Now he broadened and extended the argument for which 'The Tamworth Reading Room' strikes one as, in parts, a cartoon. The intellect, apart from disciplined religion, tended towards 'intellectualism' – the false belief in its own autonomy. Academic institutions working on this premiss would become hostile to revealed truth: 'They are employed in the pursuit of Liberal Knowledge, and Liberal Knowledge has a special tendency, not necessary or rightful, but a tendency in fact, when cultivated by beings such as we are, to impress us with a mere philosophical theory of life and conduct in the place of Revelation.'[39] The church must therefore oversee the university, and see that secular knowledge does not get the upper hand. Small wonder that one recent writer has questioned the accepted notion of Newman's 'Christian humanism', and concluded a re-examination of *The Idea of a University* by asserting that for Newman the great enemy of the day was not the Philistines, but Culture.[40] What has Newman's recourse to authority to do with those proponents of liberal education who were not trying to claim it for Roman Catholicism? The answer is that they too feel the 'nostalgia for revelation', for a static order of truth and a sound authority. In their valuable insistence on learning to penetrate behind surface appearances they tend, so to speak, to overshoot and suggest the existence of a static world of ideas; in the same way, their equally valuable insistence on seeing relations between the objects of knowledge becomes, once detached from the ordinary processes of cognition and action, a kind of striving towards the Parmenidean One. The gravitational attraction of permanent knowledge and authoritative science is pertinent also to the continued identification of classical and liberal education.

We have already noted that, for Copleston, liberal and classical education were the same. While philosophy was the end to which the liberally educated man aspired – the way so to speak in which he looked at the world – Greek and Latin continued to be regarded as the fundamental subject, or as in some way a fundamental discipline. Thus John Stuart Mill, on any account an advocate of modern studies, argued quite late on in his life that classical language and literature should be kept in the place they already occupied in liberal education. Saying that 'The only languages ... and the only literature to which I would allow a place in the ordinary curriculum, are those of the Greeks and Romans'[41] he argued on their behalf both as mental disciplines and for the content of their philosophy and history. In the same year as Mill's St Andrews address, F. W. Farrar edited the volume of *Essays on a Liberal Education*. Half of the essays in this book were devoted to the use of the classics. I have in all fairness to add that one of these was Henry Sidgwick's splendidly pragmatic essay on 'The Theory of Classical Education', which in fact debunks very effectively the claims of the classics to an exclusive place in the preparation of young men, and demands that physical science and English literature be taught as necessary parts of a liberal education. But the fact that Sidgwick had to engage in the argument at all is in itself indicative. The claim died hard that classics formed the best road to that mental culture which was the goal of education; this is amply demonstrated by all the debates on the introduction into university curricula of physical sciences, modern history, modern languages, and English literature. I think we can explain this fact about the history of the theory of higher education in the nineteenth century in the terms I suggested above. For in a world of challenge to accepted educational norms, in a world where intellectual operations were becoming increasingly disparate, in the world of the Society for the Diffusion of Useful Knowledge, the new geology, the Library of Anglo-Catholic Theology, and the Great Exhibition, the classics represented an unbroken tradition; represented above all a corpus of studies of attested value. In a hierarchy of intellectual activities they naturally occupied a high place. I would like to quote Whewell, whose testimony – from *On the Principles of English University Education* (1837) – is all the more striking because as an advocate of mathematical studies, a loud opponent of the teaching of philosophy, and a pioneer in the historiography of the inductive sciences, he might be supposed to have been biased against Greek and Latin. Greek and Latin, he wrote, are 'peculiar and indispensable elements of a liberal education'. How, he asked (and we should take note of this emphasis on continuity) was the connection of the generations, 'requisite to the transmission and augmentation of mental wealth', to be maintained? The answer was by 'living upon a common intellectual estate'. The argument is continued in a passage which I hope makes clear why I have insisted both on the ambiguity of the idea of liberal education and on its connection with classical education:

In nations, as in men, in intellect as in social condition, true nobility consists in inheriting what is best in the possessions and character of a line of ancestry. Those who can trace the descent of their own ideas, and their own language, through the race of cultivated nations; who can show that those whom they represent or reverence as their parents, have everywhere been foremost in the fields of thought and intellectual progress, – these are the true nobility of the world of the mind; the persons who have received true culture; and such it should be the business of a liberal education to make men.[42]

Whewell was a snob, but this passage is nevertheless suggestive in its association of a classical curriculum with a social argument. The feudal metaphor becomes a model. By liberal education you could send into society from the universities men with a common intellectual heritage, even a common tone: 'There is an intellectual freemasonry by which liberal minds recognise each other,' noted Pattison. 'We call it intellectual sympathy, but it is strictly moral, for it is the love of truth which such minds have in common.'[43] And it is tempting to conclude that classics retained their importance because they provided a common intellectual background, a common language indeed, both in fact and in aspiration for the members of the lettered elite. We have not in fact strayed far from the subject of the universities as intellectual centres. The vision with which we are dealing is of the universities as the source for a class of the liberally educated, diffused as a kind of spiritual authority in society. This was the contribution of the university theorists to the problem of cultivating an enlightened opinion with which Coleridge, Mill, and

Arnold strove. And Mill, like Arnold, recognised that the universities could make a contribution to this end. There was no incompatibility, he said at St Andrews, between knowing the leading truths of a number of subjects and some one subject in detail:

It is this combination which gives an enlightened public: a body of culti-vated intellects, each taught by its attainments in its own province what real knowledge is, and knowing enough of other subjects to be able to discern who are those who know them better. ... The elements of the more important studies being widely diffused, those who have reached the higher summits find a public capable of appreciating their superiority, and pre-pared to follow their lead. It is thus, too, that minds are formed capable of guiding and improving public opinion on the greater concerns of practical life.[44]

THE FORTRESSES OF THE HIGHER LIFE

We have now examined the notion of 'liberal education' upon which rested the theory of the university as 'seminary' (to borrow Sir William Hamilton's word),[45] as an institution for the production of an enlightened public. But the university had another function beyond giving a 'broad healthy culture' to those who came as students. This was the production and maintenance of scholars. A formulation from late in our period, and from outside Oxbridge, may help to make the point. In his inaugural lecture as Professor of Humanity at Aberdeen (1882), James Donaldson set about answer-ing the question 'What part does the work of the scholar occupy in the work of the nation?'. The scholar, he replied, produces ideas, while the normal tendency of society is to deaden the mind. 'The world is ruled by ideas', he observed, 'The world is itself a great idea. ... It is the intellectual and spiritual life that constitutes our real life. And the man who makes the current of our intellectual and spiritual life flow vigorously, adds to our life and brings out its power and nobler phases.' This clerisy, which Donaldson associated with the university, had a quite imperial destiny:

Now surely no one will deny that it is essential that a nation should possess such a band of thinkers and investigators as I have described. They form the very life blood of a nation. A nation which contributes nothing to the circulation of ideas is tending to barbarism. A nation which is well pro-vided with such thinkers is in the van of nations. And is it an ignoble ambition for a nation to wish to be foremost in the world of thought, fore-most in influencing the minds of men?[46]

And hence – if we follow out Donaldson's logic – we have a general hegemony. We should now examine the argument for the university as the home of the clerisy. Afterwards, by examining theories of the social role of intellect, I shall hope to show what both approaches to the idea of a university have in common.

Once again, we start from the presupposition that the universities are national institutions, and exist, however indirectly, for the good of society as a whole. This was the main point of Hamilton's argument when, in 1831, he heralded the case for reform in the *Edinburgh Review*. That the state, acting in society's interest, had the right to intervene in the affairs of the universities was the (not undisputed) starting place of the Commissions of 1850. Clerisy theories were put forward by the reformers, and they were in vogue during the debate over the development of the professorial system. We find, as by now we have come to expect, that advocacy of the clerisy implies an attack on certain aspects of orthodox liberalism – in this instance the doctrine of the free market as applied to education. The ideal of liberal education, Pattison reported

is one which, as it originated in a profound study of the nature of the mind, can only be appreciated by the maintenance of that study and knowledge. It needs protection therefore. There is no natural demand for it. The pressure and competition of actual life not only do not call for such an education, but have a continual tendency to substitute for it the more immediately available education of professional skill and accomplishment. To secure this popular education the state has only to remove intellectual obstacles, and leave it to the operation of the law of supply and demand. Remove restrictions on the Universities, and they will contribute their share towards popular education. But this is not their proper business, and has never been regarded so among us. The higher education is that which the Universities seek at once to give, and to give the means of appreciating, and in this function they need protection.[47]

Bulwer and Whewell spoke in the same vein.[48] An institutionally based clerisy is necessary because the prevailing social pressures are inimical to enlightenment; in the face of a materialist civilisation, high mental culture (which is that civilisation's hope) does not stand a chance. When he reviewed the first volume of Buckle's *History of Civilization in England*, Pattison criticised positivist optimism which, 'having resolved the study of what may be called the dynamics of society into the study of the laws of the mind',[49] saw knowledge, and consequently social progress, as cumulative and progressive. There were, declared Pattison in a passage from which I have already quoted, no certain grounds for optimism, even though

it is not questioned that intellectual progress is a fact; that its course can be traced; that it is an element of national history – perhaps the most attractive element. But what is of vital consequence for us to know is, if intellectual advance is an inevitable necessity. Will society be regenerated by its Intellect in spite of its Passions? The condition of every society yet known to us has been a small minority of educated persons in a combination either of conflict or harmony, with an overwhelming unenlightened mass. The enlightened minority who are in possession of the knowledge, have, more or less, leavened the whole. Where this practice of leavening has proceeded, unchecked, for any considerable time, an appearance is presented which may easily be mistaken for an intrinsic power in Knowledge to conquer every other motive of action. But is it more than an appearance? What security have we that the sleeping volcano of Passion will not flame forth with irresistible violence? That the ocean of Imagination, and False Opinion, will not break in, submerge a continent, and sweep away every trace of the Palace of Truth?[50]

Liberalism offers guarantees neither of the preservation of culture, nor of control over the mass. The image, once again, is that of a disinterested, pure minority pitted against the masses who represent – in some sense *are* – the passions. And with those dark forces stands imagination, widely mistrusted by the advocates of the clerisy. The model for the social operation of intellect could hardly be more apparent.

For Pattison, the whole matter of national education and of the cultivation of the intellect was involved in the question of professorial extension. In 1850–2 he was the only liberal in Oxford to defend the tutorial against the professorial system – on the same grounds, as will appear, on which he later supported the latter: 'The Professorial and Tutorial methods represent respectively the education which consists in accomplishment and current information, and that which aims at disciplining the faculties, and basing the thoughts on the permanent ideas proper to the human reason.' The practical bearing of the distinction he illustrated (as will scarcely surprise us) from the case of America where, despite striking material development, we find 'a poverty of thought, a soulless literature ... rhetorical feebleness, and all the vices of a decaying civilisation', all due to 'a want of that higher idea of education which this country has kept alive, even through periods of mental torpor, in our Universities'. The pressure of civilisation would inevitably be in the direction of 'current information'; the 'more popular notion of education', Pattison noted, was spreading here, as in France and Germany, and popular education had much in common with the 'facile process of lecture-hearing' that would be encouraged by the professorial system. The argument and assumptions will not come as a surprise to readers of this book. Here, in his evidence to the Commissioners, Pattison spells out his Coleridgean position clearly:

But I have no wish to depreciate this species of education, which I would willingly see much more widely diffused in this country, but in its proper sphere, for the classes, that is, whose callings in life will not admit of the more protracted process which a solid education requires. But I fear that we are in danger of forfeiting one of the greatest privileges which this country derives from its still holding on to the traditions of the older civilizations, if we think to substitute in the Universities this lecture-room polish for the much more athletic discipline of our old grammar-school system. Each system has its own place; they should not be rivals; the one for the mass of the people, the other for a cultivated *clerisy*.[51]

There are two kinds of education, both involving a specific sort of intellectual activity, and the higher sort is suitable for the clerisy alone. The recurrence of Coleridge's word is not accidental.

Pattison was not alone in giving evidence to the Commission on the value of the university as a home for the clerisy. Henry Halford Vaughan, then Regius Professor of Modern History and subsequently author of a manifesto on 'Oxford Reform and Oxford Professors', spoke from the professorial side, but as an advocate of far more than mere lecturing. From our point of view, Vaughan's evidence (which the Commission found so valuable that they reproduced part of it in the Report) is interesting because it describes the manner in which the putative clerisy was to operate. Lecturing to undergraduates was not the

only nor indeed the chief use which professors may answer in our Universities. The great want of Oxford hitherto has not been merely nor chiefly that the Professors have not been sufficiently active in teaching, but that the system has disfavoured the existence, and missed the general effects of Professorial learning. Some powerful men we have had; a considerable body, or a constant succession of such we have not had; men who could give authoritative opinions in matters connected with the sciences; whose words when spoken in public or private could kindle an enthusiasm on important branches of learning, or could chill the zeal for petty or factitious erudition; men whose names and presence in the University could command respect for the place, whether attracting students of all kinds and ages to it, or directing upon it the sight and interest and thought of the whole learned world; men whose investigations could perpetually be adding to knowledge, not as mere conduits to convey it, but as fountains to augment its scantiness, and freshen its sleeping waters. Of such men we desire more than we have had. The first care must be to promote the creation of such.

This was not to be done by salaries alone. Nor should such men, once obtained, be obliged to lecture, though those with a real enthusiasm for knowledge would usually be only too delighted to share their findings. Nevertheless, even those with no bent for teaching could make their contribution:

They will investigate, reflect, and write, even if they do not very actively lecture: they will address the world if not the students of the academy, and their words will come back to the University in some form, 'after many days'. They may not irrigate the ground immediately beside them, but the abundance of their spring heads and the larger volume of their pent-up waters must go forward to feed and cleanse the cities of the earth, or to move the vaster wheels of European literature, or to deepen the main sea of the world's knowledge. Much, too, in spite of recluse habits, must insensibly evaporate and fall again in showers, seasonable ever, though capricious, upon the spot.[52]

The clerisy has found a home.

Pattison went on thinking about the problem that the Commissioners expressed thus: 'It is generally acknowledged that both Oxford and the country at large suffer from the absence of a body of learned men devoting their lives to the cultivation of science, and to the direction of academical education.'[53] In the early 1860s he went to Germany, and was impressed by the fact that the German universities were 'centres of mental activity in science'.[54] As he observed the working of the revised examination and fellowship systems, he started to believe that the university ought primarily to be a scholarly institution. Facing the Commissioners of 1877, he spoke bitterly of the rise of the lucrative business of 'taking boarders'. Commercial habits were obscuring the 'spiritual ends' for the sake of which the university existed:

So entirely are these ends sunk out of sight now, that I must seem to the practical tutor to be siring an unfruitful paradox when I say that the office of an academical teacher is a spiritual administration. Yet no one has left a name in the annals of education who has not conceived of his office as such.[55]

The Commissioners were plainly worried that Pattison was putting forward an idea of the university as an institution for learned study rather than for education. There was an ambiguity about the final exchange; when, the Earl of Redesdale asked 'Do you consider that the great object of a university ought to be to produce the greatest number of useful members of society, whereby the nation at large may be most extensively benefitted?', Pattison replied – 'Certainly'.[56] Actually, Pattison had stated his views very clearly the year before, in his contribution ('Review of the Situation') to the *Essays on the Endowment of Research*, when he had called upon the newly-announced Commission to control the prize system and endow research. What is done at Oxford in the next two years, he wrote, would set the tone for the whole country. The choice was between the university which attracted those with a vocation, and a 'great national lycée' bound to routine and examinations.[57] Eight years earlier still, he had made his longest statement on behalf of the university as a centre of study rather than as a school. This was his *Suggestions on Academical Organisation* (1868), in which he argued that examinations and the competitive 'prize system' were destroying genuine studies:

The object of these 'Suggestions' has been to insist that the university shall be no longer a class-school, nor mainly a school for youth at all. It is a national institute for the preservation and tradition of useful knowledge.

It is the common interest of the whole community that such knowledge should exist, should be guarded, treasured, cultivated, disseminated, expounded.[58]

The mixed metaphors are interesting, and carry at least a suggestion of a mercantilist economy for learning (intellectual activity is the accumulation and maintenance of knowledge as substance) which exists in tension with Pattison's habitual emphasis on the dynamics of philosophical thought.

Philosophical thought should be the object of university studies, yet, between the 'upper millstone of ecclesiastical terror and the lower millstone of the competition machine', it led a precarious existence at Oxford.[59] Philosophy, we note, is urged as a kind of *regina scientiarum*. It is not, I think, going too far to say that the proponents of a spiritual power moved towards philosophy (the word still meant more than it does now after fifty years of linguistic positivism have presided over the dismantling of philosophy's empire) as a unifying discipline, a mental activity which would encompass all the otherwise divergent sciences. We find a widespread hope that logic, the science of thought, could pave a way to a grasp of the

'leading truths', the uniform 'laws' of all sciences. We find a desire
not, it is true, so much to build vast syntheses, but to assert identical
modes of operation in all areas open to the intellect. Henry Sidgwick,
giving up his attempt to read Hegel in German, wrote that there
were after all some great truths there with which he sympathised
strongly: 'That the universe is essentially, and fundamentally
rational; the laws of the subject and the object harmonious; history
the evolution of the human spirit, etc. etc. – all this is well enough.'[60]
Pattison struggled bravely to keep physical science within the realm
of reason attainable by the philosopher. The successes of physical
science had, he pointed out, gained a general recognition of the
importance of mind. He continued, gallantly, and rightly: 'It is
unphilosophical to talk of the materialist tendency of modern
science – a superficial inference from the fact that what is known is
matter. What is known in science is not matter but the laws of
matter; and law is ideal, is an abstract cognition.'[61] But Pattison is
doing more than asserting the symbolic nature of all our knowledge.
His adherence to the idea of science as the comprehension of uniform
laws offers to organise, to render practically susceptible of inclusive knowledge, a disparate intellectual universe; to show that
social science, biology, physiology, geology, or what have you are all
ultimately one in being science and are consequently accessible to
the philosopher. The claim for an organising science of the sciences
does not rule out natural science from a place in university education, but, as used by Pattison, it does insist that natural science
should be subordinate to the humanities: his is very much a
classicist's and philosopher's account of science. The same drift is
apparent in Matthew Arnold:

The study of letters is the study of the operation of human force, of human
freedom and activity; the study of nature is the study of the operation of
non-human forces, of human limitation and passivity. The contemplation
of human force and activity tends naturally to heighten our own force and
activity; the contemplation of human limits and passivity tends rather to
check it. Therefore the men who have had the humanistic training have
played, and yet play, so prominent a part in human affairs, in spite of their
prodigious ignorance of the universe; because their training has powerfully
fomented the human force in them. And in this way letters are indeed
runes.[62]

Arnold went on to urge that natural sciences should play a part in
education, because in relation to the humanities they would assume

their appropriate, subordinate place. The whole passage may be instructively compared with Huxley's brilliant Romanes Lecture, 'Evolution and Ethics', where so much greater weight is given to the actual processes of scientific knowledge. Pattison's and Arnold's arguments, however, illustrate my point that for an articulate group of nineteenth-century thinkers, the humanities represented the assertion of the human mind, trained in philosophy, over the partial results of the branches of knowledge. Thus Pattison fought to keep the word 'science' for the humanities, insisting on using it throughout the *Suggestions* in the sense of *scientia*. Like Matthew Arnold, he sought an English equivalent for *Wissenschaft*, and, like Arnold again, he associated *Wissenschaft* with the task of the spiritual power and, more explicitly, with the task of the universities:

Beyond the circles of scientific men ... there is no public appreciation of abstract science or profound learning. The dependence of culture and civilisation on the maintenance somewhere in the body-politic of the theories of the various arts of life is not understood among us. We have in English no word by which to render the German *Wissenschaft*. We mean by *science* that which admits demonstrative or experimental proof, as opposed to art, practice, or literature. But the German term is much more comprehensive, and is applicable to the methodical and abstract treatment of any matter whatsoever. *Wissenschaft* expresses the purpose and aims for which a university exists.[63]

University and the *scientia* that contains and organises knowledge are thus found in association.

Pattison was not alone in working out the idea of a national philosophic culture. Sometimes the enterprise is allied with a kind of intellectual nationalism that laments England's philosophical dependence on the Continent. Henry Halford Vaughan argued in his evidence to the 1852 Commission that the absence of the 'Professorial element in its vigour' was the reason for the silence of Oxford on philosophical subjects. We were dependent on foreign books just because, unlike their Continental counterparts, our universities had no class of professors:

Had we a Professorial system of our own embracing all the great subjects of instruction, the national character and genius would assert itself in their works. The spirit of our own institutions, intellectual character, domestic life and moral qualities, would necessarily be at work in the minds of our Professors to form a literature and philosophy independent, native, and in the truest and most valuable sense congenial; it would, therefore, not tend to make us copyists of foreign systems either in form or spirit, but would open for us a new source of independence in these things.[64]

To Francis Newman, a few years earlier, it was a matter of deep regret that

Of Mental and Moral Philosophy, it is enough to say that those who desire to study these subjects, look every where else, rather than to our Universities; and that if it be inquired, what Aristotle and Plato held, we have to apply to Germany, not to Oxford for information.

The continuation is entirely characteristic of the argument:

How large an item of mischief in our material condition is ascribable to the feebleness and low rank of Moral Science in our Universities, cannot here be discussed: else it might perhaps be made probable, that what are called by some 'the material and mechanical tendencies of *the Age*', are in no small measure ascribable to this neglect.[65]

The most astonishing metaphor was, however, left to J. R. Seeley, later to become Regius Professor of Modern History at Cambridge. In his contribution to Farrar's volume of *Essays on a Liberal Education*, entitled 'Liberal Education in Universities', he attacked the tripos and 'examining system' as pernicious, and advocated instead the 'teaching system' under which teachers could integrate their scholarship and teaching responsibility. If the universities were to renounce learning, the 'intellectual rank and character' of the country would be left to chance: 'Private thinkers and amateur writers may by accident rise to support our credit, just as, if we should disband our army, volunteers might succeed in defending our coasts.' If we sought a reason why, 'instead of overrunning the Continent with our ideas, as in the days of Locke, Newton, and Bentley', we had been invaded by French and German philosophies, we would find among the causes that 'in the warfare of thought we have hoped to resist regular troops by volunteers'.[66] As it happened, of course, English ideas were to be massively deployed in the next few decades in lands less well equipped to defend themselves than our Continental neighbours. The easy acceptance which we have noted before in educational rhetoric of military and imperial metaphors seems noteworthy. Pedagogy, too, nursed imperial aspirations. While asserting the disinterestedness of the elite, the theorists became entangled in contradictions generated by the society over which they intended to exercise independent and beneficent influence. In the final stage of my present argument I want to examine the association between the theory of the active powers of the mind and a prescriptive theory of the elite.

Proposals on behalf of a clerisy entered, we have seen, into the arguments of the nineteenth-century university reformers. Both the diffusionist school, and the party who believed that the university should be a community of scholars which performed its social function incidentally, shared a belief in society's need for a spiritual power. Late in the century an aetiology is suggested by the rationalist Henry Sidgwick's remark that, while he found it increasingly incomprehensible how anyone akin to himself in mental habits could find his religion in Christianity, 'I grow more and more . . . to regard Christianity as indispensable and irreplaceable – looking at it from a sociological point of view'.[67] Further, they shared certain underlying assumptions about the nature of mental life and educational process, and it is this common core that we have now, at last, briefly to consider. This entails paying further attention to a paradox apparent in Coleridge's work: that is that a theory of mind which stresses the dynamic nature of intellectual activity, and sees education in terms of the active apprehension of underlying relationships between phenomena, also advocates the existence of an intellectual elite to which the 'higher' mental functions are reserved. A hierarchy of values is enforced by virtue of which prestige is accorded to some forms of cognition rather than to others.

In the 1840s and 1850s, we remember, there were men who, attentive to the social ferment around them, and distressed by the factional embroilment of the church, started to seek a centre of spiritual authority in the university. Henry Halford Vaughan noted the lack of a body of men in Oxford who 'could give authoritative opinions in matters connected with the sciences; whose words when spoken in public or private could kindle an enthusiasm on important branches of learning, or could chill the zeal for petty or factious erudition'.[68] Something more is sought than when we say that so-and-so is an 'authority' on Tudor agrarian problems, or an 'authority' on Milton. There is a feeling that the authority of what Jowett, speaking to the same Commission, called a 'body of eminent men . . . who might have formed the centres of opinion and knowledge'[69] extends to the moral life of the intellectual community and hence of the community as a whole. Reconciliation, the drawing together in harmony of those jarring forces that it pleased theoretical liberalism to set at the centre of social dynamics, was at once intellectual and social. The parallel (or even identity) between the growth of new subject matters and the growth of an unprecedented kind of industrial society was often asserted. So when Francis Newman asked that the universities learn to accommodate the material sciences in order that the modern and ancient knowledge might grow up together in mutual friendship, he argued that the alternative ('two national minds generated under two hostile systems') was a preparation for a 'war of opinions' in which 'crude "industrialism" will prove much stronger than speculative acuteness or profound erudition, as the wants of the body are more craving than those of the spirit'.[70] The national good requires the harmonious development and maintenance of systematic learning. But although the health of the social organism depends upon the health of high-level intellectual enterprise, society cannot unaided generate its own intellectual organs. Against the liberal shibboleths of unlimited competition and free trade, the university reformers urged the necessity of institutional protection for those steadying influences without which liberal society would prove ultimately self-destructive.

The provision of minds which see beyond the phenomena, which penetrate into principles where ordinary minds leave off, is an imperative of the idealism which attracts minds as diverse as those of Mill, Pattison, Newman, and T. H. Green. The role of the intellectual, free in proportion as he exercises mental power over his environment, is defined as against those who are held to live at the mercy of sense and history. Coleridge had formulated a number of problems with which his successors still had to cope – even though the concept of influence is here of marginal importance. Pattison, for example, confessed in his *Memoirs* to having been interested in Coleridge as a young man.[71] Despite his return to nominalist rectitude, his educational thought displays elements which can be discussed in the terms in which we discussed Coleridge. Clearly, the transcendent world of reason attracts him. It permits an overlap with John Henry Newman's idea of how philosophy could aid the pastors of the church in rescuing man from 'that fearful subjection to sense which is his ordinary state'.[72] In the asceticism of Pattison's college sermons we glimpse the adoption of the cognitive and moral elite by the university:

Thus to complete education is the profession of a university; here the crown and apex is placed on all previous instruction; all the knowledge we have previously acquired, all that we have been taught of science, art, or accomplishment, has been preliminary, introductory, subordinate. Hitherto the established social and material order in which we find ourselves placed has imposed itself upon our nature. On entering within the sphere of the superior education we are for the first time called upon to exert a force in the opposite direction – a reaction of the human soul against the barrier outside. A reaction – not a rebellion. The understanding and the will remain as before the passive instruments of society and nature. But we become conscious of a personal force, we obtain glimpses of a new world underlying the world of sense, law, and custom; we find ourselves members at once of two worlds, worlds distinct and yet connected, one of which contains the key to the other.[73]

Here are the vestiges of the opposition between the reason – the faculty which permits us to rise above the phenomenal world – and the 'understanding and will which remain . . . the passive instruments of society and nature'. Like Coleridge, Pattison wants to assert the active powers of mind as against an apparently deterministic universe. Earlier in the same sermon, he noted that man 'has an active or creative power, by whatever name we are to call it. Mind is a reagent against society, a personality counteracting organisation, a judgement exercising a dissolving force upon received opinion.'[74] Yet, like Coleridge again, he offers an epistemological theory applicable to 'man' only to convert it into a justification for confining the higher mental activity to an elite whose members alone have the freedom to move between both worlds. When we enter 'within the sphere of the superior education we are *for the first time* called upon to exert a force in the opposite direction – a reaction of the human soul against the barrier outside' (my italics).[75] Those lacking this educational experience are, presumably, trapped at the level of mere understanding, incapable of doing more than responding in an automatic way to the pressures of nature and society which, significantly, have been conflated. Knowledge is progressive – that is the ground on which Pattison distinguishes between education and propaganda – but the active apprehension of laws which marks progressive knowledge and is fundamental to reaction against the social and material order is the prerogative only of the few. In the nature of the case, those few are intellectuals.

The university, it was coming to be said in the nineteenth century, holds the key to that kingdom upon which, as a feature of a dual model for intellectual activity, we have commented so often. The social and material world is painful, divisive, and obtrusive. To dwell there is to live in a state of subjection to bodily and emotional need. To transcend that state and find your way home is the prerogative of the philosopher, the model product of higher education, whose right to extrinsic moral influence rests upon his interior condition. T. H. Green, whom no one could accuse of lack of social conscience, wrote of that

anticipatory anticipation of the world as spiritual which is the privilege of the philosopher, and which he shares with the saint and the poet.... The results of art and science, of religion and law, are all to him 'workings of one mind, features of the same face'; yet are the workings and the features infinite. No longer a servant, but a son, he rules, as over his own house. In it he moves freely, and with that consciousness that comes of freedom.[76]

At the risk of seeming cheap, it seems unavoidable to observe that those who have not (as Green put it) 'ascended the courts of the intelligible world' remain servants – often in all too literal a sense. The correlative of the contemplative serenity of the few is that, for the many, social forms (which are to be transcended rather than altered) will remain inescapably alien.

A road through despair was mapped out for the knower. Pattison, like many other highly-literate Victorians, spoke of the fearful pressures of all there was to be known; the ramifying sciences, history, the 'whole train of social evils and necessities loudly calling for aid and cure'. The finite understanding, he went on, 'is crushed when it is brought into the presence of the infinite expanse of the knowable, and turns aside in despair'. Yet at this point the learner

becomes conscious of a force within himself; he feels the stirring of an innate power unknown before. His position with regard to things without, to other men, is from this moment altered. His intelligence is not only the passive recipient of forms from without, a mere mirror in which the increasing crowd of images confuse and threaten to obliterate each other; it becomes active and throws itself out upon phenomena with a native force, combining or analysing them – anyhow altering them, reducing them, subjecting them, imposing itself upon them. *Vivida vis animi pervicit*; it has broken the bonds which held it captive, the spiritual principle within is born; we begin to live with a life which is above nature. The point of time in our mental progress at which this change takes place cannot be precisely marked; it is a result gradually reached, as every higher form of life is developed by insensible transition out of a lower. As physical life passes into psychical life by a succession of steps in which there is no break, so does psychical life into spiritual. This is the life that the higher education aspires to promote, this is the power which it cherishes and cultivates, this is the faculty to which it appeals.[77]

As Sparrow, who quotes this passage, notes, this appears to be the vision that sustained Pattison throughout his life. It is a fact of considerable significance for this study that such a theory of the intellectual life – defined at each point as against the passive subjection to phenomena – should be current during the early period of the modern university. For to make the pure intellectual life the paradigmatic mode of escape from an oppressive reality is to identify society with nature in its operations upon the rest of mankind, and hence (directly or indirectly) to assert the impossibility of seriously changing a society whose alien nature is taken for granted. A Pauline intimation of an elite existing within an unregenerate world is near the surface. The 'greater part of mankind', said Pattison as he spoke on his deathbed of the philosopher's vision,

have no mind, or circumstances have not developed it. Yet the whole of this ideal order of intellect is only a scaffolding on which is built up the grand conception of the universe as a totality governed by fixed laws. The true slavery is that of the 'doers' to the free idle philosopher who lives not to do, or enjoy, but to know.[78]

The fatal distinction between knowing and doing (and, we might add, between knowing and enjoying) is one to which theorists of the clerisy seem typically prone. Needless to say, this ideological inheritance was not without implications for the modern university.

The distinction between two types of intellectual experience has worked itself out in a number of ways, and in my diagnosis of it I have made selective use of the work in educational sociology of Basil Bernstein and his followers.[79] High prestige has been assigned to certain forms of knowledge (both at the level of content and that of the manner in which they are learned) which are regarded as pure, that is as relatively insulated from the pressures of social history and as relatively independent of the subjective experience of the student. Low prestige is correspondingly accorded to impure forms of knowledge – those pertaining to day-to-day life and the organic and economic processes which sustain it. Learning (with a capital L) has thus been typically dissociated from learning (with a small l), and esoteric forms of learning cherished at the expense of a recognition that learning is a general human need. In the university, two types of consequence can be observed. One concerns curriculum. Because purity was at a premium, strong boundaries (homologous with the boundaries between subject matter and social world) were set up between disciplines. In such terms we can, I believe, explain a paradox which I have not had space to study here – that the specialised honours system was instituted and developed as standard equipment in the very period when liberal education (which empha- sised the acquisition of method rather than of content) enjoyed high favour. Henceforward each new subject had to present its credentials of purity and intellectual rigour before being officially accepted as a discipline; obviously 'impure' subjects, such as sociology had (and in places still have) to battle their way in to the university in the teeth of sustained resistance. Next, of course, attempts to establish inter-disciplinary courses still have to face entrenched opposition on the part of the supporters of specialised honours – this at a time when at the level of research many traditional boundaries are being abandoned as untenable. To mix subjects at first degree level can be seen as a sign of low intellectual status, a fact to which the 'pass' and 'ordinary' degrees of the older universities bear melancholy witness.

The second type of consequence concerns the propagation of an esoteric image of the university. Since learning and the higher func- tions of intellect come to be associated with specific institutions, those institutions should be insulated as far as practicable from the society around them. This tendency to appropriate the values of objectivity, detachment, and a degree of seclusion from socialisation for the university entails emphasis on the internal student, who is in a position to be immersed in the values and conditions of the univer- sity. Hence the practical restriction of university students to the limited age and experience group of those culturally and econom- ically prepared to attend full time. Correspondingly, a situation in which most people have no time, opportunity, or inducement for study was taken for granted. Only the few, ran the theory, could achieve the kind of intellectual activity for the advancement of which the university stood. Therefore it was perfectly reasonable that only a few should be offered the chance to try; and the method by which those few were selected need not be too closely scrutinised. The organisation of knowledge paralleled and reinforced the strati- fication of society.

Valuable as was the exposure of the social and cultural limitations of liberalism to which the proponents of the clerisy contributed, it had serious disadvantages. Perhaps because it identified democracy and liberalism, its insistence upon the simultaneously cultural and social importance of community and of history branded the intellectual activity of the many as subjective, dependent and inconsiderable. Thus, in offering intellectuals an existential justification in terms of overcoming alienation through sustained intellectual activity, it contributed to a distinctive and questionable ideology for the university.

7

EPILOGUE:]
CULTURAL STUDIES WITHOUT A
CLERISY

We have now examined some of the arguments proposed in the nineteenth century in favour of the existence of an intellectual elite. By the end of that century, the role both of the conscious intellect and of the *pouvoir spirituel* was having to be re-defined so as to adapt to changing ideas about the nature and limitations of mental activity – ideas that made comprehensive claims inescapably anomalous – and to adapt, moreover, in the context of increasingly blatant change in the social and symbolic systems. I shall not restate my arguments here. Yet the whole of this book has been undertaken under the conviction that the theory of the clerisy is still a living issue, and that in various ways it still underlies much of our thinking about culture and education.

To have even a portion of ... illuminative reason and true philosophy is the highest state to which nature can aspire, in the way of intellect; it puts the mind above the influences of chance and necessity, above anxiety, suspense, unsettlement, and superstition, which is the lot of the many. ... But the intellect, which has been disciplined to the perfection of its powers, which knows, and thinks while it knows, which has learned to leaven the dense mass of facts and events with the elastic force of reason, such an intellect cannot be partial, cannot be exclusive, cannot be impetuous, cannot be at a loss, cannot but be patient, collected, and majestically calm, because it discerns the end in every beginning, the origin in every end, the law in every interruption, the limit in each delay; because it ever knows where it stands, and how its path lies from one point to another. It is the τετράγωνος of the Peripatetic, and the 'nil admirari' of the Stoic, –

> Felix qui potuit rerum cognoscere causas,
> Atque metus omnes, et inexorabile fatum
> Subjecit pedibus, strepitumque Acherontis avari.[1]

The argument of Newman's *Idea of a University* rested, of course, upon another and even grander vision: that of a universe whose essential order was given, and whose meaning was interfused among all the details of life. But to re-read this central claim and to be aware (even remotely) of its appeal, is to recognise that it behoves those of us who are professionally engaged in the study and interpretation of culture to bring to the level of conscious criticism a tradition that has helped to shape so many of the available ideas about our role. And, as I shall suggest, the status of that tradition does not merely concern the elite or would-be elite, but bears upon the manner in which, as a society, we institutionalise our culture and education.

The theory of the clerisy, I have argued, rested upon epistemological foundations. Now, systematic abstract thought (the kind of activity usually ascribed to 'thinkers') is a more or less sophisticated and highly verbalised version of the conceptual and rational activity that characterises the human race. Part of my argument will concern the disadvantages of treating the former as though it were different in kind – as though indeed it could exist at all without the latter. *Homo faber* and *homo sapiens*, as Gramsci, following Marx, pointed out, are one and the same animal. The importance of the 'higher' activity has been taken for granted (at least by those engaged in it) for millennia. Substantive philosophy provided and in many ways still provides the model for a cultural mode interacting with the general social discourse. Enormous claims have been made for its formative value in the world; and, even in an era when it had become clear that the various departments of a now divided philosophy could not render up general lessons about the conduct of life, its practitioners continued to find in its pursuit solace for the wearying and dispiriting experience of living in the world. Elaborate conceptual activity has even been believed to put the thinker in touch with the realm of ideas, of spirit, of the really real – with truth, in other words, not provisional, relative, and embattled, but certain and unchanging. Philosophers have been valued accordingly. On the other hand, the pedagogy of the philosopher has had its critics. Max Stirner, the anarchist theoretician, anticipated by some years Nietzsche's criticism of the 'ascetic priest', and spoke for a whole tradition whose values confront the idealist and pedagogic ethic:

He who lives for a great idea, a good cause, a doctrine, a system, a lofty calling, may not let any worldly lusts, any self-seeking interest spring up in him. Here we have the concept of *clericalism*, or, as it may be called in its pedagogic activity, schoolmasterliness; for the idealists play the schoolmaster over us. The clergyman is especially called to live to the idea and work for the idea, the truly good cause. . . .

Here we come upon the old, old craze of the world, which has not yet learned to do without clericalism – that to live and work *for an idea* is man's calling, and according to the faithfulness of its fulfillment his *human* worth is measured.[2]

What is the role of the ideal which Stirner rejects? What needs does systematised theoretical knowledge answer? On the social plane, organised abstraction can (we do not know whether it necessarily does) minister to hierarchy. It helps to allay the fear of change, of the loss of the identity either of the self or of the perceived world. For the threat of dissolution can be acceptably projected upon society as a collapse of boundaries accompanied by loss of meaning. Philosophy has, however, traditionally offered a context of meaning, and it is not difficult to see in this guarantee of orderly significance the extension of a normal human procedure. In his study of perception in relation to the visual arts, E. H. Gombrich describes the principle of 'constancy'. Our perceptions of reality are formed, he claims in an argument which I have found extremely valuable, by repeated matching of the input of undifferentiated sense data against our acquired schema. 'Constancy' is the principle by which we intuit the identity of an object however differently it may appear to us from minute to minute, or from one viewpoint to another. If we are to see at all, this is clearly an inescapable process. We have to sort out the variable appearances of things, and ascribe continuity of being to the thus discriminated components of the world. Yet it is possible to take this activity further. Gombrich observes that this 'confidence in the stability of things in a changeable world is deeply ingrained in the structure of our language and has formed the basis of man's philosophy. The Aristotelian distinction between "substance" and "accident" is nothing but the codification of this faith in a stable world.'[3] Those who have had time for sustained thought about human cognition have often been dissatisfied with the fickle world of sense data, and hankered after a world of 'real' (i.e. unchanging) qualities upon which to build their comprehension of data. This tendency – sometimes misleadingly referred to as 'Platonist' – may be found wherever we have records of elaborate thought. The necessity of accounting intellectually for the chaotic behaviour of the world's attributes is transmuted into the postulate of a reassuring ideal world whose central characteristic is its unambiguous and objective reality. Impatience with the conditions of materiality could be partially allayed by the demotion of the baser primary needs and relations to an inferior order of reality. Truth would thus emerge not as a provisional or hypothetical attribute of propositions, but as the promise of substantive reality. The flicker of the shadows on the wall of the cave need threaten no longer. The nature of the needs which this strategy meets can easily be felt. Such needs parallel and overlap with needs for coherence and certainty which have traditionally found religious fulfilment. Some words from Peter Berger and Thomas Luckman's *The Social Construction of Reality* are applicable to the social as well as the individual identity:

> By the very nature of socialization, subjective identity is a precarious entity. It is dependent upon the individual's relations with significant others who may change or disappear. . . . The 'sane' apprehension of oneself as possessor of a definite, stable and socially recognized identity is continually threatened by the 'surrealistic' metamorphosis of dream and fantasies, even if it remains relatively consistent in everyday social interaction.[4]

Sanctioned truth plays a part in diminishing the fearful sensual and fantastic elements of living. Nietzsche's analysis of the links between suffering, guilt, and asceticism is apt. As a comparatively succinct source, I quote the peroration from *The Genealogy of Morals*:

> Man, the most courageous animal . . . does not deny suffering *per se*: he wants it, he seeks it out, provided it can be given a meaning. Finally the ascetic idea arose to give it meaning – its only meaning so far. But any meaning is better than none and, in fact, the ascetic ideal has been the best stopgap that ever existed. Suffering has been interpreted, the door to all suicidal nihilism slammed shut. No doubt that interpretation brought new suffering in its wake, deeper, more inward, more poisonous suffering; it placed all suffering under the perspective of *guilt*. . . . All the same, man had saved himself, he had achieved a meaning, he was no longer a leaf in the wind, a plaything of circumstance . . . he was now able to will something. . . . We can no longer conceal from ourselves what exactly it is that this whole process of willing, inspired by the ascetic ideal, signifies – this hatred of humanity, of animality, of inert matter; this loathing of the senses, of reason even; this fear of beauty and happiness; this longing to escape from illusion, change, becoming, death, and from longing itself. It signifies, let us have the courage to face it, a will to nothingness, a revulsion from life, a rebellion against the principal conditions of living.[5]

Such a 'rebellion against the principal conditions of living' has been a recurrent feature of idealist and quasi-idealist philosophies, and has left its mark upon our understanding of culture and culture's agencies. We have built upon an impoverished notion of human life.

The appeal of idealism, in the sense in which I defined it in chapter 1, was that it offered a coherent cosmic and social identity that lightened the burden of history and granted the reflective individual a comprehensible role. As a philosophic disposition it has, I suggested, been likely to find adherents in periods of rapid and perplexing symbolic change. Behind the instability of nineteenth-century society, it could be claimed, lay the world of which the visible world was but the vesture, and of which a few, through their enlarged understandings, could obtain a fleeting apprehension.

Nevertheless, it would plainly be very inadequate to maintain that all abstract thought represented a neurotic need to keep chaos at bay by casting spells upon the world. The value of concentrated and systematic thought is not in serious doubt. I am concerned here with theoretical thought carried to the extreme of being used to justify a scheme which asserts the authoritative nature of highly conceptual and verbal operations at the expense both of the phenomenal world and of less 'intellectual' human behaviour. Periodically we need to remind ourselves that our ideas are provisional only.

A man is rarely content to rest in the wholly implicit. . . . He is driven by a necessary, yet specious passion for structure, a rage of annexation lest the richly implicit escape him along with the moment that contains it. He wants what is now, and wholly true, to be hereafter and forever Truth. And in the pursuit of substantive doctrine he is liable to lose the meaning.[6]

That drive may result in large-scale intellectual organisation of the world; and the promulgation of a system tends to foster thoughts rather than thinking, tends to delude us with the promise of entirely accounting for whatever set of phenomena to which it is applied. Precipitated thinking may constitute an unavoidable moment of our capacity to think at all, but we should remember the solution in which that precipitate was an element.

I suggested earlier that idealism and nostalgia for system is a characteristic of periods when the structures of assumptions and the very paradigms for thought are undergoing radical alteration. But there is a further underlying tendency of all mental operation towards monism, springing from the desire that all should turn out to be fundamentally one. This drive is one moment of the dialectic of thought itself: without the impulse to simplify, to recognise similarities amid difference, to identify one phenomenon with another, or to make one symbol stand for a number of percepts, thought could not exist. My argument is thus faced with a problem both epistemological and, in the broadest sense, political. For the other moment of the dialectic must be a pluralist intention – the recognition of and making adjustment for difference, inconsistency, discontinuity, and the ultimately irreducibly alien nature of the mind's objects. To emphasise and foster such openness is perhaps a prime task of cultural studies at the present time; though it is an openness threatened by constraints grimly present in our institutional structures, forces from whose stature we shall remove no cubits merely by taking thought.

Mental activity is caught in a perpetual paradox. It has as a precondition that the mind should strive to make sense of the non-stop bombardment of stimuli by selecting and editing in a manner compatible with the intuited unity of the self. This activity goes on in the context of socially generated and sustained symbols and meanings. Yet at the same time the mind has implicitly to doubt its own premises, to adapt by continually modifying its own achievements or by changing the screens through which reality is interpreted. It is my case that systematic thought – while developing the orderings upon which so much of our thinking (at least in the study and interpretation of culture) is based – has tended to favour monism, the single rather than the multiple strategy. Thus it has connived at the debasement of the ordinary activities of life (which, I would argue, ought not to be divorced from the intellectual and cultural) by insisting that the alternative to imperial intellectual activity was passive capitulation to an unassimilable world – the lot of animals, or of ordinary human beings, but not of philosophers. Only the few, it has been claimed, can exercise significant intellectual force over their environment. The counter-move is to ask whether omniscience-directed activity *is* the only alternative to being a feather for each wind of circumstance or appetite that blows. The imposing facade of intellectual structure does, it is true, seem to put the threatening actual in perspective, yet, as Schiller noted, the speculative spirit is itself impoverished by lack of contact with the practical.

There is, however, another, more relaxed notion of order, a version of which is discussed by Anton Ehrenzweig in *The Hidden Order of Art*, a seminal discussion of modern art in relation to psychiatry. Here order is seen as emerging from creative activity, and I shall risk extracting a 'lesson' germane to my argument. It is that by culture and training most of us are too apt to dread the possibly overwhelming effect of the resurgence of undifferentiated material; to be afraid of the 'primary process' of our psyche, preferring that it be strictly controlled and ordered by the 'secondary process'. The greater our unwillingness to relax, to risk engagement in possibly dangerous give and take (whether with others, with our unconscious, or, like artists, with our material) – in a word, the more anxious we are – the less are we capable of creativity in the broadest sense.[7] One hallowed consequence of the fear of breakdown has been the drive towards a conceptual system and towards the ideas associated with the clerisy argument, many of which have been inherited by our cultural studies. A clerisy represents a kind of social secondary process, a bulwark against symbolic collapse. It maintains strong boundaries and a clearly defined status system between the different kinds of potential knowledge; and, like its analogue, it implies that the modification of its structures is equivalent to total breakdown. A clerisy affirms the validity of institutions that maintain strong boundaries and status differences, and would assert its control by despising those forces which it cannot entirely dominate or write off. Contempt is an all-too-frequent, and by no means incidental aspect of would-be intellectual establishments.

We have commented previously both on the ambivalence of the clerisy theorists towards poetry and on their neglect of the non-verbal arts. It seems possible that this ambivalence is connected with a suspicion of the fantasy in which all art has its springs. The parallel between the psyche and society is quite explicit in Plato's discussion of the poets. Both poet and painter are accused of producing works which are at two removes from reality. Further, the poet, like the painter, appeals to that part of the mind which it is the wise man's task to subordinate:

We are therefore quite right to refuse to admit him to a properly run state, because he stirs up and encourages and strengthens the lower elements in the mind at the expense of reason, which is like giving power and political control to the worst elements in the state and ruining the better elements.[8]

So the work associated with the intellectual elite is to a large extent that of ensuring the dominance of the higher elements of the mind so as to avert the collapse of boundaries and consequent irruption of pre-rational or fantasy elements. Thus it is supposed to guarantee the continuity of rational society. When in 1866 Pater wrote his essay on Coleridge, he found the thought of his own day to be characterised by what he called the 'relative spirit', and saw Coleridge's commitment to the 'absolute spirit' as something of an admirable anachronism.[9] Yet we might question Pater's suggestion that ancient philosophy is distinguished by the fact that it 'sought to arrest every object in an eternal formula' and so to lead the world back to primordial unity. The tendency has, in one form or another been perennial, and we need not go as far as a Coleridge or a Schelling to look for it. In a complicated world of social, political, and symbolic pluralism, monism (whether at the everyday or the elaborate level) retains its consolatory function.

What is the relevance to culture of the constellation of ideas that I have been observing – to culture in the traditional sense, though with some reference to the anthropologists' uses of the word? I hope to suggest why I regard the form of cultural criticism derived from the nineteenth-century clerisy tradition as inadequate. The idea of culture, then, of the body of cultivating influences that typically emerged from the clerisy argument, was one that both emphasised the normative aspect of culture, and attempted to isolate the cultural work from its context of cultural and social activity. In this tradition, culture, it is true, is not identified with works – for it consists of an inward condition – but it rests upon and is defined by a canon of works. The achievements of contemporary society can be judged in the light of the timeless canon, and 'great' works are typically praised for their very separateness from ordinary human activity. The beautiful – as in Kant's aesthetics – is an object of delight apart from any interest: that is, it provokes delight that involves no reference to the suspect faculties of feeling and desire. Freedom, in the idealist tradition, consists of liberation from the claims of feeling, and thus the act of aesthetic appreciation (one important stage in that liberation) becomes the model for all intellectual operation. Kant's thought-provoking account of the imagination arises within the dialectic generated by a model of the mind in which the intellectual part is regarded as separate from and superior to the passionate part – a model which (though still from an idealist standpoint) Schiller made a brave attempt to rebuild in the *Letters on the Aesthetic Education of Mankind*. But the idealist tradition resisted his efforts, and persisted in asserting the dichotomy between form (which has to do with the moral realm) and content (which has to do with the historical world of appetite and need) to the detriment of the latter. The clerisy, we have seen, is required to codify consciousness. Its philosophical and literary base is the canon of great works. The accompanying mental set reads literature for 'truths', and ascribes transcendent value to doctrines excised from their literary and historical contexts. Further, at the level of curriculum, the drive to insulate culture from history leads to the erection of strong boundaries between 'subjects', separating, say, the study of literature from that of social history or sociology – boundaries that in the universities we are only now, and with considerable difficulty, learning to cross. Sometimes one such purified subject is asserted by its practitioners as the definitive mode of cultural or critical discourse.

The desire to make of culture a surrogate religion, and to offer its products as generically endowed with transcendent importance, colours attitudes towards past, present, and future. When looking back, it not only tends to diminish the alien, unassimilable aspects of the past, but also fuels the impulse to endow discrimination with absolute rightness in selecting from the mass of available materials certain works to be approved as 'greats'. Not that the value for certain purposes of some sort of selective canon in philosophy and the arts is in doubt. But I would question the sectarian intolerance of selection that puts its preferences beyond the reach of argument. In the end, rigorous insistence on the superiority of the selected work does service neither to culture at large, nor to the chosen work, which is required to bear the burden of moral consistency and didactic weight traditionally demanded of gospels. Attention to thinking as a social activity, and to 'everything that passes for "knowledge" in society' characterises the new intellectual history and the new sociology of knowledge.[10] Translated into cultural studies, such an approach could – while not denying the educational value of distinguished texts – enrich our understanding of cultural matters, and would certainly represent a shift away from the clerisy model.

In wishing to question the validity of a normative philosophic and literary culture, I am not denigrating the well-wrought, or ejecting Shakespeare and Aeschylus in favour of doing your own thing. Rather I am suggesting that 'great' works should not be accorded unquestioned superiority of the kind parodied in the institution of 'set books', an institution with roots in a conception of the 'great' which came to the fore in the nineteenth century. In his account of the 1966 Dartmouth Seminar on the teaching of English, John Dixon quotes one speaker as saying

It is through ... talk that children can best find out in exchange with one another what are their responses to an experience, real or symbolic, and help one another to come to terms with it. ... Works of literature enter this talk as voices contributing to the conversation, and the talk in its turn provides a context for literature, which helps the children to take in what the voices have to say.[11]

And when commenting on this passage, Patrick Creber in *Lost for Words,* his book on the role of language teaching in combating educational failure, remarks that the teacher has to 'set up a situation into which the literary voice can enter without interrupting or drowning the rest of the conversation'.[12] We might with advantage learn to look on outstanding cultural works as 'voices contributing' to (and arising from) ongoing social dialogue. This is not to reduce them to the level of mere chattiness, but to replace them in their context of human strivings after shared meanings. The psychologist Denys Harding contrasts 'respect' and 'deference' as two modes of human attitude towards others.[13] The tendency of contemporary culture is to command (or seek to command) deference rather than respect, and so entrenched is deference with its attendant snobberies and inhibitions in our social life, that to change this emphasis would be no easy matter. But those who study and teach cultural subjects could make a small beginning by weaning themselves from the residual assumption (cheering as it is) that they are the agents and mediators of a homogeneous realm of superior wisdom.

The cultivation of catholicity as to what constitutes culture also requires us to see culture as a process. In connection with existing works, this entails the recognition that their interaction with life is continued and varied; also that man's relationship to his creation is not unambiguous. And if culture is not to be seen as an autonomous body of definitive wisdom, but a continued making and re-making, then every one is in some sense (and not necessarily deliberately) engaged in it. For it is meaningful to say of individual works that they are re-created in each seeing, reading, or performance. Even more so is it meaningful of the symbolic world at large. Our object could be the 'homo significans' which Roland Barthes describes as the new man of structuralist research. For structuralism, he claims, is a mode of thought 'that seeks less to assign fulfilled meanings to the objects which it discovers, than to understand how meaning is possible. ... In the end we could say that the object of structuralism is not man in possession of meanings, but man as the maker of meanings.'[14] Even high culture relies for its maintained significance upon the generality of human symbolising activity. This in itself would be reason enough for its practitioners to pay more attention to that less specific, more pervasive process.

I have been talking about one aspect of a culture of deference – a set of cultural norms and works to which, it could be implied in the nineteenth century at least, other symbolic activity was inferior. In attitudes towards the present, too, the constellation of ideas associated with the clerisy argument suggests the erection of boundaries not only between the subjects of the curriculum but also between 'culture' and what ordinarily goes on in society. There is therefore a tendency to welcome the product rather than the process by which the product emerges, or by which its significance is sustained. Gutenberg technology, McLuhan tells us, has reinforced this tendency towards reification, towards treating cultural objects as though they could exist independently of human action. His argument deserves to be taken seriously, but at the same time technology itself cannot altogether account for the uses to which it is put. A long while ago, Buber alerted us to the dangers of detaching 'creativity' from our experience of creativity in living situations, which he called 'immediacy'. Detached from immediacy, creativity, he argued, turned into 'productivity' – was channelled, that is to say, into product. Thus we risk a situation in which no experience or perception can be valued for itself, but only in so far as it contributes to or can be used to attain some other good.[15] This variety of insight has, of course, an important nineteenth-century tradition behind it, to which Marx's Paris writings made a significant contribution. As the earliest and most explicit source for Marx's theory of alienation (itself the subject of considerable commentary), the so-called 1844 Manuscripts have played a formative part in the making of this book. In them, cultural and economic life is treated as an interconnected set of relations intimately linked to human needs and potentials. Thus human symbolising activity is not arbitrarily to be dissociated from the economic and biological modes. Hence, in turn, the prevailing organisation of society can be related to that society's culture in the narrower sense. Empirically, Marx's critique still has much to say to us today. For, he argues, our social organisation offers us false goals. Through the division of labour and the institution of private property it has insisted that we channel our capacities for making into limited, productive ends. Nor is it the factory worker alone who is trapped in this way: we all surround ourselves with things and chain ourselves physically and mentally to their maintenance. We become largely incapable of valuing anything – least of all our own energies – for any purpose except a limited usefulness, and consequently stultify our own potential to 'appropriate our being in a manifold way'.[16] Without going into detail, it is clear that here there is a provocative account of the constraints our social state places upon our imagination. The relevance to my general argument is, I think, clear. For, to accord with clerisy theory, culture – which originates in the creative activities of everyone – risks being specialised and objectified in institutional forms to be offered back to society by the guardians as an alienated force.

A related consequence of the arguments for a clerisy-maintained culture is emphasis on the verbal and on the central importance of literacy. This is a precondition of faith in the powers of linear argument and in intellectual structure. High verbality seems to be a prerequisite of the arguments for a clerisy, and theorists of the intellectual elite have been notably reticent about music, and dismissive at times of dancing and the visual arts. Within the intellectual hierarchy, not only non-verbal modes of communication, but also varieties of experience that cannot be or can be only tangentially verbalised are tacitly demoted to an inferior position. Book learning is accepted as the paradigm for all learning, and a familiar pattern of exclusion emerges. The rational coherence represented by verbal (and above all, written) language, with its persuasive powers and its capacity for storage, is invoked to distance the shifting and anxiety-generating world of sense. The further transition to essentialism appears rather like a case of large-scale sour grapes – if the world denies us the satisfaction and stability to which we feel ourselves entitled, we will despise it, and set up an ideal world in its stead. Given the aspects of language that foster essentialism, it is easy enough to see how it comes to be believed that written words can transmit exactly what is thought, or that all significant modes of individual or social experience can be adequately and without remainder characterised in words. The longing for an ideal (and that is to say stable) symbolic organisation tends to sanction anything that looks like an authoritative interpretation of reality. And the normative culture proposed as a result of this desire is to command not respect (as one mode of human enrichment among others), but deference as the definitive model for symbolic construction.

Education, the institutional fashion in which culture is transmitted and validated, is clearly crucial in any discussion of the social role of intellectual activity. The set of dispositions that has been the subject of this book has been and still is highly influential in creating the climate of thought about education. Its idealist bent has legitimated – that is, sanctioned and rendered widely acceptable – the compartmentalisation by which education is seen as the preserve of certain specific institutions. To have doubts about this situation is to begin to ask questions of the kind which the American controversialists Paul Goodman, Ivan Illich, John Holt, and others are asking. For the clerisy model organises consciousness on a hierarchical scale, and proposes that the highest achievement of education is the creation of an elite capable of understanding and transmitting the 'higher' forms of knowledge. It operates with the aid of a culture of deference, a symbolic curriculum for which homogeneity and authority are claimed. Thus it helps make current educational patterns and institutions acceptable. Curriculum, discipline, and the layout and timetabling of schools stress certain forms of social and pedagogical relationship. The clerisy theory – modelled as it is upon traditional structures of authority – endorses this insistence. And the model is widely acceptable to teachers for reasons which suggest an intensified version of the argument I have advanced. Faced with the possibility of breakdown into chaos, with the denial of the authority which constitutes your existential life-raft, you cling (understandably enough) to the symbolic relief afforded by the cognitive scale which assures you of your own relative importance. Your trained access to knowledge places you intellectually (and thus, by residual implications which we have already traced, socially and morally) above those whom it is your job to educate. The situation can scarcely encourage humility.

Historically, to be tempted by the clerisy argument has generally been to idealise education and educational institutions, as also to idealise culture, at the cost of ignoring the entanglement of those institutions and that culture with the very social system which in other respects you were drawn to criticise. Thus the authority model and the intellectual value hierarchy affirm another aspect of education. The thrust towards a clerisy, we have seen, involves the willingness not only to structure consciousness (which is, of course, inevitable) but also to claim transcendent truth for whatever structuring the proponent believes in. The importance of those who are not committed to that structure is thereby diminished: they do not appear so real, and what they say partakes of an inferior order of truth compared to those on the inside. Faith in correctness, and narrow criteria of validity thus enter. While the binary system of right versus wrong does not now enjoy quite the supremacy accorded to it in the lower forms of Victorian education, it is still a hardy perennial, and, coupled with a latent positivism that encourages us to look for comprehensive objectivity, sustains our vastly elaborate examination system. The obsessive drive towards rightness (assuming, as it must, that there are significant questions to which, in any but a provisional sense, there can be a right answer) wards off one kind of anxiety (the existential fear of breakdown into an undifferentiated state), but contributes to another (the dread of rejection, of the devaluation of your being consequent upon giving the wrong answer). There is industrial value in being able to exercise selection so simply and cheaply.

The systematised drive towards rightness, towards approved solutions to approved questions, represents the antithesis of creativity. From the immense and steadily growing literature of creativity we might generalise and applaud the spread of the notion that creativity can be defined as that capacity to innovate, to exercise the imagination, which is a general human potential, rather than just the prerogative of a few great creators. Inventiveness can thus be observed and fostered in our relationships, our work, our arrangements for daily living.[17] At the same time, it is obvious that such a broad conception of creativity does not square with the clerisy tradition whose emphasis is likely to be placed on the superior function of the elite and the primacy of spirit over matter. In relation to creative play, the Platonic ambivalence persists: in the *Republic* the artist is seen as a dealer in counterfeits who encourages the perverse and irrational part of the mind. In the *Ion*, on the other hand, he is held to be inspired. But it is not difficult to recognise that the theory of inspiration represents small threat to the model, since it suggests both the existence of a transcendent source for the breath of inspiration, and also that this experience is reserved for a band of choice spirits. Imagination is too much akin to fantasy to meet the whole-hearted approval of those who seek, as a matter of social urgency, rational control in the mind. Better, therefore, that it be restricted to an elite. To succumb to the clerisy temptation and hope for a place among the philosophic guardians will be to connive at the non-recognition of imagination in ordinary human affairs, and at its isolation as a specialised attribute. Correspondingly, the maintenance of society's symbolic life will be seen as a task for experts. There are all sorts of social-historical reasons why our society requires (even if it does not always get) an educational system whose values are those of conformity, deference, specialisation, and the supposedly established order. But a would-be member of the clerisy should be urged to hesitate before endorsing, in the name of the higher order, those values and the operations which realise them. Whether we like it or not, people are continuously engaged in creating and re-creating values and meanings. To assert this is simultaneously to assert the pervasiveness of cultural activity; a form of cultural history and study that ignores this continuous creation of value and meaning and hankers after a metaphysical reference world upon which truth could safely depend, risks (at the very least) its own debilitation.

I began this essay by suggesting that those of us engaged in cultural studies needed to re-evaluate what we were doing, and in particular to ask how far we still depended upon a residual conception of the clerisy. True, the clerisy's supporters have in this country, as in the United States, given up the comprehensive claims that I described earlier. They have given them up partly because the conscious intellect has been publicly forced to amend its claims to psychic hegemony, partly because of the progress of specialisation in their professional activity, partly because of the continued diversification of society. The kind of confidence in the intellectuals' role manifested in Mannheim's *Ideology and Utopia*, with its argument that an economically independent intellectual class could be the agent of disinterested criticism in society, mediating between the forces of reaction and progress, is apt to sound naive today. And similar, though less sociologically defined aspirations enhance for us now the slightly archaic feeling of the socio-cultural proposals of Eliot or Leavis.[18] Yet, as anyone who has worked in a British university knows, the assumption of the unproblematic social validity of the intellectual's role, the self-importance co-existing with supposed enlightenment, is not confined to those who actually publish the clerisy's claims. There is still a good number who would endorse Jacques Barzun's claim that 'intellect is the capitalized and communal form of live intelligence', and go on to bank that capital at the academy.[19]

What implications does the rejection of the clerisy ideal have for those who study and interpret the traditional cultural subjects? Catholicity about subject matter, for one thing. Those whose domain has been letters, for example, would have to become more attentive to the work of social historians and sociologists, and all would need to question the validity of the traditional subject boundaries. Beyond seems to lie an ethic of limitation. At the end of the First World War, Max Weber, confronting the apparently irreconcilable value spheres into which the world was divided, told his audience of Munich students:

Science [i.e. *Wissenschaft*] today is a vocation organized in special disciplines in the service of self-clarification and knowledge of interrelated facts. It is not the gift of grace of seers and prophets dispensing sacred values and revelations, nor does it partake of the contemplation of sages and philosophers about the meaning of the universe.[20]

To renounce the clerisy would be to renounce the dream of a social potency based upon your expertise in the symbolic field. It would be to carry on intellectual operations in a world of painful uncertainty, ambiguity, and mixed motive without the consolation of a purified (because undivided) self or subject. And it would be to substitute what, in a companion lecture, Weber called an 'ethic of responsibility' for an 'ethic of ultimate ends' – even though that stance would permit no definitive view of past, present, and future.

Let me repeat that I am denying the value neither of theoretical or abstract thought, nor of scholarship and learning. Scholars of the highest quality, noted Gramsci, are necessary to every civilisation.[21] The enrichment of our present and our future requires the painstaking investigation and, so far as is possible, the availability of our past. But, since everyone in fact thinks, since everyone plays his part in the ongoing creation of the symbolic world, so professional intellectual activity must – if its practitioners are prepared to forgo their larger claims – learn to accept a limited role, learn to explore continuities rather than erect boundaries, and to object to the devaluation of other types of life and experience implicit in over-emphasising the value of the intellectual. Chronic inattention to basic human activities has frequently been a hallmark of the intellectual class. With this contraction of the boundaries of significance belonged one of the most outstanding features of the liberal tradition as interpreted by the intellectual class in the last century and into the present one: a quality of innocence, an Arnoldian disdain for machinery passing into a comparatively general refusal to consider too curiously its own economic and social position.

The division of labour has in a way been fundamental to the argument pursued in this book. In particular, the supposed or actual division between intellectual and non-intellectual activities has been the result of the existence of an intellectual class. Dissatisfaction with at least some of the results of the division of labour has been voiced since the late eighteenth century, and proponents of the intellectual elite were, we have seen, particularly alarmed about some effects of specialisation. But a qualification is crucial: specialisation of function can be seen either in a social context in terms of classes and their sub-divisions, or, on the other hand, as pertaining to the mind. The campaign against specialisation carried on by the initiates of *Bildung* in Germany, and of 'liberal education' in England, was waged at the intellectual level alone. The practising intellectual could thus be proffered as the type of the undivided, unalienated life – a free man, in a position to oversee and judge between the various specialisms that crowded upon his attention, the harbinger of the patrician detachment that Wilhelm Meister envied in the nobleman. The new road to freedom began in disciplined mental activity. But this aspiration – the key to the intellectual's putative superiority over other, fragmented life forms – contained a fatal flaw. To pursue a praxis as an intellectual is only possible because of the division of labour. It was all too easy to argue that, while specialisation was deplorable at the intellectual level, it was unavoidable at the level of economic work. To know nothing of a science, Madame de Staël observed, but 'that portion of it which individually belongs to us, is to apply the division of labour (inculcated by Smith) to the liberal studies, when it is only adapted to the mechanic arts'.[22] On the assertion that the intellectuals were capable, indeed the sole group capable, of overcoming the effects of this division, rested the right (the obligation even) to guide society. For they alone possessed the freedom to attend to society's true needs. Anyone else spoke merely from a class position.

Because he believed that mental work was the highest, least dependent form of activity, and the intellectual life the highest form of earthly existence, Fichte did not consider the possibility that intellectuals could (like anyone else) be victims of the division of labour. The other thinkers with whom we have been concerned did not attain such a pinnacle of assurance. But they did believe that the divisions of existence and the pressures of partial interest could be transcended at the level of intellect. With their faith in the disinterestedness and freedom of the rational mind, they evaded the suspicion that intellectuals, too, could have sectional interests of their own, or that their interests might not be entirely of their own making. Thus Coleridge appears to believe in the possibility of a clerisy that would not violate the true requirements of cultivation or of the community. Mill does not consider that his ideal intellectual elite could constitute what (in Benthamite vocabulary) they called a 'sinister interest'. Selfishness was, after all, the mark of the unenlightened. That the prescribed intellectual class could be less than disinterested, less than perfectly attuned to its society's needs, is quite overlooked by the tradition. Whether the elite was to act as guardian or opposition, it was to be the agent of needs which no one with sectional interests of his own could justly assess, and the custodian of a form of discourse capable of comprehending and arbitrating between all other forms. After Coleridge, the economics of the intellectual elite were for a long time demoted as a subject of little relevance. Thus the theory of the clerisy, in offering as an ideal that which was furthest removed from organic and economic life, was a good deal less radical, and less of a threat to the existing order, than was sometimes imagined.

I am well aware of the risks undertaken in this attempt to spell out an argument about the nature and status of cultural studies that seems to me to have been implicit in the earlier parts. There is, I acknowledge, a danger amongst others of falling victim to a prevalent orthodoxy in English literary criticism with its theoretical commitment to Dionysian values, its delight in ambivalence and irony, its propensity for finding paradox and dubiety beneath every surface, and its eruptions of Lawrentian disdain for modes of discourse other than the particularity and concreteness of fiction. For one consequence of my argument must surely be a recognition of the irresponsibility of treating any one mode of discourse – be it historical, fictional, anthropological, or structuralist – as definitive. We have to teach (and to learn) the relativity of our terms; to strive after sense – even in an age when data about the physical and social worlds seem to be proliferating with bewildering complexity – and yet resist the temptation of exclusive system. To say this is not to connive at the capitulation which Benda dreaded of the universal and rational in the face of the subjective and romantic. For to grant limited authority to conscious intellect, to deny that it is a faculty that converges with the ideal world, is not to relegate mind to the status of pure reflex of psychological or social reality, but rather to commit oneself to dialogue, and to the formation of theories and concepts not absolute and definitive, but dialectical and in tension. In conclusion I want to emphasise this sense of a sustained and necessary dialectic between forms of discourse, and (both at a personal and a social level) between on one hand the highly rationalised and highly formed and on the other the serial activities of day to day living. As Schiller said in his discussion of the sensuous and formal drives, to watch over the operations of both and

secure for each of these two drives its proper frontiers, is the task of culture, which is, therefore, in duty bound to do justice to both drives equally: not simply to maintain the rational against the sensuous, but the sensuous against the rational too. Hence its business is twofold: first, to preserve the life of Sense against the encroachments of Freedom; and second, to secure the Personality against the forces of Sensation. The former it achieves by developing our capacity for feeling, the latter by developing our capacity for reason.[23]

In this spirit we should denigrate neither theory nor practice. We should recognise and promote the creative interaction of intellect and the greater self, of institutions and persons, words and actions, or written and oral culture. This entails seeing for what it is the sectarian arrogance by which cultural specialists, trusting in their own purity, and convinced of the self-sufficiency of good intentions, could dream of setting themselves up as the mentors and judges of the world.

NOTES

The following abbreviations are used in these notes:

CCS   Samuel Taylor Coleridge, *On the Constitution of the Church and State according to the Idea of Each*, ed. J. C. Barrell (Everyman's Library edn, 1972)

CL   *Collected Letters of Samuel Taylor Coleridge*, ed. E. L. Griggs (6 vols., Oxford, 1956–71)

CPW   Matthew Arnold, *Complete Prose Works*, ed. R. H. Super (Ann Arbor, Michigan, 1961–)

CW   *Collected Works of Samuel Taylor Coleridge*, ed. Kathleen Coburn (Princeton and London, 1969–)

HHW   Thomas Carlyle, *Heroes and Hero Worship* in *Complete Works of Thomas Carlyle*

MCW   *Collected Works of John Stuart Mill* (Toronto, 1963–)

NB   *The Notebooks of Samuel Taylor Coleridge*, ed. Kathleen Coburn (1957–)

Works   *Complete Works of Thomas Carlyle*, ed. H. D. Traill (Centenary edn, 30 vols., 1895–9)

The place of publication is London unless noted otherwise.

Chapter 1. Introduction

1. *Ideology and Utopia* (1936). In brief, Mannheim argued that a 'free-floating' (i.e. economically non-aligned) intelligentsia could remain independent of and hence mediate between the progressive and conservative forces in society. Cf. T. S. Eliot's paper 'On the Place and Function of the Clerisy' in Roger Kojécky, *T. S. Eliot's Social Criticism* (1971), and Kojécky's book, esp. ch. 9. General studies with a bearing on this part are G. B. de Huszar (ed.), *The Intellectuals: a Controversial Portrait* (Glencoe, Illinois, 1960); Philip Rieff (ed.), *On Intellectuals: Theoretical Studies and Case Studies* (Garden City, N.J., 1969); and essays by Edward Shils collected in *The Intellectuals and the Powers* (Chicago, 1972).

2. *From Max Weber*, eds. H. H. Gerth and C. Wright Mills (1948), p. 147. Cf. Mill, writing to Littré of his own candidacy for Parliament: 'si je consentais à y siéger, ce serait pour n'y exercer qu'un pouvoir spirituel', *Letters of John Stuart Mill*, ed. H. Elliot (1910), II, p. 31.

3. *CL*, VI, p. 629. The version in Lucy Watson, *Coleridge at Highgate* (1925) is abbreviated.

4. *NB*, II, entry 2955 (1806).

5. Quoted in C. F. Harrold, *Carlyle and German Thought* (New Haven, 1934), p. 222.

6. *Culture and Anarchy*, *CPW*, V, p. 224.

7. In Mill's essays on 'Genius' (1832) and 'Civilization' (1836).

8. *Exposition de doctrine de Saint-Simon*, eds. C. Bouglé and E. Halévy (Paris, 1924), p. 486.

9. Northrop Frye, 'The Problem of Spiritual Authority in the Nineteenth Century' in *Backgrounds to Victorian Literature*, ed. R. A. Levine (San Francisco, 1967); and cf. H. B. Acton, 'The Idea of a Spiritual Power' (Auguste Comte Memorial Lecture, 1974). Translations from French are mine unless otherwise stated.

10. *Works*, XXV, p. 200.

11. Henry Nelson Coleridge's introduction to the 1839 edn of *CCS*, p. xxviii.

12. *The German Ideology* (Moscow and London, 1965), pp. 60–1.

13. Carl L. Becker, *The Heavenly City of the Eighteenth-Century Philosophers* (New Haven, 1932), ch. 4; cf. Denys Harding on the symbolic support afforded by the sub-group, in *Social Psychology and Individual Values* (revised edn, 1966), **pp. 61–2.**

14. *The Friend*, *CW*, IV, pp. i, 61.

15. 'The Tamworth Reading Room' (1841), in *Discussions and Arguments* (4th edn, 1882), p. 288. Lord Brougham was a founder of the *Edinburgh Review*, a leading politician and educational reformer.

16. *The Note-Books of Matthew Arnold*, eds. H. F. Lowry, K. Young and W. H. Dunn (Oxford, 1952), p. 83. Christian Karl Josias von Bunsen (1791–1860) was a Prussian theologian whose diplomatic employment brought him to England where he met Thomas Arnold.

17. See, for example, Eugene F. Rice, *The Renaissance Idea of Wisdom* (Cambridge, Mass., 1958).

18. *Rambler*, no. 78. My attention was drawn to this passage by Dr Heather Glen.

19. Diary for 1854 in *Letters of John Stuart Mill*, II.

20. See J. D. Culler, *Structuralist Poetics* (1975), ch. 9; cf. Lionel Trilling on narrative, *Sincerity and Authenticity* (1974), pp. 134–9.

21. Introduction to Wilhelm von Humboldt, *The Limits of State Action*, ed. and trans. J. W. Burrow (Cambridge, 1969), p. xxxiv.

22. Acton, 'Spiritual Power', p. 20.

23. T. S. Eliot, 'Arnold and Pater' in *Selected Essays* (*1917–32*), (1932); on secular religions see, for example, W. M. Simon, *European Positivism in the Nineteenth Century* (Ithaca, 1963); D. G. Charlton, *Positivist Thought in France during the Second Empire* (Oxford, 1959), and *Secular Religions in France 1815–70* (Oxford, 1963).

24. *Sartor Resartus, Works*, I, pp. 201–2.

25. 'Réflexions sur l'état des esprits' (1849), *Questions Contemporaines* in *Oeuvres* (10 vols., Paris, 1898), I, p. 219.

26. Review of H. T. Buckle's *History of Civilization in England, Westminster Review*, NS, XII (1857), p. 398.

27. 'George Orwell and the Politics of Truth' in *The Opposing Self* (1955), p. 163.

28. *CPW*, V, p. 255.

29. *The Republic*, trans. H. D. P. Lee (Harmondsworth, 1955), p. 334.

30. *Émile*, eds. F. and P. Richard (Garnier, Paris, 1964), p. 10.

31. I have received valuable help on German thought and thinkers in this period from the following books: W. H. Bruford, *Germany in the Eighteenth Century* (Cambridge, 1935) and *Culture and Society in Classical Weimar 1775–1806* (Cambridge, 1962); Herbert Marcuse, *Reason and Revolution* (revised edn, 1955); G. A. Kelly, *Idealism, Politics and History* (Cambridge, 1969).

32. *De l'Allemagne* (anon. English trans., 3 vols., 1813), I, p. 46.

33. 'State of German Literature' (1827), *Works*, XXVI, 74. Cf. *De l'Allemagne* I, p. xiv; III, pp. 8–9, 31, 73.

34. He was to speak of 'Kantism, or German metaphysics generally' 'Novalis', *Critical and Miscellaneous Essays, Works*, XXVII, pp. 201 *et seq*. Harrold, *Carlyle and German Thought*, is throughout useful on the limitations of Carlyle's German interests.

35. See, for example, René Wellek, *Immanuel Kant in England 1793–1838* (Princeton, 1931); A. O. Lovejoy, *The Reason, the Understanding and Time* (Baltimore, 1961); Harrold, *Carlyle and German Thought*; C. N. G. Orsini, *Coleridge and German Idealism* (Southern Illinois U.P., 1969); Norman Fruman, *Coleridge, the Damaged Archangel* (1971); Donald MacKinnon, 'Coleridge and Kant' in John B. Beer (ed.), *Coleridge's Variety* (1975).

36. *Statesman's Manual, CW*, VI, p. 62. A fascinating commentary by a symbolic anthropologist on the role of body imagery is to be found in Mary Douglas, *Natural Symbols* (2nd edn, 1973), esp. ch. 5.

37. *Characteristics of the Present Age* in J. G. Fichte, *The Popular Works*, trans. William Smith (4th edn, 2 vols., 1889), II, p. 37.

38. Arthur Penrhyn Stanley, *The Life and Correspondence of Thomas Arnold* (10th edn, 2 vols., 1881), I, p. 147.

39. *The New Science*, trans. T. G. Bergin and M. H. Fisch (Ithaca, 1967), p. 64.

40. *Ibid.* p. 414.

41. *The Republic*, p. 251.

42. *Ibid.* p. 255.

43. *Ibid.* p. 262.

44. *Ibid.* pp. 284–5.

45. *Ibid.* p. 245, and see K. R. Popper, *The Open Society and its Enemies* (5th edn, 1966), I, ch. 8.

46. *Present Age, Popular Works*, II, p. 115.

47. Cf. A. O. Lovejoy's discussion of the 'temporalisation of the chain of being' in *The Great Chain of Being* (1960), ch. 8.

48. Quoted in Karl Loewith, *Meaning in History* (Cambridge, 1950), p. 209. The whole book comprises a critical essay from a liberal Protestant standpoint on some of the ideas discussed here.

49. In F. G. Klopstock, *Werke in Einem Band* (Munich, 1954), pp. 233–45.

50. *On the Vocation of a Scholar*, lectures 1, 2 and 3, *Popular Works*, I.

51. *Ibid.* p. 188.

52. *Ibid.* p. 193.

53. *Present Age, Popular Works*, II, p. 5 and lecture 1 in general.

54. *On the Nature of the Scholar, Popular Works*, I, p. 211.

55. *Ibid.* p. 213.

56. *Ibid.* p. 249.

57. *Ibid.* pp. 258–63 and cf. *Present Age, Popular Works*, II, lecture 3.

58. *Present Age, Popular Works*, II, p. 43 and cf. pp. 45–7 on the role of the missionary activities of pious and holy men in the transition from the barbarous to the civilised state.

59. *Wilhelm Meister's Apprenticeship*, trans. Carlyle, Bk v, ch. 3.

60. See, for example, *Present Age, Popular Works*, II, pp. 115, 160.

61. *On University Studies*, trans. E. S. Morgan (Athens, Ohio, 1966), p. 30.

62. *Ibid.* p. 55.

63. *Present Age, Popular Works*, II, p. 282. 'Thoughtlessness' Fichte defined as 'mute and blind surrender of ourselves to the stream of phenomena, without even entertaining the thought of any unity or foundation therein', *ibid.*

64. *Autobiography*, trans. E. Michaelis and H. Keatley Moore (1886), p. 69. Friedrich Froebel (1782–1852) was an educational philosopher, a follower of Pestalozzi, and pioneer of the Kindergarten movement.

65. *Characteristics of Men, Manners, Opinions, Times*, ed. J. M. Robertson (2 vols., 1900), I, p. 193.

66. *On the Aesthetic Education of Man in a series of Letters*, eds. Elizabeth Wilkinson and F. A. Willoughby (Oxford, 1967), p. 19. I have found the introduction to this edition extraordinarily useful. My reading of Schiller (and, indeed, the argument of the book as a whole) owes much to the writings of Herbert Marcuse, whose assessment of the 'explosive quality of Schiller's conception' in the *Aesthetic Letters* will be found in ch. 9 of *Eros and Civilization* (1955 and 1961).

67. Shaftesbury, *Characteristics* I, pp. 182 *et seq.*

68. *Ibid.* p. 201.

69. *Ibid.* p. 202.

70. Quoted in *University Studies*, p. 156.

71. Dated to December 1801; *NB*, I, entry 1072. My attention was drawn to this note by Humphrey House, *Coleridge* (1953), ch. 1.

72. *University Studies*, p. 120.

73. *Ibid.* p. 142.

74. *Religion and the Rise of Modern Science* (Edinburgh, 1972), p. xiii and chs. 2 and 4.
75. E.g. 'Throughout this book it will be shown that as much as the poets had first sensed in the way of vulgar wisdom, the philosophers later understood in the way of esoteric wisdom; so that the former may be said to have been the sense and the latter the intellect of the human race.' *The New Science*, p. 110; cf. Ernst Cassirer, *Language and Myth*, trans. Susanne Langer (1946), chs. 1, 3 and 6.
76. *Critique of Judgement*, trans. J. C. Meredith (Oxford, 1952), p. 127.
77. See 'The Spirit of Philosophy' in *The Complete Works of William Hazlitt*, ed. P. P. Howe (21 vols., 1930–4), xx, pp. 369–76. This aspect of Hazlitt's work has been thoroughly explored by Roy Park in *Hazlitt and the Spirit of the Age* (Oxford, 1971).
78. *Aesthetic Letters*, p. 107; and see Letters 14 and 15 *passim*.
79. *University Studies*, p. 144.
80. *Aesthetic Letters*, p. 217.
81. *Ibid*. Introduction, p. cxxxiii.

Chapter 2. The idea of the clerisy: Samuel Taylor Coleridge

1. *The Friend, CW*, iv, pp. i, 336–7.
2. *CL*, iv, p. 762; and see R. J. White, *Waterloo to Peterloo* (Harmondsworth, 1968), pp. 58–9; *Political Thought of Coleridge*, ed. R. J. White (Cambridge, 1938), p. 210.
3. *CL*, iv, p. 761.
4. *Edmund Burke and the Revolt against the Eighteenth Century* (1929); and cf. David Cameron's *The Social Thought of Rousseau and Burke* (1973) – an effective antidote to some of the glibber generalisations about 'eighteenth-century thought'.
5. *Philosophical Lectures*, ed. Kathleen Coburn (1949), p. 221.
6. *CL*, iv, p. 759.
7. *The Friend, CW*, i, p. 494; see the discussion in Raymond Williams' *Culture and Society* (Harmondsworth, 1963), Introduction and pt 1.
8. *The Friend, CW*, i, p. 494.
9. *CCS*, pp. 33–4.
10. *The Table Talk and Omniana of Samuel Taylor Coleridge*, ed. H. N. Coleridge (1917), *sub* 10 April 1832.
11. *Philosophical Lectures*, p. 166.
12. Letter to Lord Liverpool, *CL*, iv, p. 762; *Philosophical Lectures*, p. 196.
13. *CCS*, p. 41; as John Barrell notes in his introduction, this is a 'remarkable contribution to the theory of political obligation'.
14. In particular, I have gained most from the following: J. H. Muirhead, *Coleridge as Philosopher* (1930); René Wellek, *Immanuel Kant in England 1793–1838* (1931); T. B. McFarland, *Coleridge and the*

Pantheist Tradition (Oxford, 1969); Norman Fruman, *Coleridge, the Damaged Archangel* (1971); Donald MacKinnon, 'Coleridge and Kant' in *Coleridge's Variety*, ed. John B. Beer (1975).

15. Walter Jackson Bate, *Coleridge* (New York, 1968), p. 31.
16. McFarland, *Coleridge*, p. 110.
17. *CL*, IV, p. 778.
18. Cf. *Biographia Literaria*, ed. J. Shawcross (Oxford, 1907), I, p. 100.
19. *CL*, IV, p. 792; cf. *Biographia*, I, p. 101.
20. *CL*, IV, p. 688.
21. *Ibid.* p. 761.
22. *Ibid.* p. 768.
23. *Philosophical Lectures*, p. 264.
24. *CCS*, p. 53.
25. *Friend*, I, p. 441; repeated in *CCS*.
26. See McFarland, *Coleridge*, ch. 3.
27. *The Life of John Sterling* (1851), pp. 69 *et seq.*
28. F. J. A. Hort, 'Coleridge' in *Cambridge Essays contributed by members of the university* (1856).
29. See, for example, R. J. White's introduction to *The Political Tracts of Wordsworth, Coleridge and Shelley* (Cambridge, 1953) or F. R. Leavis in *A Selection from Scrutiny* (Cambridge, 1968), I, pp. 268 *et seq.*
30. *Friend*, I, pp. 520–1.
31. Cf. Introduction to *Second Lay Sermon*; and Owen Barfield, *What Coleridge Thought* (Middletown, Connecticut, 1971), chs. 2 and 4.
32. *NB*, III, entry 3935 (June–July 1810).
33. On Coleridge's ideas of vision (applicable to the social as to the individual organism) see, for example, *Philosophical Lectures*, p. 113; *CCS*, pp. 46–7; and cf. Plato's *Timaeus*, 45, 46.
34. *CCS*, p. 69.
35. *Ibid.* p. 46.
36. *Statesman's Manual* in *Lay Sermons*, ed. R. J. White, *CW*, VI, pp. 678; Coleridge is quoting from *Friend*.
37. See *Friend*, I, p. 156.
38. See *Aids to Reflection* (Bell's 'new edn', 1884), p. 148.
39. *CCS*, p. 46.
40. *Ibid.* p. 47.
41. In 'Coleridge's and Kant's Two Worlds', *Essays in the History of Ideas* (Baltimore, 1948), p. 270.
42. *Republic*, pp. 344–5.
43. For an account, see T. B. McFarland, 'Coleridge's Anxiety' in *Coleridge's Variety*, ed. John B. Beer, pp. 134–65.
44. *Statesman's Manual*, p. 75.
45. *Friend*, I, p. 185.
46. *NB*, II, entry 2598 (1805).
47. *De l'Allemagne* (anon. English trans., 3 vols., 1813), III, pp. 18, 44.

48. MS 'Logic' in Alice D. Snyder, *Coleridge on Logic and Learning* (New Haven, 1929), pp. 126–7.
49. *Ethics*, trans. J. A. K. Thompson (Harmondsworth, 1955), pp. 303–4.
50. McFarland, *Coleridge*, p. 117.
51. *CL*, IV, p. 893; cf. Keats on 'Negative Capability': 'that is, when a man is capable of being in uncertainties, mysteries, doubts, without any irritable searching after fact and reason – Coleridge, for instance, would let go by a fine isolated verisimilitude caught from the Penetralium of mystery, from being incapable of remaining content with half-knowledge. This pursued through volumes would perhaps take us no further than this, that with a great poet the sense of Beauty overcomes every other consideration or rather obliterates all consideration.' *The Letters of John Keats*, ed. H. B. Forman (3rd edn, Oxford, 1947), p. 72.
52. *CL*, IV, p. 585; cf. De Quincey's observation: the 'restless activity of Coleridge's mind in chasing abstract truths, and burying himself in the dark places of human speculation, seemed to me, in a great measure, an attempt to escape out of his own personal wretchedness'. *Recollections of the Lakes and the Lake Poets*, ed. David Wright (Harmondsworth, 1970), p. 55.
53. *CCS*, p. 4.
54. For Coleridge's work on logic see Snyder *On Logic and Learning*, pp. 50–103 and Muirhead, *Coleridge as Philosopher*, ch. 2. Muirhead quotes the MS 'Logic' where Coleridge, working towards the principle of 'trichotomy' in place of the traditional dichotomy, argues that we have (instead of starting with opposing concepts) to 'seek first for the Unity as the only source of Reality, and then for the two opposite yet correspondent forms by which it manifests itself', p. 86.
55. *A Pluralistic Universe* (New York and London, 1909), pp. 113–14.
56. *Friend*, I, p. 61.
57. *Ibid.* I, p. 190.
58. M. Lazerowitz, *The Structure of Metaphysics* (1955), pp. 69–70.
59. *Poetical Works*, ed. E. H. Coleridge (Oxford, 1969), p. 487.
60. *Statesman's Manual*, p. 69.
61. *Biographia*, I, lxxxiii.
62. Lazerowitz, *Metaphysics*, p. 70.
63. White, *Political Tracts*, p. xvi.
64. *CCS*, p. 5.
65. *Statesman's Manual*, pp. 42–3.
66. *Second Lay Sermon*, p. 173.
67. John B. Beer, *Coleridge the Visionary* (1959), p. 39 and ch. 1 generally.
68. *Poetical Works*, pp. 108–25. The relation of 'Religious Musings' to the idea of the clerisy is suggested by Lewis Patton and Peter Mann in their introduction to *Lectures 1795: On Politics and Religion*, *CW*, I, p. xxvi.
69. *Aids to Reflection*, p. 161.

70. *CL*, I, pp. 296–7.
71. *Friend*, I, pp. 61–2.
72. *CCS*, pp. 36–7.
73. *CL*, IV, p. 714.
74. *Statesman's Manual*, p. 42.
75. As in 'Essays on the Principles of Method', *Friend*, I, pp. 448 *et seq.*
76. *Autobiography*, p. 70; see ch. 1 of this book.
77. *Friend*, I, p. 500.
78. *CL*, VI, p. 628; cf. Schelling, *On University Studies* (1802), trans. E. S. Morgan (Athens, Ohio, 1966), pp. 10–11.
79. *CL*, III, p. 414.
80. *Statesman's Manual*, p. 41.
81. *Friend*, I, p. 540.
82. Reprinted in *Friend*, I, p. 335.
83. *CCS*, p. 43.
84. *Second Lay Sermon*, p. 217; *CCS*, p. 59.
85. *CCS*, p. 53; cf. *Friend*, I, p. 447.
86. *Statesman's Manual*, p. 38; cf. Coleridge's strictures on the reading public and the 'eruditulorum natio' in *Biographia*, I, pp. 34–5; *Statesman's Manual*, pp. 36–8.
87. *Statesman's Manual*, pp. 39–40.
88. *Ibid.* p. 7. The source of Coleridge's quotation is untraced, and he may have made it up.
89. Ed. Lewis Patton (*CW*, II), p. 4. Largely capitalised in the original. As the rest of the Prospectus suggests, we are also charting here a shift in the meaning Coleridge attaches to the word 'freedom'.
90. *CL*, I, p. 277.
91. *CCS*, p. 29.
92. *Biographia*, I, p. 154.
93. *Ibid.*, I, pp. 155–6; *CCS*, pp. 59–61.
94. See the epigraph to the ninth essay in the revised *Friend*, which was taken from Erasmus' letters: 'Hoc potissimum pacto felicem ac magnum regem se fore judicans: non si quam plurimis sed si quam optimis imperit. Proinde parum esse putat justis praesidiis regnum suum muniisse, nisi idem viris eruditione juxta ac vitae integritate praecellentibus ditet atque honestet. Nimirum intelligit haec demum esse vera regni decora, has veras opes: hanc veram et nullis unquam seculis cessuram gloriam' (*Friend*, I, p. 251).
95. *Philosophical Lectures*, p. 201; cf. *Biographia*, II, 31, 40.
96. Literary Lectures, 1818, in *Literary Remains*, ed. H. N. Coleridge (4 vols., 1836), I, pp. 238–9. This is the earliest occasion known to me on which Coleridge makes use of this word, though he is obviously near it in adverting to the *clerum* to which the *Statesman's Manual* was addressed in 1816 (*Statesman's Manual*, p. 36).
97. *Anima Poetae* (1895), p. 228. I have been unable to trace this in *NB*.
98. *CCS*, p. 98.

99. *CL*, IV, pp. 51, 455; Snyder, *On Logic and Learning*, pp. 7–8; R. F. Brinkley, *Coleridge on the Seventeenth Century* (New York, 1968), gives the text of a manuscript note (unfortunately undatable) on Donne's sermons (*Literary Remains*, III, pp. 119–20; Brinkley, pp. 181–2) in which Coleridge exclaims over the consequences of conflating the Christian with the national church, and actually uses the word 'clerisy'. When Kathleen Coburn's edition of the *NB* reaches the 1820s it will undoubtedly provide much information on the development of the argument of *CCS*.

100. *Coleridge, the Damaged Archangel* – to judge at least by the paucity of his references to that work.

101. *Table Talk*, pp. 167, 214.

102. *CL*, IV, p. 711.

103. *CCS*, p. 91.

104. *Ibid.* pp. 16, 22, and ch. 2 in general; cf. *Philosophical Lectures*, pp. 86–7.

105. *Second Lay Sermon*, p. 169.

106. *Ibid.* pp. 173–4.

107. *CCS*, p. 70.

108. *Ibid.* ch. 5, which, with ch. 6, contains the central account of the national church, and on which the following account is based.

109. Respectively 'Fears in Solitude' and 'France, an Ode', *Poetical Works*, pp. 256, 243.

110. MacKinnon, 'Coleridge and Kant', p. 198.

111. *Biographia*, I, p. 194; Beer, *Coleridge the Visionary*, ch. 9.

112. *Biographia*, I, pp. 95–6; Fruman, *Coleridge, the Damaged Archangel*, p. 81.

Chapter 3. The hero as man of letters: Thomas Carlyle

1. R. H. Horne, *The New Spirit of the Age* (2 vols., 1844), II.

2. My account of Carlyle's exploration of himself and his role owes much to A. J. LaValley's *Carlyle and the Idea of the Modern* (New Haven, 1968).

3. *HHW*, p. 78.

4. See, for instance, the description of Abbot Samson in *Past and Present*, *Works*, X, p. 92.

5. *HHW*, p. 1.

6. See W. H. Bruford, 'The Idea of "Bildung" in Wilhelm von Humboldt's Letters' in *The Era of Goethe: Essays Presented to James Boyd* (Oxford, 1959); cf. ch. 1 of this book.

7. *Wilhelm Meister's Apprenticeship*, *Works*, XXIII, pp. 76–7. There is a suggestive criticism of Carlyle's silence-equals-health doctrine in Sterling's essay 'On the Writings of Thomas Carlyle', reprinted in *Essays and Tales*, ed. J. C. Hare (2 vols., 1848), I, pp. 252–381.

8. *Correspondence between Goethe and Carlyle*, ed. C. E. Norton (1887), p. 279.
9. See, for example, W. H. Bruford, 'Goethe and some Victorian Humanists', *Publications of the English Goethe Society*, NS, XVIII (1949); or the opening of G. H. Lewes's *Life and Works of Goethe* (1855).
10. *Correspondence*, p. 7. Goethe's role in Carlyle's spiritual crisis of 1824 is played down by W. Witte in his essay 'Carlyle's Conversion' in *The Era of Goethe*.
11. *Correspondence*, pp. 34–5.
12. Edward Caird, 'The Genius of Carlyle' (1892), reprinted in *Essays in Literature and Philosophy* (2 vols., Glasgow, 1892), I, p. 267. A wealth of evidence on Carlyle's impression on his contemporaries is now to be found in J. P. Seigel, *Thomas Carlyle, the Critical Heritage* (1971).
13. *The Life of John Sterling* (1851), p. 344. LaValley excels on the subject of Carlyle's development of a 'totalitarian self', but I cannot agree that in *Sterling* Carlyle, having by then 'explored the futility of the heroic strain', turned towards a 'more realistic assessment of the role of selfhood in the modern world'. *Carlyle and the Idea of the Modern*, p. 235 and see pt 3 generally.
14. *Sybil* (1926), p. 431.
15. *Arthur Coningsby* (1967), p. 396.
16. See, for example, Kingsley's introductions to the first and revised edns of *Alton Locke*.
17. J. A. Froude, *Thomas Carlyle: a History of his Life in London* (1902), I, p. 316. Cf. George Eliot's testimony (1855) that 'there is hardly a superior or active mind of this generation that has not been modified by Carlyle's writings; there has hardly been an English book written for the past ten or twelve years that would not have been different if Carlyle had not lived.' *Leader*, VI, pp. 1034–5.
18. *Sterling*, p. 57.
19. *Sterling*, p. 50.
20. *Sterling*, p. 80; see Graham Hough, 'Coleridge and the Victorians' in *The English Mind*, ed. H. S. Davies and George G. Watson (Cambridge, 1964), pp. 185–6; Robert Preyer, *Bentham, Coleridge and the Science of History* in *Beiträge zur Englischen Philologie*, XLI (1958).
21. *Sterling*, p. 126.
22. 'Boswell's Life of Johnson' (1832), *Works*, XXVIII, p. 119.
23. *Life of Friedrich Schiller* (1825) in *Works*, XXV, p. 157.
24. *Works*, XXVII, p. 75.
25. E.g., *Sartor Resartus* in *Works*, I, p. 31; *HHW*, p. 165.
26. *Wotton Reinfred* in *Last Words of Thomas Carlyle* (1892), p. 21.
27. *Sartor*, pp. 142–5. See J. L. Halliday's methodologically dubious but highly suggestive *Mr Carlyle, My Patient* (1949), pp. 69–72.
28. 'The State of German Literature' (1827), *Works*, XXVI, p. 83.
29. *Wotton Reinfred*, p. 62.

30. 'Novalis' (1829), *Works*, XXVII, p. 27.
31. *Schiller*, p. 43.
32. *Ibid.* p. 41.
33. *Ibid.* pp. 200–1.
34. 'Death of Goethe' (1832), *Works*, XXVII, p. 377.
35. *Correspondence*, p. 163.
36. *HHW*, p. 114.
37. 'Historic Survey of German Poetry' (1831), *Works*, XXVII, pp. 369–70.
38. See, for example, the poem 'Ecce Homo' in the 'Prelude in Rhymes' to *The Gay Science*. Nietzsche's view of Carlyle was, however, scarcely complimentary – see aphorism 97 of *The Gay Science* where he refers to a 'garrulousness due to an inner pleasure in noise and confused emotions: for example, in Carlyle', (trans. Kaufmann, p. 150).
39. *HHW*, pp. 1–2.
40. *Past and Present*, p. 92.
41. *Ibid.* p. 69. Cf. Leslie Stephen's *Cornhill* obituary: 'Carlyle's life would serve for a better comment than even his writings upon his title, "the hero as man of letters",' Seigel, *Carlyle, the Critical Heritage*, p. 481.
42. *Past and Present*, p. 92.
43. *Ibid.* p. 34.
44. *Sterling*, p. 285.
45. Quoted by Froude in *Carlyle in London*, II, p. 441.
46. *Ibid.* II, pp. 284 *et seq.*
47. *Ibid.* I, p. 102.
48. 'Characteristics' (1831), *Works*, XXVIII, p. 16, 23–4.
49. *Latter-Day Pamphlets* (1850), *Works*, XX, p. 191.
50. *HHW*, pp. 1–2.
51. To Emerson, *The Correspondence of Emerson and Carlyle*, ed. Joseph Slater (New York, 1964), p. 105.
52. 'Shooting Niagara' (1867), *Works*, XXX, p. 24.
53. *Sterling*, p. 221.
54. Leszek Kolakowski, 'The Priest and the Jester' in *Marxism and Beyond* (1971), p. 44.
55. 'Death of Goethe', p. 377, and again in *HHW*, pp. 80–1. The seer could detect what Carlyle, following Goethe, liked to call *das offenbare Geheimnis*, the 'open secret' of the universe.
56. 'Novalis', p. 41.
57. *HHW*, p. 80. There is clearly an affinity with Arnold's repeated description of the role of criticism being to 'see the object as in itself it really is'.
58. *HHW*, p. 157; cf. pt I, ch. 2, pp. 35–7.
59. *HHW*, p. 162.
60. *Ibid.*
61. *HHW*, p. 171.

62. *Sartor*, p. 127.
63. *HHW*, p. 168.
64. *HHW*, p. 166.
65. As, for example, in 'Shooting Niagara'.
66. *HHW*, p. 152.
67. *Marxism and Beyond*, pp. 55–6; see also Ralf Dahrendorf, 'The Intellectual and Society: the Social Function of the Fool in the Twentieth Century' in Philip Rieff (ed.), *On Intellectuals: Theoretical Studies and Case Studies* (Garden City, N.J., 1969). H. B. Acton, *The Idea of a Spiritual Power* (1974), finds the concept distasteful.
68. *Schiller*, p. 44.
69. *Ibid.* p. 195.
70. *Sartor*, p. 150.
71. *Ibid.* pp. 153–4.
72. *Characteristics of the Present Age* in *The Popular Works*, trans. William Smith (4th edn, 2 vols., 1889), pp. 43, 58 and lectures 3 and 4 in general.
73. *Sartor*, pp. 153–4.
74. See C. F. Harrold, *Carlyle and German Thought* (New Haven, 1934), pp. 82 *et seq.*
75. *HHW*, pp. 91–2.
76. *Sartor*, p. 156.
77. Eugene Goodheart, *The Cult of the Ego* (Chicago, 1968), p. 80.
78. 'Novalis', p. 35.
79. Goodheart, *The Cult of the Ego*, pp. 86–7, and cf. p. 74.
80. 'Characteristics', p. 16; cf. L. L. Whyte, *The Unconscious Before Freud* (1962), esp. pp. 115–29 and 131–52.
81. *HHW*, p. 2. Cf. 'Intellect, the power man has of knowing and believing, is now nearly synonymous with Logic, or the mere power of arranging and communicating.' ('Signs of the Times', p. 74.) In this region of his thinking, Carlyle is once again very close to Nietzsche and other exponents of what John Carroll has in his book (*Break-Out from the Crystal Palace*, 1974) called the 'anarcho-psychological critique' of classical liberal rationality. Carlyle's sceptical anti-nomianism was, however, to be resolved in an authoritarian direction.
82. *HHW*, pp. 2–3.
83. 'Characteristics', p. 22.
84. *HHW*, pp. 106–7.
85. 'Curious, I say, and not sufficiently considered: how everything does cooperate with all; not a leaf rotting on the highway but is indissoluble portion of solar and stellar systems; no thought, word or act of man but has sprung withal out of all men, and works sooner or later, recognisably or unrecognisably, on all men!' *HHW*, p. 102.
86. John Ruskin, *Time and Tide by Wear and Tyne, Works*, ed. E. T. Cook and A. D. O. Wedderburn (39 vols., 1903–12), XVII, p. 376, and cf. p. 415. Some of Ruskin's ideas on spiritual hierarchy may be

gathered from *Time and Tide* chs. 13, 22 and 25, or *Sesame and Lilies*, pt 2.

87. Cf. the cases of Mill and of Sterling. Evidence for Carlyle's relations with other intellectuals may be found in Froude, *The First Forty Years*, in M. St. J. Packe's *Life of John Stuart Mill* (1954), in Emery Neff's *Carlyle and Mill* (New York, 1926), and in Hill Shine's *Carlyle and the Saint-Simonians* (Baltimore, 1941).

88. Froude, *Carlyle in London*, ii, p. 469.

89. 'Shooting Niagara', pp. 39, 41. My italics.

90. In Emerson's *Complete Works* (Bohn's Standard Library edn, 2 vols., 1879), ii, p. 174–89.

91. In formulating this point I have been helped by D. W. Harding, *Social Psychology and Individual Values* (revised edn, 1966), e.g. pp. 109, 164.

Chapter 4. The majority and the remnant: Matthew Arnold

1. See Kathleen Tillotson, 'Matthew Arnold and Carlyle' in *Mid-Victorian Studies* (1965); D. J. DeLaura, 'Arnold and Carlyle', Publications of the Modern Language Association, lxxix (1964).

2. 'The Bishop and the Philosopher', *CPW*, iii, pp. 43–4.

3. Frederic Harrison, 'Culture, a Dialogue', *Fortnightly Review*, NS, ii (1867).

4. *Letters of Matthew Arnold 1848–88*, ed. G. W. E. Russell (2 vols., 1895), i, p. 280.

5. *Literature and Dogma, CPW*, vi, p. 332.

6. *Ibid.* p. 189; cf. for example, the argument of ch. 3 of *Culture and Anarchy, CPW*, v.

7. *Five Uncollected Essays*, ed. Kenneth Allott (Liverpool, 1953), p. 2.

8. His only explicit reference to Coleridge's idea of a national church is in 'The Bishop and the Philosopher', where he called it a 'beautiful theory' – *CPW*, iii, p. 51.

9. 'Numbers; or The Majority and the Remnant' in *Discourses in America* (1885), pp. 2–3. On Arnold's reception in America, see J. H. Raleigh, *Matthew Arnold and American Culture* (Berkeley and Los Angeles, 1957).

10. 'Numbers', p. 6.

11. *Ibid.*

12. *Parochial and Plain Sermons* (8 vols., 1899), iii, p. 256; for the influence of Newman on Arnold see D. J. DeLaura, *Hebrew and Hellene in Victorian England* (Austin, Texas, 1969), esp. ch. 9.

13. 'Numbers', p. 8.

14. *Ibid.* p. 71.

15. *Ibid.* pp 7–8.

16. *Ibid.* p. 10.

17. 'Numbers', pp. 15 *et seq.*
18. *Ibid.* p. 17.
19. *Ibid.*
20. *Ibid.* pp. 24–5.
21. *Ibid.* p. 27.
22. *Ibid.* p. 30.
23. *Ibid.* pp. 30–1.
24. On the implications of Arnold's style see John Holloway, *The Victorian Sage* (1953), ch. 7.
25. 'Numbers', p. 56.
26. *Ibid.*
27. *Ibid.* p. 64.
28. *Ibid.* p. 63.
29. *Ibid.* p. 66.
30. *Letters*, I, p. 115.
31. 'Numbers', p. 67.
32. *Ibid.* p. 68.
33. Cf. Seymour Lipset's remark, 'I have considered as intellectuals all those who create, distribute, and apply *culture*, that is the symbolic world of man, including art, science, and religion.' (*Political Man*, 1960, p. 311.)
34. *Democracy in America*, trans. George Lawrence (2 vols., 1968), I, p. 10. My italics.
35. 'The Prophet of Culture' (1867) reprinted in *Miscellaneous Essays and Addresses* (1904), p. 58.
36. 'Equality' in *Mixed Essays* (1879) (Popular edn, 1903), p. 70.
37. *CPW*, IV, p. 5; and see p. 109 of this book.
38. See, for instance, the glowing account of Burke's work in Arnold's *Academy* review of Renan's *La Réforme intéllectuelle et morale CPW*, VII, pp. 40–1.
39. Arthur Penrhyn Stanley, *The Life and Correspondence of Thomas Arnold* (hereafter Stanley) (10th edn, 2 vols., 1881), I, p. 94.
40. The affinities between Rousseau and Burke are the subject of David Cameron's recent book, *The Social Thought of Rousseau and Burke* (1973).
41. *Culture and Anarchy*, *CPW*, V, p. 122.
42. *CPW*, IV, p. 5 (Arnold's italics). Quoted by Coleridge in *CCS*, pp. 84–5.
43. Cf. Lionel Trilling, *Matthew Arnold* (1963), pp. 280–7.
44. Stanley, I, p. 228.
45. *Ibid.*
46. *Democracy in America*, I, pp. 5, 9.
47. 'Democracy', *CPW*, II, pp. 7–11.
48. Stanley, *Whether States, like Individuals, after a certain period of Maturity, inevitably tend to Decay* (Oxford, 1840), p. 25.
49. *Literature and Dogma*, *CPW*, VI, p. 332.

50. *God and the Bible, CPW*, vii, p. 229.
51. *The Note-Books of Matthew Arnold*, ed. H. F. Lowry, K. Young and W. H. Dunn (Oxford, 1952), pp. 84, 107.
52. Trilling, *Matthew Arnold*, p. 342.
53. *Literature and Dogma, CPW*, vi, p. 294.
54. *Politics*, trans. Jowett, introd. by H. W. C. Davies (Oxford, 1959), p. 33.
55. Stanley, i, p. 194.
56. *Introductory Lectures on Modern History* (1845), p. 10.
57. *Ibid.* p. 13.
58. *Note-Books*, p. 83.
59. Stanley, i, p. 119.
60. *Miscellaneous Works* (1845), p. 108.
61. *Ibid.*
62. In *Miscellaneous Works*, pp. 226–35. On the class terminology, see Asa Briggs, 'Middle Class Consciousness in English Politics', *Past and Present* (1956).
63. 'Equality', pp. 94–5.
64. *Essays in Criticism, CPW*, iii, pp. 109–10.
65. *Questions Contemporaines* (1868) in *Oeuvres Complètes* (10 vols., Paris, 1899), i, p. 214. My trans.
66. 'Democracy', p. 18.
67. *Ed.* P. E. Charvet, *La Réforme intéllectuelle et morale* (Cambridge, 1950), p. 46.
68. *Note-Books*, pp. 481–2.
69. 'Civilisation in the United States', *Five Uncollected Essays*, p. 64.
70. 'Emerson' in *Discourses in America* (1885), p. 145.
71. 'Civilisation in the United States', p. 48.
72. *Ibid.*, pp. 53–4.
73. *Letters*, ii, p. 346.
74. 'Civilisation in the United States', p. 3.
75. *Ibid.* p. 64.
76. 'The Literary Influence of Academies' in *Essays in Criticism*, pp. 232–57.
77. *An Appeal from the New to the Old Whigs* in *Burke's Works and Correspondence* (8 vols., 1852), iv, p. 466.
78. 'Equality', p. 89.
79. Preface to *Poems* (1853).
80. *Parochial and Plain Sermons*, iii, p. 266.
81. *CPW*, v, p. 224; cf. E. Alexander, *Matthew Arnold and John Stuart Mill* (1965), esp. ch. 2.
82. 'Democracy', p. 6.
83. *Ibid.* p. 25.
84. 'Equality', pp. 69–70.
85. Cf. Newman – of 'real cultivation of mind, I do not deny that the characteristic excellencies of the gentleman are included in it', in the

preface to *The Idea of a University Defined and Illustrated*, ed. I. T. Ker (Oxford, 1976).
86. 'Equality', pp. 59–60.
87. *North America* (2 vols., 1862), I, p. 413. Coleridge used a version of this phrase when proposing the educational role of the national church – *CCS*, p. 85. It comes from Ovid's *Epistolae ex Ponto*, II, ix.
88. 'Equality', p. 68.
89. *Ibid.*
90. *Ibid.* pp. 89–90.
91. *Plays, Prose Writings and Poems* (1930), p. 60.
92. *Essays in Criticism*, 2nd series is not yet complete in the *CPW*. Some references are therefore given to the Everyman's Library edn, here p. 301. For a contrasting conception of culture as embodying tragic contradiction, see Georg Simmel's 'Der Begriff und die Tragödie der Kultur' in *Philosophische Kultur* (Leipzig, 1911), pp. 245–77.
93. *Essays in Criticism*, 2nd series, p. 303.
94. Annotations to Boyd's *Dante* (written *c.* 1800?), *Complete Writings*, ed. Geoffrey Keynes (Oxford, 1969), p. 412.
95. 'Milton', *Essays in Criticism*, 2nd series, p. 262.
96. 'The Study of Poetry', *Essays in Criticism*, 2nd series, p. 237.
97. *Culture and Anarchy*, p. 97.
98. *Ibid.* p. 111.
99. 'The Prophet of Culture', p. 55.
100. *Note-Books*, p. 26.
101. *CPW*, III, p. 54.
102. *Note-Books*, p. 238.
103. *CPW*, III, p. 275.
104. *Ibid.* p. 274.
105. *Culture and Anarchy*, pp. 147–50.
106. *Ibid.* p. 150.
107. *Schools and Universities on the Continent*, *CPW*, IV, p. 252.
108. *Culture and Anarchy*, p. 146. The alien from the populace sounds rather like Felix Holt.
109. *Culture and Anarchy*, p. 228.
110. *Essays in Criticism*, p. 12.
111. *Essays in Criticism*, 2nd series, p. 381.
112. *Causeries du lundi*, trans. E. J. Trechmann (nd), I, p. 298.
113. *Culture and Anarchy*, p. 119.
114. *Ibid.* p. 117.
115. Stanley, II, pp. 233–4. My attention was drawn to this passage by Robert Preyer, *Bentham, Coleridge and the Science of History* in *Beiträge zur Englischen Philologie*, XLI (1958) 47.
116. *Culture and Anarchy*, pp. 133 *et seq.*
117. *Schools and Universities*, p. 305.
118. *Ibid.* pp. 34–5.
119. *Ibid.* pp. 314–15.

120. *Ibid.* pp. 29–30.
121. *Ibid.* p. 147.
122. *Ibid.* p. 182.
123. *Culture and Anarchy*, p. 149.
124. *Ibid.* pp. 243–4. Cf. Thomas Arnold's 'Principles of Church Reform'.
125. *Criticism*, p. 235. My italics.
126. *Ibid.*
127. *Parochial and Plain Sermons*, III, p. 286.
128. *Culture and Anarchy*, p. 149. Once again, Arnold is very close to Newman in his attack on liberalism. Thus, in connection with the Gorham case when the civil authority had intervened to decide on a point of doctrine, Newman had written with bitter irony: 'May not the free-born, self-dependent, animal mind of the Englishman, choose his religion for himself? ... are we to obtrude the mysteries of an objective, of a dogmatic, of a revealed system, upon a nation which ultimately feels and has established, that each individual is to be his own judge in truth and falsehood in matters of the unseen world?' *Certain Difficulties felt by Anglicans in Catholic Teaching Considered* (1850) (2 vols., 1888), I, p. 24.
129. *Questions Contemporaines*, p. 213.
130. Thomas Arnold, too, sometimes approached this position. See his letter on the July 1830 Revolution in Paris, where he speaks of a 'royal rebellion against society, promptly and energetically suppressed'. (Stanley, I, p. 235.)
131. *Culture and Anarchy*, p. 223. My italics. For an analogous transition on the part of liberal intellectuals during the Home Rule crisis, see John P. C. Roach, 'Liberalism and the Victorian Intelligentsia', *Cambridge Historical Journal*, XIII (1957). That the 'view of the intellectual as a "natural" dissenter is to a large extent an optical illusion, produced by the greater visibility of dissenting intellectuals' is argued by Ralph Miliband in his *State in Capitalist Society* (1969), p. 260; and see ch. 8 generally.

Chapter 5. The reconstruction of opinion: John Stuart Mill

1. *Mill and Liberalism* (Cambridge, 1963), esp. p. 105 *et seq.* Cf. the accounts of Mill by R. J. White in 'John Stuart Mill', *Cambridge Journal*, V (1951), and by Shirley R. Letwin in *The Pursuit of Certainty* (Cambridge, 1965), pt 3.
2. *Autobiography* (World's Classics, 1924), p. 138; 'Guizot', *Dissertations and Discussions* (2 vols., 1859), II, p. 218. The *Autobiography* should be checked against *The Early Draft of John Stuart Mill's Autobiography*, ed. J. Stillinger (Urbana, Illinois, 1961) which contains valuable material on Mill's relationship with Comte.
3. *Autobiography*, p. 91.

4. Third thesis against Feuerbach.
5. See Eli Halévy, *The Growth of Philosophic Radicalism*, trans. M. Morris (1928), pt 1, ch. 3; pt 2, ch. 1.
6. *Introduction to the Principles of Morals and Legislation*, ed. W. Harrison (Oxford, 1948), p. 126.
7. *Mill on Bentham and Coleridge*, ed. F. R. Leavis (1950), p. 121.
8. *Utilitarianism, MCW*, x, p. 233.
9. *On the Aesthetic Education of Man in a series of Letters*, eds. Elizabeth Wilkinson and F. A. Willoughby (Oxford, 1965), p. 119.
10. *Early Draft*, p. 171 and cf. *Autobiography*, p. 194.
11. See essay on 'Nature' in *Three Essays on Religion, MCW*, x.
12. *Letters of John Stuart Mill*, ed. H. Elliot (2 vols., 1910), I, p. 15.
13. 'Considérations sur le pouvoir spirituel' (1826), reprinted in *Système de Politique Positive* (4 vols., Paris, 1851–4), IV, p. 205.
14. *System of Logic* (4th edn, 1861), II, p. 516.
15. See W. H. Bruford, 'The Idea of "Bildung", in Wilhelm von Humboldt's Letters' in *The Era of Goethe: Essays Presented to James Boyd* (Oxford, 1959).
16. *Letters*, I, p. 47; M. St. J. Packe, *Life of John Stuart Mill* (1954).
17. *The Spirit of the Age*, ed. F. A. Hayek (Chicago, 1942), pp. 35–6.
18. See, for example, Edward Lytton Bulwer's *England and the English* (1833), ed. Standish Meacham (Chicago and London, 1970), p. 319.
19. *On Liberty* (Everyman's Library edn, 1910), pp. 127–8.
20. *Spirit of the Age*, p. 16.
21. *Ibid.* pp. 25–6.
22. *Ibid.* p. 31.
23. *Ibid.* p. 19.
24. *Ibid.* p. 21. I have here found three books particularly useful: F. A. Hayek, *The Counter-Revolution in Science* (Glencoe, Illinois, 1955); Leszek Kolakowski, *Positivist Philosophy*, trans. Norbert Guterman (Harmondsworth, 1972), and Jürgen Habermas, *Knowledge and Human Interests*, trans. Jeremy J. Shapiro (1972).
25. *Early Draft*, pp. 188–9.
26. *Earlier Letters 1812–48*, ed. F. E. Mineka, *MCW*, XIII, p. 574.
27. *Spirit of the Age*, pp. 61–2.
28. *Ibid.* p. 76.
29. *Ibid.* p. 78.
30. *Ibid.* pp. 92–3.
31. *Autobiography*, chs. 4 and 6. A thorough account of the political activities of the philosophic radicals is to be found in J. Hamburger, *Intellectuals in Politics* (New Haven, 1965).
32. *Earlier Letters*, XII, pp. 91–2.
33. *Ibid.* p. 108.
34. *Dissertations and Discussions*, I, p. 192.
35. *Logic*, II, p. 515; and cf. *MCW*, VIII, pp. 925–6 which lists only minor variants.

36. 'Plan des travaux scientifiques nécessaires pour réorganiser la société', reprinted in *Système de Politique Positive*, IV, pp. 47–136.
37. *Cours de Philosophie Positive* (6 vols., Paris, 1830–42), IV, p. 648.
38. *Ibid.* IV, p. 221 n.
39. In 'Considérations sur le pouvoir spirituel', Comte argued that the critical epoch had had its day, and that the proper task facing the spiritual power was the government of opinion, and the establishment and maintenance of the principles which ought to regulate social relationships.
40. Eds. M. and F. Hincker (Paris, 1966), pp. 90–1, 206.
41. Ed. P. Van Tieghem (Paris, 1959), p. 374.
42. *Earlier Letters*, XIII, pp. 563–4.
43. Cf. M. H. Abrams, *The Mirror and the Lamp* (Oxford paperback, New York, 1971), pp. 23 *et seq.*, 320–2.
44. Diary, in *Letters*, II, Appendix A, *sub* 11 April.
45. *Ibid. sub* 27 January.
46. Comte availed himself of a model for intellectual operations that looks curiously Kantian. Thus in the *Cours* we read: 'In the true system of human economy, individual or social, the aesthetic faculties are in some fashion intermediaries between the purely moral faculties and the intellectual faculties proper.' They thus played a part in education. But – perhaps needless to say – in the education of the individual as of the race, 'the ultimate aim is so far as possible to transfer the decisive influence to the reason, not to the imagination', *Cours*, V, pp. 148, 150.
47. *Earlier Letters*, XII, 76.
48. *Ibid.* XII, 38–43.
49. *Ibid.*
50. See W. O. Chadwick, *The Victorian Church* (1966), I, pts 1 and 2. On the subject of the pamphleteers I am indebted to Mr Peter Moore.
51. *Earlier Letters*, XI, p. 221.
52. *Dissertations and Discussions*, I, p. 2; Graeme Duncan, ch. 8 of whose study *Marx and Mill* (Cambridge, 1973) contains a balanced account of Mill's elite, does not consider this essay.
53. *Ibid.* p. 12.
54. *Ibid.* p. 28.
55. *Ibid.*
56. *Ibid.* p. 31.
57. *Ibid.* p. 38.
58. *Bentham and Coleridge*, p. 148.
59. *London Review*, I (1835) 258.
60. *Ibid.* p. 293.
61. *On Bentham and Coleridge*, ed. F. R. Leavis (1950), p. 88; see I. W. Mueller, *John Stuart Mill and French Thought* (Urbana, Illinois, 1956), chs. 5 and 6.
62. *Earlier Letters*, XIII, p. 434; the stagnation of Chinese society was

more or less proverbial in nineteenth-century thought, and instances of its currency can be found in the works of thinkers as diverse as Condorcet and Nietzsche.

63. *Dissertations and Discussions*, I, p. 188.
64. In *Mill's Essays on Literature and Society*, ed. J. B. Schneewind (New York, 1965), p. 362.
65. *Dissertations and Discussions*, I, p. 200.
66. *Dissertations and Discussions*, I, pp. 95–9; Sedgwick's *Discourse* had been published in 1834. As an expansion of an address given at Trinity, it was aimed especially at an undergraduate audience, and concerned the growth in tandem of the intellectual and moral powers. The study of the laws of nature, of ancient literature, and of 'ourselves as individuals and as social beings' all conduced to this dual development.
67. *Dissertations and Discussions*, II, pp. 62 *et seq.*
68. *Ibid.* p. 71.
69. *Exposition de doctrine de Saint-Simon* in *Collection des economistes et reformateurs Français*, eds. C. Bouglé and E. Halévy (Paris, 1924), p. 210.
70. *Letters*, I, p. 20.
71. *Bentham and Coleridge*, p. 140.
72. *Ibid.* p. 104. My italics.
73. *Ibid.* p. 140.
74. *Autobiography*, pp. 140–1.
75. *Earlier Letters*, XII, pp. 40–1.
76. *Letters*, II, pp. 252–3.
77. See *The Triumph of Time: a Study of the Victorian Concepts of Time, History, Progress and Decadence* (Cambridge, Mass., 1966), ch. 2.
78. *Cours*, V, p. 328.
79. *Ibid.* pp. 432–3.
80. *Cours*, V, pp. 351–4.
81. *Ibid.* pp. 198–9.
82. *Ibid.* p. 474.
83. *Earlier Letters*, XIII, pp. 501–4.
84. *Cours*, V, p. 285.
85. *Ibid.* p. 321.
86. *Lettres inédites de John Stuart Mill à August Comte publiées avec les réponses de Comte*, ed. L. Lévy-Bruhl (Paris, 1899), p. 35.
87. *Earlier Letters*, XIII, p. 508.
88. Mueller, *Mill and French Thought*, pp. 105 *et seq.*; W. M. Simon, *European Positivism in the Nineteenth Century* (Ithaca, 1963), pp. 172–201.
89. *Comte and Positivism, MCW*, X, pp. 316–17.
90. *Ibid.* pp. 309, 314.
91. *Ibid.* p. 314.

92. *Liberty, Equality, Fraternity* (1873), ed. R. J. White (Cambridge, 1967), pp. 123 *et seq.*

93. *Dissertations and Discussions*, II, pp. 237–8.

94. *On Liberty*, p. 110; cf. p. 105.

95. Duncan, *Marx and Mill*, p. 276.

96. *Comte and Positivism, MCW*, X, pp. 314–15.

97. *Ibid.* pp. 334–5. There is a useful discussion of the Religion of Humanity in its historical context in D. G. Charlton, *Secular Religions in France 1815–70* (Oxford, 1963).

98. *Representative Government* (Everyman's Library edn, 1910), pp. 267–268.

99. Mueller, *Mill and French Thought*, p. 251.

100. *Letters*, II, pp. 202–3.

101. *Liberty*, p. 111.

102. *Ibid.*

103. *Autobiography*, p. 215.

104. *Liberty*, p. 117.

105. *Ibid.* p. 119.

106. *Ibid.* p. 130.

107. *Representative Government*, p. 265.

108. *Ibid.* p. 268.

109. *Ibid.*

110. *The English Constitution* (1867) (Fontana Library, edn, 1963), p. 247; cf. the introduction, by R. H. S. Crossman to this edn, pp. 5–10.

111. *Representative Government*, p. 288.

112. *Ibid.* pp. 288–9.

113. *Earlier Letters*, XII, p. 37.

114. *Representative Government*, p. 289.

115. *Letters*, II, p. 223.

Chapter 6. The idea of a university

1. *Principles of Political Economy* (1848), Bk V, xi, para. 15. Cf. his friend, Alexander Bain's review 'Of a Liberal Education in General' (*Westminster Review* XLIX, 1848), pp. 141–63 which represents another contribution to the mounting pressure on the government to take steps to reform the universities. There Bain argues that we are 'reckless of the progress of civilization' in leaving science (i.e. systematic knowledge) to take care of itself, and that next to 'the maintenance of the peace and good order of society, the government is bound to support an instrumentality of progress, or to see that there exists in full efficiency a staff of scientific explorers, with all the requisite aids and furtherances.'

2. *Collected Essays* (9 vols., 1894), III, pp. 239, 261.

3. 'A Liberal Education and Where to Find It' (1868), *Collected Essays*, III, p. 105.

4. Jowett's introduction to the *Republic*, in his edn of Plato's *Dialogues* (3rd edn, Oxford, 1892), III, pp. lxxxviii–lxxxix.

5. 'On the Classification and Framing of Educational Knowledge' (1971), reprinted in *Class, Codes and Control* (3 vols., 1975), III, pp. 97–8.

6. Northrop Frye, 'The Problem of Spiritual Authority in the Nineteenth Century' in *Backgrounds to Victorian Literature*, ed. R. A. Levine (San Francisco, 1967).

7. V. A. Huber, *The English Universities*, ed. and trans. by Francis Newman (2 vols., 1843), II, p. 348.

8. For information about Francis Newman and his career, see W. Robbins, *The Newman Brothers* (1966).

9. Preface to *The English Universities*, pp. ix–x.

10. *Ibid.* pp. xi–xii.

11. As late as 1870 it was possible for J. R. Seeley, then just appointed as Kingsley's successor to the Regius Chair of History at Cambridge, to call on the clergy to act as the spiritual power of the nation. The terms plainly parallel the arguments on behalf of the intellectual estate. 'Besides the general duty of proclaiming political first principles, there seems to be a more special function belonging to the clergy. Taken indifferently from all classes, and addressing assemblies composed indifferently from all classes, they are the natural mediators in the perpetual warfare between class and class. . . . Nothing can be more plainly written in the New Testament than the mission of the Church to reconcile all such differences, to pull down all barriers, and to establish unity among men. No institution would seem better adapted to forward this perpetual process of reconciliation than the institution of a clergy. An order of men taken from all the warring classes, and removed, as it were, from the arena of conflict, expected to have intercourse with the poor and admitted to intercourse with the rich, enabled to hear both sides of the controversy, highly educated, so as to form an intelligent opinion, not dependent (that is, where the Church is well ordered) on the favour of either side, and provided with frequent opportunities of addressing both sides together, – such an order should do much to remove the principal cause of discord between classes – which is ignorance of each other's interests and feelings, – and they should be able to pronounce with more authority p. 278). See also C. R. Sanders, *Coleridge and the Broad Church Movement* (Durham, North Carolina, 1942), esp. chs. 4–10; W. Owen Chadwick, 'Charles Kingsley at Cambridge' (*Historical Journal*, XVIII.2 (1975) 303–25).

12. Cf. Sheldon Rothblatt, *The Revolution of the Dons: Cambridge and Society in Victorian England* (1968), esp. ch. 6; Arthur Engel, 'The

Emerging Concept of the Academic Profession at Oxford 1800–1854' in Lawrence Stone (ed.), *The University in Society* (2 vols., 1975), I, pp. 305–51.

13. 'Evidence', *Report of Her Majesty's Commissioners appointed to inquire into the State, Discipline, Studies and Revenues of the University and Colleges of Oxford* (1852), p. 212.

14. *CPW*, IV, p. 330.

15. See, for example, W. C. Perry, *German University Education* (2nd edn, 1846); Newman's translation of Huber, *English Universities*; Arnold's *Schools and Universities on the Continent* (1868); Pattison's *Suggestions on Academical Organisation* (Edinburgh, 1868).

16. The Cambridge Union was founded in 1815. On intellectual societies in the universities some information may be gathered from A. and E. M. Sidgwick, *Henry Sidgwick, a Memoir* (1906), pp. 33 *et seq.*; Carlyle, *Life of Sterling* (1851), ch. 4; Hallam Tennyson, *Alfred Lord Tennyson, a Memoir* in *The Life and Works* (12 vols., 1898–9), I, chs. 2 and 3; Sanders, *Coleridge and the Broad Church Movement*, chs. 5 and 7; David Newsome, *Godliness and Good Learning* (1961), pp. 1–10.

17. Arthur Penrhyn Stanley, *The Life and Correspondence of Thomas Arnold* (10th edn, 2 vols., 1881), I, p. 37.

18. *The Correspondence of Arthur Hugh Clough*, ed. F. L. Mulhauser (2 vols., Oxford, 1957), I, p. 38. Liddell and Scott give 'self-sufficiency' and 'independence' as equivalents for the Stoic quality of αὐταρκεῖα.

19. *Ibid.* p. 49.

20. Mill, *Political Economy*.

21. My account of the older universities is largely owing to W. R. Ward, *Victorian Oxford* (1965); D. A. Winstanley, *Early Victorian Cambridge* (Cambridge, 1955) and *Later Victorian Cambridge* (Cambridge, 1947); Rothblatt, *Revolution of the Dons*; and E. G. W. Bill, *University Reform in Nineteenth-Century Oxford; a Study of Henry Halford Vaughan* (Oxford, 1973).

22. *The Idea of a University Defined and Illustrated*, ed. I. T. Ker (Oxford, 1976), p. 5.

23. 'The Grading of Secondary Schools' (1877) in T. H. Green, *Works*, ed. R. L. Nettleship (3 vols., Oxford, 1885), III, pp. 409–10. Cf. R. C. Jebb on the subject of university extension: the universities should desire to be 'mother-cities of intellectual colonies, and to spread the influence of their teaching throughout the land'. *The Work of the Universities for the Nation, Past and Present* (Cambridge, 1893), p. 2; on university extension and the history of the extra-mural movement see J. F. C. Harrison, *Learning and Living* (1961).

24. F. W. Farrar (ed.), *Essays on a Liberal Education* (1867), p. 78.

25. Huxley, 'A Liberal Education and Where to Find It', 'Science and Culture', 'On the Educational Value of the Natural History Sciences' and 'Address on University Education', all in *Collected Essays*, III; cf.

The Oxford English Dictionary, s.v. 'liberal' (adj.) 1; Aristotle, *Ethics*, trans. J. A. K. Thomson, pp. 303–9.

26. *Sermons* (1885), p. 72.
27. Attribution from *Wellesley Index of Victorian Periodicals*, I. On Sydney Smith see Leslie Stephen's article in the *Dictionary of National Biography*.
28. *Edinburgh Review*, xv.29 (October, 1809) 51.
29. *A Reply to the Calumnies of the Edinburgh Review against Oxford* (Oxford, 1810), pp. 105–6.
30. *Ibid*. p. 107–8.
31. *Ibid*. p. 111.
32. *Ibid*. pp. 111–12.
33. *Ibid*. pp. 170–1.
34. *Idea of a University*, pp. 146–53.
35. *Ibid*. pp. 120–1.
36. *Ibid*. p. 186.
37. 'Newman and Education', *Cambridge Journal*, IV (1951) 660–78.
38. 'The Tamworth Reading Room' (1841), reprinted in *Discussions and Arguments* (4th edn, 1882). Newman noted, incidentally, that Brougham had borrowed the Christian idea of 'an aristocracy of exalted spirits' for his 'new Pantheon' (p. 288).
39. *Idea of a University*, p. 185.
40. Peter A. Dale, 'Newman's *The Idea of a University*: the Dangers of a University Education', *Victorian Studies*, XVI.1 (1972).
41. 'Inaugural Address at St Andrews' in *Mill's Essays on Literature and Society*, ed. J. B. Schneewind (New York, 1965), p. 364.
42. *On the Principles of English University Education* (Cambridge, 1837), p. 37.
43. Pattison, *Sermons*, p. 59.
44. 'Inaugural Address at St Andrews', p. 363.
45. *Discussions on Philosophy and Literature, Education and University Reform* (1852), pp. 743, 763.
46. *Culture and Scholarship* (Aberdeen, 1892), pp. 19–20.
47. 'Evidence', p. 45.
48. *Principles*, p. 119; much of Edward Lytton Bulwer's *England and the English* (1833), ed. Standish Meacham (Chicago and London, 1970) is relevant to the discussion of the intellectual and moral life of the nation. See in particular II, ch. 2; III, chs. 6 and 7; IV, chs. 2 and 6–8. In observing the vitality of German and Scottish metaphysics, Bulwer alludes to the endowment of professorships, and remarks that 'such a system is far more necessary in the loud and busy action of a free commercial people, than it is in the deep quiet of a German state. With us it is the sole means by which we shall be able to advance a science that *cannot* by any possible chance remunerate or maintain its poorer disciples in all its speculative dignity.... Professorships compel a constant demand for ethical research, while they afford a

serene leisure for its supply; insensibly they *create* the taste upon which they are *formed*, and maintain the moral glories of the nation abroad, while they contribute to rectify and elevate its character at home.' p. 321.

49. H. T. Buckle, *History of Civilization in England* (2 vols., 1857–61), I, p. 207.
50. *Westminster Review*, NS, XII (1857) 396.
51. 'Evidence', pp. 45–6.
52. *Ibid.*, p. 274, and see pp. 97–8 where part of Vaughan's statement is reproduced. On Vaughan's part in the discussion on the Commission see Bill, *University Reform in Nineteenth-Century Oxford*, chs. 8 and 10.
53. Quoted by Pattison in *Suggestions*, pp. 152–5.
54. *Suggestions*, p. 162.
55. 'Evidence', p. 256.
56. *Ibid.* p. 257.
57. *Essays on the Endowment of Research* (various authors) (1876), p. 25.
58. *Suggestions*, pp. 325–6.
59. 'Philosophy at Oxford', *Mind*, I.I (1876).
60. In *Henry Sidgwick, a Memoir*, p. 238.
61. *Suggestions*, p. 147.
62. *CPW*, IV, p. 292.
63. *Suggestions*, p. 226.
64. 'Evidence', p. 86.
65. Preface to Huber, *English Universities*, p. xxviii.
66. *Essays on a Liberal Education*, p. 178.
67. *Henry Sidgwick, a Memoir*, p. 455.
68. 'Evidence', p. 274.
69. *Ibid.* p. 37.
70. Preface to Huber, *English Universities*, pp. xxxiii–xxxiv.
71. *Memoirs*, ed. Mrs Pattison (1885), p. 164; see Graham Hough, 'Coleridge and the Victorians' in *The English Mind*, eds H. S. Davies and George Watson (Cambridge, 1964), pp. 175–92; and A. Dwight Culler, *The Imperial Intellect* (New Haven, 1955), pp. 176–8.
72. *Idea of a University*, p. 160.
73. *Sermons*, pp. 111–12; three of these are particularly relevant to university education: those preached on 3 November 1861, 18 October 1863 and 30 April 1865.
74. *Ibid.* p. 109.
75. On a smaller scale, the same movement is apparent in Leavis's conflation of 'intelligence' with 'criticism', and hence with 'critics'; e.g. 'The Function of Criticism at Any Time' in *Selections from Scrutiny* (Cambridge, 1968), II, pp. 280–303.
76. R. L. Nettleship, *Memoir of Thomas Hill Green* (1906), p. 94.
77. *Sermons*, pp. 112–14.

78. Quoted in John Sparrow, *Mark Pattison and the Idea of a University* (Cambridge, 1967), p. 131.
79. I have found particularly valuable the essays of Bernstein contained in *Class, Codes and Control*, III, and essays by Young, G. M. Esland and others in M. F. D. Young (ed.) *Knowledge and Control: New Directions for the Sociology of Education* (1971).

Chapter 7. Epilogue: cultural studies without a clerisy

1. John Henry Newman, *The Idea of a University Defined and Illustrated*, ed. I. T. Ker (Oxford, 1976), pp. 123–4.
2. *The Ego and its Own*, ed. John Carroll (1971), pp. 80–1. On what he sees as the alternative nineteenth-century tradition, see John Carroll, *Break-Out from the Crystal Palace* (The anarcho-psychological critique: Stirner, Nietzsche, Dostoevsky) (1974), esp. chs. 1 and 2.
3. *Art and Illusion* (4th edn, 1972), p. 230, and cf. p. 46.
4. *The Social Construction of Reality* (1966), (Harmondsworth 1971), pp. 117–18.
5. As trans. by Francis Golffing (1956), pp. 298–9.
6. J. W. Sanders, *John Donne* (Cambridge, 1971), p. 96. Cf. the argument of Lawrence's great essay 'Morality and the Novel' (1925) where, however, there is a marked tendency to assert the novel as the only form of discourse capable of 'revealing to us the changing rainbow of our living relationships'.
7. *The Hidden Order of Art* (1970), pt 1. Cf., once again, Nietzsche: 'Those moralists who command man first of all to gain control of himself thus afflict him with ... a constant irritability in the face of all natural stirrings and inclinations. ... Whatever may henceforth push, pull, attract, or impel such an irritable person from inside or outside, it will always seem to him as if his self-control were endangered. No longer may he entrust himself to any instinct or free wingbeat; he stands in a fixed position with a gesture that wards off, armed against himself, with sharp and mistrustful eyes – the eternal guardian of his castle, since he has turned himself into a castle. ... [He] has certainly become insufferable for others, difficult for himself, and impoverished and cut off from the most beautiful fortuities of his soul. Also from all further *instruction*. For one must be able to lose oneself occasionally if one wants to learn something from things different from oneself.' (*The Gay Science*, trans. Walter Kaufmann (New York, 1974), pp. 244–5.)
8. *Republic*, p. 382.
9. 'Coleridge's Writings', *Westminster Review*, NS, xxix (1866).
10. P. L. Berger and T. Luckmann, *The Social Construction of Reality* (1967), p. 26. See, for example, Clifford Geertz, 'Ideology as a Cultural System' in David Apter (ed.), *Ideology and Discontent* (Glen-

coe, Illinois, 1964); Michael Walzer, 'On the Role of Symbolism in Political Thought', *Political Science Quarterly* (June 1967); John Dunn, 'The Identity of the History of Ideas', *Philosophy*, XLIII (1968); and Quentin Skinner, 'Meaning and Understanding in the History of Ideas', *History and Theory*, VIII (1969).

11. *Growth through English* (National Association for the Teaching of English, 2nd edn, 1969), p. 36.
12. *Lost for Words* (Harmondsworth, 1972), p. 155.
13. *The Impulse to Dominate* (1941), pp. 209 *et seq.*
14. *Essais Critiques* (Paris, 1971), p. 218.
15. 'Productivity and Existence' (1911) in *Pointing the Way*, trans. M. S. Friedman (1957).
16. This is an extremely bald summary of the richly suggestive passages on the subject in the Paris MSS. See *Karl Marx: Early Writings*, trans. T. B. Bottomore (1963), pp. 120–34, 137–9, 157–72; discussions in István Mészáros, *Marx's Theory of Alienation* (1970), esp. pp. 217–311, and Bertell Ollman, *Alienation: Marx's Conception of Man in Capitalist Society* (Cambridge, 1971), esp. pp. 131–228.
17. In this area I owe a lot to Carl Rogers, *On Becoming a Person* (1961), and in this paragraph especially to the paper reprinted as ch. 19, 'Toward a Theory of Creativity'.
18. See T. S. Eliot, *Notes towards a Definition of Culture* (1948); 'On the Place and Function of the Clerisy' (1944), reprinted in Roger Kojécky, *T. S. Eliot's Social Criticism* (1971); F. R. Leavis, *Mass Civilisation and Minority Culture* (Cambridge, 1930), and *English Literature in our Time and the University* (1969); and a number of other works.
19. *The House of Intellect* (1959), p. 4. Barzun's spirited defence of the ideal of the intellectual elite is throughout relevant to my argument.
20. *From Max Weber*, eds H. H. Gerth and C. Wright Mills (1948), p. 152.
21. *Prison Notebooks*, sel. and trans. by Q. Hoare and G. Nowell Smith (1971), p. 37.
22. *Germany*, trans. anon (3 vols., 1813), III, pp. 16–17. (Smith is of course Adam Smith of *The Wealth of Nations* fame.) See Roy Pascal, ' "Bildung" and the Division of Labour' in *German Studies presented to W. H. Bruford* (1962), and ch. 1 of this book.
23. *On the Aesthetic Education of Man in a series of Letters*, eds. Elizabeth Wilkinson and F. A. Willoughby (Oxford, 1965), p. 85.

SELECT BIBLIOGRAPHY

Where the first cited work of an author was published before 1900, I have included the works published after that year in the 'Before 1900' section. The place of publicaton is London unless noted otherwise.

Before 1900

Arnold, Matthew, *Complete Prose Works*, ed. R. H. Super (Ann Arbor, Michigan, 1961–) (*CPW*)
  Discourses in America (1885)
  Five Uncollected Essays, ed. Kenneth Allott (Liverpool, 1953)
  Letters of Matthew Arnold 1848–88, ed. G. W. E. Russell (2 vols., 1895)
  Letters of Matthew Arnold to Arthur Hugh Clough, ed. H. F. Lowry Oxford, 1932)
  Mixed Essays (Popular edn, 1903)
  The Note-Books of Matthew Arnold, eds. H. F. Lowry, K. Young and W. H. Dunn (Oxford, 1952)
Arnold, Thomas, *Introductory Lectures on Modern History* (1842)
  Miscellaneous Works (1845)
Arnold, William Delafield, *Oakfield, or Fellowship in the East* (1853)
Bacon, Francis, *The New Atlantis* (1629), in *Ideal Commonwealths*, ed. H. Morley (nd)
Bain, Alexander, 'Of a Liberal Education in General', *Westminster Review*, XLIX (1848) 441–63.
Buckle, H. T., *History of Civilization in England* (2 vols., 1857–61)
Bulwer, Edward Lytton, *England and the English* (1833), ed. Standish Meacham (Chicago and London, 1970)
Caird, Edward, 'The Genius of Carlyle' (1892), in *Essays in Literature and Philosophy* (2 vols., Glasgow, 1898)
Cambridge, University of, *Report of Her Majesty's Commissioners appointed to inquire into the State, Discipline, Studies, and Revenues of the University and Colleges of Cambridge* (1852)
Carlyle, Thomas, *Complete Works of Thomas Carlyle*, ed. H. D. Traill (Centenary edn, 30 vols., 1895–9) (*Works*)
  Correspondence between Goethe and Carlyle, ed. C. E. Norton (1887)
  The Life of John Sterling (1851)
  Wotton Reinfred in *Last Words of Thomas Carlyle* (1892)
Clough, Arthur Hugh, *The Correspondence of Arthur Hugh Clough*, ed. F. L. Mulhauser (2 vols., Oxford, 1957)
  'A Review of the Oxford University Commissioners' Report', *North American Review* LXXVI (1853)

Coleridge, Samuel Taylor, *Aids to Reflection* (Bell's 'new edn', 1884)
Biographia Literaria, ed. J. Shawcross (2 vols., Oxford, 1907)
Collected Letters of Samuel Taylor Coleridge, ed. E. L. Griggs (6 vols., Oxford, 1956–71) (*CL*)
Collected Works of Samuel Taylor Coleridge, ed. Kathleen Coburn, (Princeton and London, 1969–)
On the Constitution of the Church and State according to the Idea of Each, ed. J. C. Barrell (Everyman's Library edn, 1972) (*CCS*)
Literary Remains, ed. H. N. Coleridge (4 vols., 1836)
The Notebooks of Samuel Taylor Coleridge, ed. Kathleen Coburn (1957–) (*NB*)
Philosophical Lectures, ed. Kathleen Coburn (1949)
The Table Talk and Omniana of Samuel Taylor Coleridge, ed. H. N. Coleridge (1917)
Comte, Auguste, *Cours de Philosophie Positive* (6 vols., Paris, 1830–42)
Système de Politique Positive (4 vols., Paris, 1851–4), esp. vol. IV which contains Comte's early essays in an appendix
Condorcet, Marquis de, *Esquisse d'un tableau historique des progrès de l'esprit humain* (1795), eds M. and F. Hincker (Paris, 1966)
Copleston, Edward, *A Reply to the Calumnies of the Edinburgh Review against Oxford. Containing an account of the studies pursued in that University* (Oxford, 1810)
D'Israeli, Isaac, *An Essay on the Manners and Genius of the Literary Character* (1795), revised as *The Literary Character* (1818)
Donaldson, James, *Culture and Scholarship* (Aberdeen, 1892)
Emerson, Ralph Waldo, *Complete Works* (Bohn's Standard Library, edn, 2 vols., 1879)
Essays on the Endowment of Research by various writers (1876)
Farrar, F. W. (ed.), *Essays on a Liberal Education* (1867)
Fichte, J. G., *The Popular Works*, trans. William Smith (4th edn, 2 vols., 1889)
Addresses to the German Nation, trans. R. F. Jones and G. H. Turnbull (1922)
Froebel, Friedrich, *Autobiography*, trans. E. Michaelis and H. Keatley Moore (1886)
Froude, J. A., *Thomas Carlyle's Early Life* (2 vols., 1903)
Thomas Carlyle: a History of his Life in London (2 vols., 1902)
Green, T. H., *Prolegomena to Ethics*, ed. A. C. Bradley (Oxford, 1883)
Works, ed. R. L. Nettleship (3 vols., Oxford, 1885)
Hamilton, Sir William, *Discussions on Philosophy and Literature, Education and University Reform* (1852)
Harrison, Frederick, 'Culture: a Dialogue', *Fortnightly Review* VIII (1867)
Hazlitt, William, *The Complete Works of William Hazlitt*, ed. P. P. Howe (Centenary edn, 21 vols., 1930–4)

Herder, J. G., *Herder on Social and Political Culture*, ed. and trans. F. M. Barnard (Cambridge, 1969)

Horne, R. H., *The New Spirit of the Age* (2 vols., 1844)

Hort, F. J. A., 'Coleridge' in *Cambridge Essays contributed by members of the university* (1856)

Huber, V. A., *The English Universities*, ed. and trans. Francis Newman (2 vols., 1843)

Humboldt, Wilhelm von, *The Limits of State Action*, ed. and trans. J. W. Burrow (Cambridge, 1969)

Huxley, T. H., *Collected Essays* (9 vols., 1893–4)

James William, 'On Some Hegelisms' (1882) in *Essays in Popular Philosophy* (New York, 1896)
    A Pluralistic Universe (Hibbert Lectures) (New York and London, 1909)
    Principles of Psychology (2 vols., 1890)

Jebb, R. C., *The Work of the Universities for the Nation, Past and Present* (Cambridge, 1893)

Jowett, Benjamin, 'Introduction to Plato's *Republic*' in *Dialogues* (3rd edn, 5 vols., Oxford, 1892)

Lessing, G. E., *Die Erziehung des Menschengeschlechts* (1780) in *Gesammelte Werke*, ed. P. Rilla (Berlin, 1968)

Marx, Karl, *Karl Marx: Early Writings*, ed. T. B. Bottomore (1963)

Marx, Karl and Engels, Friedrich, *The German Ideology* (Moscow and London, 1965)
    Selected Works (Moscow and London, 1968)

Maurice, F. D., *Has the Church or the State the Power to Educate the Nation?* (1839)

Mill, James, 'Education' (1824) in *James Mill on Education*, ed. W. H. Burston (Cambridge, 1969)
    An Essay on Government, ed. E. Barker (Cambridge, 1937)
    'The State of the Nation' and 'The Reform of the Church', *London Review*, 1 (1835)

Mill, John Stuart, *Autobiography* (World's Classics edn, 1924)
    On Bentham and Coleridge, ed. F. R. Leavis (1950)
    Collected Works of John Stuart Mill (Toronto, 1963–) (*MCW*)
    Dissertations and Discussions (2 vols., 1859)
    'De Tocqueville on Democracy in America', *London Review*, 1 (1835)
    The Early Draft of John Stuart Mill's Autobiography, ed. J. Stillinger (Urbana, Illinois, 1961)
    Letters of John Stuart Mill, ed. H. Elliot (2 vols., 1910)
    Lettres inédites de John Stuart Mill à Auguste Comte publiées avec les réponses de Comte, ed. L. Lévy-Bruhl (Paris, 1899)
    On Liberty and *Representative Government* (Everyman's Library edn, 1910)
    Mill's Essays on Literature and Society, ed. J. B. Schneewind (New York, 1965)
    Principles of Political Economy (1848)

Mill, John Stuart, *The Spirit of the Age*, ed. F. A. Hayek (Chicago, 1942)
  System of Logic (4th edn, 1861)
Newman, John Henry, *Certain Difficulties felt by Anglicans in Catholic Teaching Considered* (2 vols., 1888)
  Discussions and Arguments (4th edn, 1882)
  The Idea of a University Defined and Illustrated, ed. I. T. Ker (Oxford, 1976)
  Parochial and Plain Sermons (8 vols., 1899)
Oxford, University of, *Report of Commissioners of 1877* (1881)
  Report of Her Majesty's Commissioners appointed to inquire into the State, Discipline, Studies, and Revenues of the University and Colleges of Oxford (1852)
Pater, Walter, 'Coleridge's Writings', *Westminster Review*, NS, XXIX (1866)
Pattison, Mark, 'History of Civilisation in England', *Westminster Review*, NS, XII (1857)
  Memoirs, ed. Mrs Pattison (1885)
  'Philosophy at Oxford', *Mind*, I.I (1876)
  'Review of the Situation' (1876) in *Essays on the Endowment of Research* (1876)
  Sermons (1885)
  Suggestions on Academical Organisation (Edinburgh, 1868)
Renan Ernest, *L'avenir de la science* (1848) and *Questions Contemporaines* (1868) in *Oeuvres Complètes* (10 vols., Paris, 1899)
  La Réforme intellectuelle et morale, ed. P. E. Charvet (Cambridge, 1950)
Ruskin, John, *Sesame and Lilies* and *Time and Tide by Wear and Tyne* in *Works*, eds. E. T. Cook and A. D. O. Wedderburn (39 vols., 1903–12)
Sainte-Beuve, C. A., *Causeries du lundi* (1849–51), trans. E. J. Trechmann (8 vols., nd)
  Chateaubriand et son groupe littéraire sous l'empire, ed. M. Allem (Paris, nd)
  Portraits littéraires (2 vols., Paris, 1852)
Saint-Simon, *Exposition de doctrine de Saint-Simon* in *Collection des economistes et reformateurs Français*, eds. C. Bouglé and E. Halévy (Paris, 1924)
Schelling, F. W. J., *On University Studies* (1802), trans. E. S. Morgan (Athens, Ohio, 1966)
Schiller, Friedrich, *On the Aesthetic Education of Man in a series of Letters*, eds. Elizabeth Wilkinson and F. A. Willoughby (Oxford, 1965)
Sedgwick, Adam, *A Discourse on the Studies of the University* (Cambridge, 1834)
Seeley, J. R., *Introduction to Political Science* (1919)
  Lectures and Essays (1870)
Sidgwick, A. and Sidgwick, E. M., *Henry Sidgwick, a Memoir* (1906)
Sidgwick, Henry, 'John Stuart Mill', *The Academy*, IV (1873)
  'Liberal Education', *Macmillan's Magazine*, XV (1867)
  'Philosophy at Cambridge', *Mind*, I (1876)

Sidgwick, Henry, 'The Philosophy of T. H. Green', *Mind*, NS x (1901)
 'The Prophet of Culture' (1867) and 'The Pursuit of Culture as an Ideal' (1897) in *Miscellaneous Essays and Addresses* (1904)
Smith, Sydney, 'Essays on Professional Education', *Edinburgh Review*, xv (1809)
Staël-Holstein, Anne Louise Germaine de, *Germany*, trans. anon. (3 vols., 1813)
 De la littérature considérée dans ses rapports avec les institutions sociales (1800), ed. P. Van Tieghem (Paris, 1959)
Stanley, Arthur Penrhyn, *The Life and Correspondence of Thomas Arnold* (10th edn, 2 vols., 1881)
 Whether States, like Individuals, after a certain period of maturity, inevitably tend to decay (Oxford, 1840)
Stephen, James Fitzjames, *Liberty, Equality, Fraternity* (1873), ed. R. J. White (Cambridge, 1967)
Stephen, Leslie, *English Literature and Society in the Eighteenth Century* (1904)
 'Henry Sidgwick', *Mind*, NS, x (1901)
 History of English Thought in the Eighteenth Century (2 vols., 1876)
Sterling, John, *Arthur Coningsby* (3 vols., 1833)
 Essays and Tales, ed. J. C. Hare (2 vols., 1848)
Tocqueville, Alexis de, *Correspondance Anglaise*, eds., J. P. Mayer and Gustave Rudler, in *Oeuvres, papiers et correspondences* (12 vols., Paris, 1951–64)
 Democracy in America, trans. George Lawrence (2 vols., 1968)
Vico, Giambattista, *The New Science*, trans. T. G. Bergin and M. H. Fisch (Ithaca, 1967)
Ward, Adolphus W., 'Is it expedient to increase the number of universities in England?' (1878) in *Collected Papers* (5 vols., Cambridge, 1921)
Whewell, William, *Of a Liberal Education in General* (1845)
 On the Principles of English University Education (Cambridge, 1837)
Wilde, Oscar, 'The Critic as Artist' (1891) in *The Artist as Critic, Critical Writings of Oscar Wilde*, ed. Richard Ellmann (1970)

After 1900

Abrams, M. H., *The Mirror and the Lamp: Romantic Theory and the Critical Tradition* (New York, 1953)
 Natural Supernaturalism (1971)
Acton, H. B., 'The Idea of a Spiritual Power' (Auguste Comte Memorial Lecture, 1974)
Adorno, T. W., *Prisms*, trans. S. and S. Weber (1971)
Alexander, E., *Matthew Arnold and John Stuart Mill* (1965)
Annan, Noel, 'The Intellectual Aristocracy' in *Studies in Social History: a Tribute to G. M. Trevelyan*, ed. J. H. Plumb (1955)

'John Stuart Mill' in *The English Mind*, ed. H. S. Davies and G. G. Watson (Cambridge, 1964)
  Leslie Stephen: His Thought and Character in Relation to his Time (1951)
Bantock, G. H., 'Newman and Education', *Cambridge Journal*, IV (1951)
Bate, Walter Jackson, *Coleridge* (New York, 1968)
Becker, Carl L., *The Heavenly City of the Eighteenth-Century Philosophers* (New Haven, 1932)
Beer, John B., *Coleridge the Visionary* (2nd edn, 1970)
Beer, John B. (ed.), *Coleridge's Variety* (1975)
Benda, Julien, *La Trahison des clercs* (Paris, 1927)
Berger, P. L. and Luckmann, T., *The Social Construction of Reality* (1967)
Berlin, Isaiah, *Four Essays on Liberty* (Oxford, 1969)
Bernstein, Basil, *Towards a Theory of Educational Transmissions*, vol. III of *Class, Codes and Control* (3 vols., 1975)
Bibby, Cyril, *T. H. Huxley: Scientist, Humanist and Educator* (1959)
Bill, E. G. W., *University Reform in Nineteenth-Century Oxford: A Study of Henry Halford Vaughan* (Oxford, 1973)
Black, Max (ed.), *The Morality of Scholarship* (Ithaca, 1967)
Bottomore, T. B., *Elites and Society* (1964)
Bradbury, Malcolm, 'The Idea of a Literary Elite', *Critical Quarterly*, II (1960)
  The Social Context of Modern English Literature (Oxford, 1971)
Britton, Karl, *John Stuart Mill* (Harmondsworth, 1953)
Brombert, Victor, *The Intellectual Hero: Studies in the French Novel 1880–1955* (1962)
Brown, A. W., *The Metaphysical Society* (New York, 1947)
Bruford, W. H., *Culture and Society in Classical Weimar 1775–1806* (Cambridge, 1962)
  Germany in the Eighteenth Century: the Social Background of the Literary Revival (Cambridge, 1965)
  'Goethe and some Victorian Humanists', *Publications of the English Goethe Society*, NS, XVIII (1949)
  'The Idea of "Bildung" in Wilhelm von Humboldt's Letters' in *The Era of Goethe: Essays Presented to James Boyd* (Oxford, 1959)
Buckley, J. H., *The Triumph of Time: a Study of the Victorian Concepts of Time, History, Progress and Decadence* (Cambridge, Mass., 1966)
Burrow, J. W., *Evolution and Society: a Study in Victorian Social Theory* (Cambridge, 1966)
Bush, Douglas, *Matthew Arnold* (1971)
Calleo, D. P., *Coleridge and the Idea of the Modern State* (New Haven, 1966)
Cameron, David, *The Social Thought of Rousseau and Burke: a Comparative Study* (1973)
Carroll, John, *Break-Out from the Crystal Palace* (1974)

Cassirer, Ernst, *The Logic of the Humanities* (New Haven, 1961)

Chadwick, W. Owen, *The Victorian Church* (2 vols., 1966 and 1970)

Charlton, D. G., *Positivist Thought in France during the Second Empire* (Oxford, 1959)

  Secular Religions in France 1815–70 (Oxford, 1963)

Clarke, M. L. *Classical Education in Britain 1500–1900* (Cambridge, 1959)

Cobban, Alfred, *Edmund Burke and the Revolt against the Eighteenth Century* (1929)

Collingwood, R. G., *Autobiography* (1939)

Colmer, John, *Coleridge, Critic of Society* (Oxford, 1959)

Connell, W. F., *The Educational Thought and Influence of Matthew Arnold* (1951)

Coulling, S. M. B., 'The Evolution of Culture and Anarchy', *Studies in Philology*, LX (1963)

Cowling, Maurice, *Mill and Liberalism* (Cambridge, 1963)

Crook, D. P., *American Democracy in English Politics 1815–50* (Oxford, 1965)

Culler, A. Dwight, *The Imperial Intellect: a Study of Newman's Educational Ideal* (New Haven, 1955)

Davie, G. E., *The Democratic Intellect: Scotland and her Universities in the Nineteenth Century* (Edinburgh, 1961)

DeLaura, D. J., *Hebrew and Hellene in Victorian England* (Austin, Texas, 1969)

Duncan, Graeme, *Marx and Mill: Two Views of Social Conflict and Social Harmony* (Cambridge, 1973)

Eliot, T. S., *After Strange Gods: a Primer of Modern Heresy* (1934)

  'The Idealism of Julien Benda', *Cambridge Review*, XLIX (1928)

  Notes towards a Definition of Culture (1948)

  Selected Essays 1917–32 (1932)

  The Use of Poetry and the Use of Criticism (1933)

Faber, Geoffrey, *Jowett: a Portrait with Background* (1957)

Forbes, Duncan, *The Liberal Anglican Idea of History* (Cambridge, 1952)

Fruman, Norman, *Coleridge, the Damaged Archangel* (1971)

Frye, Northrop, 'The Problem of Spiritual Authority in the Nineteenth Century' in *Backgrounds to Victorian Literature*, ed. R. A. Levine (San Francisco, 1967)

Fyvel, T. R., *Intellectuals Today* (1968)

Goodheart, Eugene, *The Cult of the Ego* (Chicago, 1968)

Gramsci, Antonio, *Prison Notebooks*, ed. and trans. by Q. Hoare and G. Nowell Smith (1971)

Grierson, H. J., 'Thomas Carlyle', *Proceedings of the British Academy*, XXVI (1940)

Gross, John, *The Rise and Fall of the Man of Letters* (1969)

Halévy, Elie, *The Growth of Philosophic Radicalism*, trans. M. Morris (1928)

Halliday, J. L., *Mr Carlyle, My Patient* (1947)

Hamburger, J., *Intellectuals in Politics: John Stuart Mill and the Philosophic Radicals* (New Haven, 1965)

Harrison, J. F. C., *Learning and Living* (1961)

Harrison, J. R., *The Reactionaries: a Study of the Anti-Democratic Intelligentsia* (1967)

Harrold, C. F., *Carlyle and German Thought* (New Haven, 1934)

Hayek, F. A., *The Counter-Revolution in Science: Studies in the Abuse of Reason* (Glencoe, Illinois, 1955)

Heeren, John, 'Karl Mannheim and the Intellectual Elite', *British Journal of Sociology*, XXII (1971)

Heller, Erich, *The Disinherited Mind* (New York, 1959)

Himmelfarb, Gertrude, *Victorian Minds* (1968)

Holloway, John, *The Victorian Sage: Studies in Argument* (1953)

Hookyas, R., *Religion and the Rise of Modern Science* (Edinburgh, 1972)

Houghton, Walter, *The Victorian Frame of Mind* (New Haven, 1957)

House, Humphrey, *Coleridge* (1953)

Hughes, H. Stuart, *Consciousness and Society: the Reorientation of European Social Thought 1890–1930* (1957)

Huszar, G. B. de (ed.), *The Intellectuals: a Controversial Portrait* (Glencoe, Illinois, 1960)

Kelly, G. A., *Idealism, Politics and History: Sources of Hegelian Thought* (Cambridge, 1969)

Kojécky, Roger, *T. S. Eliot's Social Criticism* (1971)

Kolakowski, Leszek, *Marxism and Beyond*, trans. J. Z. Peel (1971)

Positivist Philosophy: from Hume to the Vienna Circle, trans. Norbert Guterman (New York, 1968)

Krieger, Leonard, 'The Intellectuals and European Society', *Political Science Quarterly*, LXVII (1952)

LaValley, A. J., *Carlyle and the Idea of the Modern* (New Haven, 1968)

Lazerowitz, M., *The Structure of Metaphysics* (1955)

Leavis, F. R., 'Elites, Oligarchies and an Educated Public', *The Human World* 4 (1971)

English Literature in our Time and the University (1970)

Mass Civilisation and Minority Culture (Cambridge, 1930)

Leavis, Q. D., 'Henry Sidgwick's Cambridge', *Scrutiny*, XV (1947)

Letwin, S. R., *The Pursuit of Certainty* (Cambridge, 1965)

Lippincott, B. E., *Victorian Critics of Democracy* (Oxford, 1938)

Lovejoy, A. O., *Essays in the History of Ideas* (Baltimore, 1948)

The Reason, the Understanding and Time (Baltimore, 1961)

Lukács, Georg, *Essays on Thomas Mann*, trans. S. Mitchell (1964)

Writer and Critic and other Essays, trans. Arthur Kahn (1970)

McFarland, T. B. *Coleridge and the Pantheist Tradition* (Oxford, 1969)

Mannheim, Karl, *Essays on the Sociology of Culture* (1956)

Essays on the Sociology of Knowledge (1952)

Ideology and Utopia (1936)

Manuel, F. E., *The New World of Henri Saint-Simon* (Cambridge, Mass., 1956)

Maurras, Charles, *L'Avenir de l'intelligence* (1905) in *Oeuvres capitales* (4 vols., Paris, 1954)

Milne, A. J. M., *Social Philosophy of English Idealism* (1962)

Mueller, I. W., *John Stuart Mill and French Thought* (Urbana, Illinois, 1956)

Muirhead, J. H., *Coleridge as Philosopher* (1930)
The Platonic Tradition in Anglo-Saxon Philosophy (1931)

Neff, Emery, *Carlyle and Mill: an Introduction to Victorian Thought* (New York, 1926)

Nettleship, R. L., *Memoir of Thomas Hill Green* (1906)

Newsome, David, *Godliness and Good Learning: Four Studies on a Victorian Ideal* (1961)

Orsini, C. N. G., *Coleridge and German Idealism* (Illinois, 1969)

Packe, M. St. J., *Life of John Stuart Mill* (1954)

Pankhurst, R. K. P., *The Saint-Simonians, Mill and Carlyle* (1957)

Park, Roy, *Hazlitt and the Spirit of the Age: Abstraction and Critical Theory* (Oxford, 1971)

Pascal, Roy, ' "Bildung" and the Division of Labour' in *German Studies Presented to W. H. Bruford* (1962)

Plamenatz, John (ed.), *Readings from Liberal Writers, English and French* (1965)

Preyer, Robert, *Bentham, Coleridge and the Science of History* in *Beiträge zur Englischen Philologie*, XLI (1958)

Rice, Eugene, F., *The Renaissance Idea of Wisdom* (Cambridge, Mass., 1958)

Richter, Melvin, 'Intellectual and Class Alienation: Oxford Idealist Diagnoses and Prescriptions', *European Journal of Sociology*, VII (1966)
The Politics of Conscience: T. H. Green and his Age (1964)

Rieff, Philip (ed.), *On Intellectuals: Theoretical Studies and Case Studies* (Garden City, N.J., 1969)

Roach, John P. C., 'Liberalism and the Victorian Intelligentsia', *Cambridge Historical Journal*, XIII (1957)
'Victorian Universities and the National Intelligentsia', *Victorian Studies*, II (1959)

Robbins, W., *The Newman Brothers: an Essay in Comparative Intellectual Biography* (1966)

Roberts, Mark, *The Tradition of Romantic Morality* (1973)

Rothblatt, Sheldon, *The Revolution of the Dons: Cambridge and Society in Victorian England* (1968)

Sanders, C. R., *Coleridge and the Broad Church Movement* (Durham, North Carolina, 1942)

Sanders, J. W., *The Profession of Letters* (1964)

Shannon, R. T., 'John Robert Seeley and the Idea of a National Church' in *Ideas and Institutions of Victorian Britain*, ed. R. Robson (1967)

Shils, Edward, *The Intellectuals and the Powers* (Chicago, 1972)

Shine, Hill, *Carlyle and the Saint-Simonians* (Baltimore, 1941)

Simmel, Georg, 'Der Begriff und die Tragödie der Kultur' in *Philosophische Kultur* (Leipzig, 1911)

Simon, W. M., *European Positivism in the Nineteenth Century* (Ithaca, 1963)

Snyder, Alice D., *Coleridge on Logic and Learning* (New Haven, 1929)

Somervell, D. C., *English Thought in the Nineteenth Century* (1929)

Sparrow, John, *Mark Pattison and the Idea of a University* (Cambridge, 1967)

Stone, Lawrence (ed.), *The University in Society* (2 vols., 1975)

Tillotson, Kathleen, *Mid-Victorian Studies* (1965)

Trilling, Lionel, *Matthew Arnold* (1939 and 1963)

Ward, W. R., *Victorian Oxford* (1965)

Watson, George G., *The English Ideology: Studies in the Language of Victorian Politics* (1973)

Weber, Max, *From Max Weber: Essays in Sociology*, eds. H. H. Gerth and C. Wright Mills (1948)

Wellek, René, 'Carlyle and German Romanticism', *Studies in Philosophy*, xxvii (1930)

Immanuel Kant in England 1793–1838 (Princeton, 1931)

Wetherby, H. L., 'Newman and Victorian Liberalism: a Study in the Failure of Influence', *Critical Quarterly*, xiii (1971)

White, R. J., *The Political Tracts of Wordsworth, Coleridge and Shelley* (Cambridge, 1953)

Willey, Basil, *Nineteenth-Century Studies* (Harmondsworth, 1964)

Williams, Raymond, *Culture and Society* (Harmondsworth, 1963)

The Long Revolution (Harmondsworth, 1965)

Winstanley, D. A., *Early Victorian Cambridge* (Cambridge, 1955)

Later Victorian Cambridge (Cambridge, 1947)

Wisdom, John, *Philosophy and Psychoanalysis* (Oxford, 1964)

Witte, W., 'Carlyle's Conversion' in *The Era of Goethe: Essays Presented to James Boyd* (Oxford, 1959)

Young, M. F. D. (ed.), *Knowledge and Control: New Directions for the Sociology of Education* (1971)

INDEX

America, United States of, 102–11, 120, 121, 126, 200
Aristotle, 23, 51, 116–17, 189, 194, 206, 216
Arnold, Matthew, *100–39*; 3–4, 12, 15, 17, 29–30, 31, 36, 64, 65, 68, 140, 159, 180–1, 184, 198, 204–5. Principal works discussed: *Culture and Anarchy*, 101, 106, 119, 128, 129, 131–2; 'Function of Criticism', 130–2, 133; 'Numbers', 102–9, 119, 129; *Schools and Universities*, 134, 135–6. On criticism, 121, 127, 129–32; on democracy, 103–9, 115, 118–25; on education, 114, 118, 121; on the remnant, 106–9, 110, 114, 121–2, 125, 129–32, 135; on the state, 111–12, 113, 114, 132–9; on timeless culture, 102, 103, 106–7, 110, 111, 118, 123, 128–9, 136; on totality, 136–8
Arnold, Thomas, 21–2, 76, 113, 114–15, 117–18, 132, 134–5, 137, 150, 185
Arts, 35, 88, 97, 153, 219–21, 225. *See also* literature, imaginative; poetry

Bagehot, Walter, 174
Benda, Julien, vii, 1, 231
Bentham, Jeremy, 142, 157, 161
Blake, William, vii, 127
Bulwer, Edward Lytton, 4, 199, 256–7
Bunsen, Christian Karl Josias von, 9, 117
Burke, Edmund, 38, 39, 102, 111, 113, 121–2, 126, 132, 134

Cambridge, University of, 181, 184–8. *See also* universities
Carlyle, Thomas, *72–99*; 3, 12, 14, 15–16, 18–19, 36, 100, 116, 120, 140, 141, 145, 153, 192. Principal works discussed: *Heroes and Hero Worship*, 72, 73–4, 86, 90–1, 94;

Past and Present, 83, 85, 90; *Sartor Resartus*, 76, 80–1, 94–5; *Sterling*, 76–9. And creativity, 87–9, 95–6; on education, 98–9; on heroism, 72–4, 80, 95, 98, 99; and literary activity, 72, 73, 74–6, 85–7, 98; on Literary Guild, 90–1, 98; on order, 82–3; and relation of spiritual to material, 80–7, 93, 94–7
Christianity, 154, 194–5, 207
Church of England, The, 15, 52, 63, 64, 65, 78–9, 155–6, 157, 158, 181–2, 183, 186, 187
classics, in education, 10, 190, 193, 196–7
clergy, 1, 63, 65, 185, 254
clerisy, *4–17, 63–71, 198–207, 214–32*; 41, 72, 73, 102, 140–1, 154–7, 164, 178–9, 184
Clough, Arthur Hugh, 185–6
Coleridge, Samuel Taylor, *37–71*; 14, 18–20, 29, 30, 32, 34, 78, 79, 113, 120, 122, 134, 140, 141, 142, 143, 144, 149, 150, 154, 155–8, 160, 161, 163, 180, 192, 193, 194, 197, 201, 207, 209, 220–1, 231. Principal works discussed: *Constitution of the Church and State*, 37, 52, 58, 60–1, 63, 65–9; *Lay Sermons*, 52, 54, 55, 60, 66. On civilisation and cultivation, 40–1, 65–7; clerisy defined, 63–8; and dynamic philosophy, 38–9, 41, 42–55; on education, 2–3, 58–71; on ideas, 51–2, 54–5, 58; on imagination, 54; theory of mind, 47–51, 53, 57–8, 69; on reason and understanding, 20–1, 48–53, 66–7, 69; on state, 41–2, 60, 62, 66
Comte, Auguste, 140, 141, 145, 147, 148, 150–4, 162–71, 176
Condorcet, Marquis de, 152
Copleston, Edward, 191–3
criticism, 1, 127, 129–32, 231
culture, 2, 9, 10, 14–15, 35, 99, 100, 102, 103–9, 110, 111–12, 119,

271